A Browser's Book of Texas History

Steven A. Jent

Republic of Texas Press
Plano, Texas

Library of Congress Cataloging-in-Publication Data

Jent, Steven A.
  A browser's book of Texas history / Steven A. Jent.
    p. cm.
  Includes index.
  ISBN 1-55622-698-5 (pbk.)
  1. Texas—History—Anecdotes. I. Title.

F386.6.J46   2000
                                99-052466
                                    CIP

Republic of Texas Press is an imprint of Wordware Publishing, Inc.
No part of this book may be reproduced in any form or by
any means without permission in writing from
Wordware Publishing, Inc.

Printed in the United States of America

ISBN 1-55622-698-5
10 9 8 7 6 5 4 3 2 1
9910

All inquiries for volume purchases of this book should be addressed to
Wordware Publishing, Inc., at 2320 Los Rios Boulevard, Plano, Texas 75074.
Telephone inquiries may be made by calling:

(972) 423-0090

To Katie and Cristin

Acknowledgments

Thousands of people helped me write this book. The morsels that fill *A Browser's Book of Texas History* came from a great variety of sources, but soon after I began collecting them I learned that anyone delving into Texas history can do no better than to start with the Texas State Historical Association's *New Handbook of Texas*. These six volumes are the work of more than 3,000 authors and editors, who have produced one of the state's intellectual treasures. If my book doesn't convince you that Texas is a special place, then the *Handbook* surely will.

For the illustrations I am indebted to two other eminent organizations, the Texas State Library and the Institute of Texan Cultures; in particular, many thanks to John Anderson of the TSL and Chris Floerke of the ITC.

I also thank all the thoughtful family members and friends who reminded me of notable people and events from Texas history; they are all in here.

Finally I must mention the DFW Writers' Workshop, a first-class resource for authors in any field. Their frank but friendly criticism is largely responsible for any felicities that appear between these covers. All blemishes I claim for my very own.

Contents

Introduction vii

January 1
February 21
March 41
April 63
May 87
June 109
July 129
August 149
September 169
October 191
November 213
December 233

Index 255

Introduction

No one seems ever to have thought of Texas as an average place; people never have neutral feelings about it. Its history is sprinkled with characterizations like "the dark abode of barbarism and vice," "an Elysium of rogues," and "a rendezvous of rascals for all the continent." One discouraged homesteader complained that from his wilderness home it was "250 miles to the nearest Post Office, 100 miles to wood, 20 miles to water, and 6 inches to hell." An admittedly mythical young emigrant said in her prayers, "Goodbye, God. This is the last chance I get to talk to you. We're moving to Texas." On the other hand, Texas has been "the most charming spot on earth," "an Eldorado of hope," and "a dream or youthful vision realized."

I don't have statistics to back it up, but I would bet with complete confidence that no other state can prompt as many vivid images in the minds of people from the other forty-nine states as Texas can. There simply isn't another state with a reputation on the scale of this one. Only California can even hope to compete with Texas, and so many of its connotations are of mere eccentricity or self-absorption—surfers, hot tubs, Beverly Hills, gurus—although one must grant them the redwoods, Yosemite, and Napa Valley. But no state is as familiar to those who live beyond its borders as Texas, and I suspect that this is true not just in this country, but around the globe. Not all the images are necessarily flattering: The windbag oilman with longhorns mounted on the hood of his Cadillac is not our best ambassador. But cowboys, Indians, Rangers, outlaws, gushers, missions, ghost towns, six-guns, mustangs, ten-gallon hats, guitars, the Lone Star, and that graceful arch above the Alamo—all these icons have combined in the American imagination to form the lasting perception of a self-reliant and adventurous spirit.

We hear a lot these days about the Spirit of Texas, and I am convinced that there is such a thing. There have been times when the Spirit was not all that friendly—Judge Lynch and Jim Crow have both flourished here. But the Spirit of Texas will never be connected with one vice, and that is thinking small. The men and women who made Texas what it is always had big plans and big ideas. They were known for great deeds, whether they were good deeds or bad. They were not afraid to take on big challenges and not afraid to let the world know when they succeeded.

Above all, Texans could claim to have joined the United States as a sort of peer: not simply another territory being absorbed by the Union, but one nation merging with another. The ten years of the Republic are a supremely fascinating decade, when Texas enjoyed all the paraphernalia to which an independent nation is entitled: an army, a navy, a foreign service, a frustrating war, and an insupportable debt. Above all, the Republic of Texas could glory in a magnificent first president who, even while he lived, was already the subject of as many legends as George Washington.

Do not be deceived by the fact that this book begins with La Salle and ends with Armadillo World Headquarters. This is not a chronological history of Texas. You may decide to work through it a day at a time over the course of a year, or you may enjoy just dipping into it at random. However you choose to read it, I trust that when you're done you'll agree with me, if you didn't already, that the centuries since this land was first named Tejas have indeed created a unique and colorful legacy.

JANUARY

JANUARY 1

1685 Three French ships commanded by explorer Rene-Robert Cavalier, Sieur de La Salle, reached the Gulf Coast of Texas near Matagorda Bay. The object of the expedition was to establish a base from which La Salle could search for the mouth of the Mississippi River, which he had discovered in 1682 by traveling downstream from the Great Lakes. But within weeks La Salle found his fleet reduced to a single ship, the *Belle*, after one vessel ran aground with crucial supplies and another set sail back to France. It was only the beginning of an inexorable progression of disasters that would keep La Salle from his goal and ultimately cost him and nearly all of his men their lives.

1928 The twenty-one-story Milam Building opened in San Antonio. It was the first air-conditioned office building in the United States and the first in the world expressly designed for air conditioning.

JANUARY 2

1922 At Dallas Fair Park Stadium, in the first Dixie Classic, a forerunner of the Cotton Bowl, the Aggies were up against the Praying Colonels of Center College from Danville,

Kentucky. The Colonels were possibly the best team in the country, top-heavy with All-Americans. When injuries had reduced the Aggies nearly to the point where they would have to forfeit the game, coach Dana Bible asked sophomore cadet E. King Gill, a baseball player no longer on the football team, to leave the press box and suit up. Gill never left the bench, but he was ready to step in if they needed him. At last the Aggies gained the lead and held on, winning 22-14. Gill was the first "Twelfth Man," beginning an Aggie tradition that has lasted ever since: The students from A&M stand throughout every football game to show that they, too, are ready to play.

❖
JANUARY 3
❖

1914 Frank M. Thayer, a Hollywood executive of the Mutual Film Corporation, met Pancho Villa in a motel room in El Paso, where Villa had invited several motion picture firms to bid for exclusive rights to film his army in action. Thayer agreed to pay $25,000 and a percentage of the profits, but he stipulated that there must be no night attacks, because in those days it was impossible to film without sunlight. For weeks a crew traveled with the army in a special rail car, but when studio executives saw the rushes, they complained that the footage showed too much of Villa on horseback and not enough action. They withdrew further funds, and the project died.

1959 Alaska was admitted as the forty-ninth state of the union, and, after more than a century, Texans could no longer boast that their state was the biggest. An especially awkward result was the necessity of revising the official state song, "Texas, Our Texas"; it would have been ludicrous to persist in calling Texas the "largest and grandest." No one would dare dispute that Texas, though smaller than Alaska, was still mightier, so today "mightiest and grandest" it is.

JANUARY 4

1904 Actress Emilie Charlotte (Lillie) Langtry, touring the United States by train, stopped in Langtry, Texas. But she had arrived too late to meet her most conspicuous admirer and correspondent, Judge Roy Bean, who had died nearly a year before. She did take time to meet other townspeople, who presented her with a memento: a revolver that had belonged to the late judge. Lillie had performed in several Texas cities when she toured the continent in 1888, and Bean supposedly attended her show in San Antonio, but it is unlikely that the two ever met, in this life at least.

1929 Bose Ikard—ex-slave, cowhand, traildriver, Indian fighter, and six decades a devoted friend of cattle baron Charles Goodnight—died in Austin at the age of eighty-five. Free after the Civil War, Ikard worked for Oliver Loving until Loving died in a fight with Comanches. Loving's friend Goodnight then hired him, and with years of trustworthy service Ikard became, in Goodnight's words, his "detective, banker, and everything else." Goodnight bought the granite stone that marks Ikard's grave in Weatherford, and he wrote his epitaph: "Bose Ikard served with me four years on the Goodnight-Loving Trail, never shirked a duty or disobeyed an order, rode with me in many stampedes, participated in three engagements with Comanches, splendid behavior."

JANUARY 5

1874 The Texas Supreme Court ruled in the case of *Ex Parte Rodriguez*, and thereby earned statewide ridicule as the "Semicolon Court." In December 1873 Joseph Rodriguez of Travis County was arrested for casting multiple votes in the state general election. Two prominent Republicans, A. J. Hamilton and C. B. Sabin, demanded a writ of habeas corpus on his behalf, claiming that the arrest was invalid because the election itself was illegal. Democrats, who had prevailed in that election by replacing Republican governor Edmund J. Davis with Democrat Richard Coke, opposed the writ, or, put more accurately, opposed this move to invalidate the election.

The controversy centered on a clause of the state constitution which required that all elections "be held at the county-seats...until otherwise provided by law; and the polls shall be opened for four days." The state legislature had created polling sites outside some county seats (which the clause expressly permitted, as both parties agreed). But it had also restricted voting to a single day, and that was the contentious point. Republicans argued that the semicolon between the two items meant that the second requirement was independent of the first, and therefore could not be amended by legislation, and that the election was therefore unconstitutional. After hearing a great deal of sophisticated debate, the court ruled against the state, and ordered Rodriguez released. But that was the only practical effect of their decision: in the subsequent confrontation between Coke and Davis, Davis blinked first, and Coke was inaugurated later that month.

❖

JANUARY 6

❖

1869 Cullen Montgomery Baker, wanton murderer or defender of Southern dignity, was gunned down by a Cass County posse led by Thomas Orr, a local politician and Baker's former rival in love. Baker and Orr had once competed for the hand of Belle Foster, and later Baker tried to hang Orr and was barely dissuaded from hanging Belle's father. Before the Civil

War, Baker had killed men in Texas and Arkansas on his own account, but it was during Reconstruction that he came into his own. He and his outcast bunch were nationally famous as the nemesis of the Freedmen's Bureau, as well as any black man or woman who had the bad luck to cross their path. But Thomas Orr, who had married Belle, won this last desperate round as well.

1892 William Caldwell Sublett—pioneer, Texas Ranger, Confederate cavalryman, and gold prospector—died in Barstow, Ward County. With him went the secret to a fortune in gold. For the past eleven years, Sublett had periodically disappeared into the wilderness and returned with gold nuggets and dust, which he said came from a mine whose location he alone knew. Despite his apparent access to immense wealth, he lived a modest life with few possessions. No one, not even his son Ross, was ever able to wheedle the information out of him or track him to the mine. After his death, Ross continued to search for the treasure, which he vaguely remembered visiting as a boy with his father. But his efforts failed, and so has every attempt since.

❖ JANUARY 7 ❖

1838 President Sam Houston bet Augustus C. Allen a $500 suit of clothes that he could go without a drink for a year. Allen, one of the founders of Houston City, apparently knew his man. Surrounded by dozens of taverns in the rugged new town, the president could not hold out that long; on San Jacinto Day he went on a patriotic toot. Only after he married the devout Margaret Lea two years later did he climb on the wagon for good.

1894 In the little town of Keene, the General Conference of Seventh Day Adventists opened the Keene Industrial

Academy, with an initial enrollment of fifty-six. The school's primary product was brooms, and other broom-makers eventually opened in Keene, which became known as the "Stick Horse Capital of the World." After "Ripley's Believe It Or Not" called Keene "the town without crime or police," some Fort Worth men perversely robbed the post office. The Adventist influence is still apparent in Keene: the post office and banks close on Saturdays rather than Sundays.

❖

JANUARY 8

❖

1836 Texas rebels hoisted a Lone Star flag, of sorts, for the first time. In 1835 Colonel William Ward led his Georgia Battalion of Permanent Volunteers to Texas. As they passed through Knoxville, Georgia, seventeen-year-old Johanna Troutman presented the unit with a new flag of white silk, with a blue five-pointed star and the inscriptions "Texas and Liberty" and *"Ubi Libertas habitat, ibi nostra patria est"* (Where Liberty dwells, there is our country). The battalion first unfurled the flag above the American Hotel in Velasco. It was accidentally destroyed at Goliad, just before Fannin's disastrous battle and surrender, where nearly all of the Georgia Battalion perished. Troutman died and was buried in Georgia in 1879. In 1913 her remains were moved to the State Ceme-

Johanna Troutman gave Texas its first Lone Star flag, although the design had little in common with the one we know today.

Photo courtesy Texas State Library and Archives Commission.

tery in Austin, where she rests beneath a bronze statue by Pompeo Coppini.

❖

JANUARY 9

❖

1719 France declared war on Spain, and naturally the New World became one theater of operations. In June an expedition of seven soldiers under Corporal M. Blondel, despatched from Louisiana, arrived at the Mission San Miguel de Linares de los Adaes, where they captured the single Spanish soldier in residence. But Blondel had not reckoned with the substantial force of loyal chickens at the post; they startled his horse and he fell off. In the uproar, the lay brother of the mission escaped and began spreading the news of a "massive" French invasion. The panicked Spanish evacuated all of East Texas and did not return for two years, although the French never made another foray into Texas. When the truth came out, disgusted inhabitants of New Spain called the affair the "Chicken War."

❖

JANUARY 10

❖

1880 The town of Nameless, in Travis County, officially received its curious name. After post office authorities rejected six of their nominations, local residents finally wrote in exasperation, "Let the post office be nameless and be damned." The post office granted the part of their wish that was in its power.

1901 Anthony Lucas drilled the first of the great Texas salt dome gushers at Spindletop, near Beaumont. Over 600 feet of four-inch pipe, weighing over six tons, shot 300 feet into the air, followed by a torrent of oil that flowed for nine days before it was capped. The discovery introduced a wild, freewheeling, boomtown epoch in the region, with many fortunes gained and quickly lost. A year later, oil veteran Joe "Buckskin" Cullinan and New York investor Arnold Schlaet formed the Texas Company and promptly struck it rich at nearby Sour Lake. The Texas Company would come to be better known as Texaco; Gulf and Humble also had their origins in the fields around Beaumont.

JANUARY 11

1874 Gail Borden, most famous for his invention of a process to condense milk, died in Borden, Texas at the age of seventy-two. Borden settled in the old Austin colony in 1829 and represented San Felipe at the Constitutional Convention of 1833. With two other partners, he founded the *Telegraph & Texas Register*, the journalistic voice of the new republic. As a customs officer, he was a key figure in promoting real estate development that would make Galveston the largest city in the state for much of the latter nineteenth century. Condensed milk was not Borden's first attempt to create an indestructible food. His meat biscuits won a gold medal at the Great Exhibition in London in 1851, but the mixture of dried beef and flour failed commercially, as the public found it disgusting. His work on condensed milk brought him to the brink of financial ruin, but the Civil War created a need for large quantities of preserved foods and finally made him a wealthy man.

JANUARY 12

1828 Joel R. Poinsett, the first U.S. minister to the new Mexican government now independent from Spain, signed a treaty in which the United States relinquished its claims to Texas. Until then the U.S. had maintained that it had acquired Texas as part of the Louisiana Purchase. The treaty was not ratified within the time limit, and the Jackson administration later resumed negotiations with Mexico, but the ultimate outcome was the same, and America's persistent but futile efforts to obtain Texas served only to increase the Mexican government's distrust of American colonists. Today the obscure ambassador's name is most familiar to us via the Christmas plant poinsettia. Poinsett, an avid and talented botanist, sent some specimens to his home in South Carolina and to fellow horticulturists in other states. The plant is now a multimillion-dollar crop in Texas.

1941 Frenchy McCormick, the legendary gambling queen of Tascosa, died in Channing. No one could be sure of her age, or of anything else about her origins, which she always kept secret, but she was probably around ninety years old. Until a couple of years before, she had defiantly lived alone, the sole resident of Tascosa, a ghost town since 1915. She refused to leave the dilapidated adobe house where she and Mickey, her beloved husband of thirty years, had lived when Tascosa was at its peak as a cattle town and they were the aristocrats of the monte tables. Mickey died in 1912 and was buried in Tascosa, just east of their home. When Frenchy finally agreed to leave, it was only after she was assured that she would be buried next to him when the time came, and so she was.

❖ JANUARY 13 ❖

1912 In the lobby of Fort Worth's Metropolitan Hotel, Amarillo rancher John Beal Sneed confronted Albert G. Boyce, retired general manager of the XIT Ranch, and gunned him down. In the previous fall, Boyce's son Al Jr. had released Sneed's wife Lena from the Fort Worth sanitarium where Sneed had committed her and had eloped with her to Winnipeg, Canada. Sneed killed the elder Boyce for assisting his son in the escapade. What today might seem like a straightforward case of premeditated murder was not that simple to a Fort Worth jury in 1912, or even to onlookers outside the courthouse; during Sneed's trial, four men were killed in disputes, and women went at each other with hatpins. The jury ended up deadlocked, with seven jurors ready to acquit Sneed, and the judge declared a mistrial. In March a farmer thought to be in league with the Boyces killed Sneed's father, and in September Sneed again avenged himself. Back in Amarillo, he waited two weeks to catch Al Boyce Jr. off guard, then hit him with three rounds from a twelve-gauge shotgun in front of Polk Street Methodist Church. He was ultimately acquitted in both killings, which juries ruled justifiable homicide. John and Lena Sneed spent the rest of their well-to-do lives together and died in Dallas in the 1960s. When incredulous reporters asked how the jury in the second murder trial could ever have reached a verdict of innocent, the foreman declared, "The best answer is because this is Texas. We believe in Texas a man has the right and the obligation to safeguard the honor of his home, even if he must kill the person responsible."

❖ JANUARY 14 ❖

1874 Governor Richard Coke's inauguration in Austin was accompanied by more than the usual excitement. Outgoing Governor Edmund Davis at first refused to vacate his office, claiming that the election was unconstitutional. The Capitol building filled with armed men of both camps, and Davis telegraphed President Grant requesting Federal troops. But Grant was not inclined to overturn what appeared to him to have been a free, legitimate election decided by a wide margin: He wrote Davis, "Would it not be prudent as well as right to yield to the verdict of the people, as expressed by their ballots?" Davis capitulated and no blood was shed, but on his way out he did lock the door to the governor's office, forcing Coke's friends to resort to an axe to break in.

JANUARY 15

1907   S. W. T. Lanham, the last Confederate veteran to serve as governor, ended his final term in office. As he left the Governor's Mansion, with him went the St. Bernard that had once belonged to Joseph D. Sayers, Lanham's predecessor. Four years before, as the Sayers household moved out, the dog had refused to leave the premises, and Lanham had cared for him through his two terms.

JANUARY 16

1973   The body of Old Rip, Eastland's famous horned frog, was kidnapped from its display case in the Eastland County Courthouse. After officials put a substitute corpse in its place, the Abilene *Reporter-News* received an anonymous letter from someone claiming to have perpetrated the original hoax in 1928. Rip was supposedly retrieved alive from the cornerstone of the old courthouse thirty years after being sealed in. But the writer of the letter, printed in the March 30, 1974 edition, said that, with the connivance of the demolition workers who knocked the old building down, he had sneaked a live horned frog into the cornerstone, and this was the animal that became nationally famous and was eventually enshrined.

JANUARY 17

1836   General Sam Houston ordered Colonel Jim Bowie to take thirty men from Goliad to San Antonio and demolish the fortifications there, in order to deny them to the approaching

Mexican army under Santa Anna. But at the same time, Governor Smith, although he had been removed from office by the General Council, ordered Colonel William Travis to defend the town. Smith's orders suited the temperamental Travis better than Houston's, and he and Bowie prepared for a siege in the Alamo. Bowie, Travis, and their entire command were killed when the improvised fortress fell on March 6.

1929 Thimble Theatre, the comic strip drawn by Elzie Crisler Segar, debuted a grotesque but oddly appealing new character named Popeye, the Sailor Man. (Of course, Popeye was no more bizarre than the other denizens of Segar's peculiar cosmos, which ultimately included, among others, Olive Oyl, Eugene the Jeep, Brutus, J. Wellington Wimpy, the Sea Hag, and Alice the Goon.) Thimble Theater first appeared in the *Victoria Advocate* years earlier, and Popeye himself regarded the paper as his birthplace. In a 1934 commemorative issue, the spinach industry's best friend thanked the editors, saying "Victoria is me ol' hometown on account of tha's where I got born'd at." Less notable figures who added their congratulations included President Roosevelt, Vice President Garner, and Governor Ferguson and her husband.

❖ JANUARY 18 ❖

1892 Chester Byers, trick roper, Rodeo Hall of Famer, and longtime Fort Worth rodeo star, was born in Knoxville, Illinois. Raised in Oklahoma, Chet Byers learned roping in his youth; among his instructors was Will Rogers. By 1905 he was touring the country, and then the world, with the top Wild West and rodeo shows. He was the world champion in trick and fancy roping in 1915, and again in 1916, and continued to take first place in rodeos at Madison Square Garden, Cheyenne Frontier Days, and around Texas the rest of his life. Eventually he made his home in Fort Worth, where he died in 1945, the best-known roper of his time and the man who literally wrote the book on the subject.

JANUARY 19

1929 Old Rip, Eastland's nationally famous horned frog, died of pneumonia. On February 18 of the previous year, Rip had ostensibly been retrieved alive from the cornerstone of the just-demolished old Eastland County courthouse, having been deliberately sealed in when it was built in 1897. His "miraculous" survival had made him a national celebrity; he toured the country and even visited President Coolidge in the White House. His embalmed body, in a plush casket, is now displayed in the lobby of the present courthouse.

JANUARY 20

1891 James S. Hogg became the first governor of Texas born in the state. At around 300 pounds, Hogg was the only governor to rival the gargantuan Richard B. Hubbard. His daughter Ima and her two younger brothers Mike and Tom loved to slide down the banister of the great circular stairway of the Governor's Mansion. But one day Tom fell off halfway down, banged his chin on the steps, and bled profusely. The governor decided to put an end to their hazardous sport; he hammered tacks into the railing. The holes are still there.

JANUARY 21

1879 Richard B. Hubbard, the biggest governor Texas ever had, ended his term in office which began when he succeeded Richard Coke, who resigned the office for the U.S. Senate. At well over 300 pounds, Hubbard was truly an enormous man. Indeed, it was said that he was probably the most polite man in the state; when he stood up, four women could sit down.

JANUARY 22

1927 In Round Rock, with visibility reduced by rain and mist, a train collided with a bus carrying the Baylor basketball team and some supporters. Ten people were killed and many others injured. In memory of the tragedy, the names of the "Immortal Ten" are recited on campus during every Homecoming Week.

1973 The United States Supreme Court ruled, in the case of *Roe v. Wade*, that the Fourteenth Amendment to the United States Constitution did guarantee women the right to an abortion. *Jane Roe* was the pseudonym of the woman who, in March 1970, filed suit in Dallas federal district court against Henry Wade, the Dallas district attorney, claiming that the Texas law against abortions was unconstitutional and seeking an injunction to stop Wade from prosecuting doctors who performed abortions. The court did rule the law in question unconstitutional, but refused to issue the injunction; both sides filed appeals. Seven of nine justices then ruled in favor of *Roe*, affecting not only Texas law but also the rest of the country. Over the years, however, as justices have come and gone, the balance has tipped for and against abortion rights, and the issue is still the subject of emotional and legal debate.

JANUARY 23

1877 In Jefferson, the proprietors of the Brooks House were surprised to find that "A. Monroe and wife," lately guests in room 4, had disappeared. It later transpired that the gentleman had boarded the morning train, eastbound, with his luggage and hers. No one had seen the lady since Sunday morning, two days before, when he had bought two picnic lunches and the couple strolled out of sight into the fog. A week later, "Mrs. Monroe's" body was found, shot in the head, with the remains of a picnic lunch nearby. At first authorities sought A. Monroe, but then they deduced that the couple were actually Abraham Rothschild and his companion Bessie Moore. By this time Rothschild had reached his home in Cincinnati, where he tried to commit suicide but only blinded himself in one eye. Texas officials had him extradited in March, but it was nearly two years before he went on trial for murder; both the defense and the prosecution had recruited the best legal minds in Texas, and they traded motions and countermotions for months. The first prosecution ended in a mistrial, and in December 1880 a second trial acquitted Rothschild.

Rumors and legends about the murder persist to this day. They say that in the 1890s a distinguished older man wearing an eye patch visited Bessie's grave, where he knelt and prayed. Whether or not this was Rothschild, the case is still unsolved, and is the subject of an annual dramatic performance in Jefferson.

❖
JANUARY 24
❖

1876 In a Sweetwater saloon, Corporal Melvin King suddenly began shooting at buffalo hunter and teamster Bartholomew Masterson as he talked to barmaid Molly Brennan. In seconds, Brennan was killed and Masterson was severely wounded, but King was also dead. The incident was the beginning of the legend of Bat Masterson the gunman, even though in his remaining forty-five years he never killed another man. Masterson had a lengthy career as a lawman in Kansas and Colorado, with many intervals in a variety of other occupations. At the turn of the century he ended up in New York and began one last successful career as a journalist. On the morning of October 25, 1921, he sat at his desk, began writing a column, then collapsed and died of a heart attack. His last words, as he wrote them: *There are those who argue that everything breaks, even in this old dump of a world of ours. I suppose these ginks who argue that way hold that because the rich man gets ice in the summer and the poor man gets it in the winter things are breaking even for both. Maybe so, but I'll swear that I can't see it that way.*

JANUARY 25

1839   The Texas legislature designated the Lone Star flag as the national flag of the Republic, specifying "a blue perpendicular stripe of the width of one-third of the whole length of the flag, with a white star of five points in the center thereof, and two horizontal stripes of equal breadth, the upper stripe white, the lower red, of the length of two-thirds of the whole length of the flag."

1878   The Denison *Daily News* printed the story of farmer John Martin, who saw a strange object traveling through the sky at high speed while he was out hunting. He likened it to a flying saucer, but if it contained little green men they were very little, for Martin, who stared at it for some time, compared it in size to an orange or "a large saucer."

JANUARY 26

1833   Sculptress Elisabet Ney was born in Muenster, Westphalia. Her rebellious nature revealed itself early, as she shocked her parents by insisting on studying sculpture in Berlin. She married Doctor Edmund Montgomery, after ten years of intimate friendship, but retained her independence;

the two occupied separate quarters, and she still chose to be addressed as Fraulein Ney. She was familiar with, and sculpted, all the great Germans of her day. In late 1870 the

couple left Germany for the United States. They traveled across much of the East and Midwest; then, as they passed through Texas, they saw Liendo, a plantation near Hempstead. They bought it on May 4, 1873. After a few years of plantation and family life, Ney resumed her career in sculpture, this time choosing for her subjects the great Texans, and became in effect the state's sculptor laureate. In her studio in Austin, she shocked the public with her knee-length working skirt. She died in her studio on January 19, 1907, and was buried at Liendo.

This youthful portrait of **Elisabet Ney** suggests that her strong will and independent nature developed early in her life.

Photo courtesy Texas State Library and Archives Commission.

❖

JANUARY 27

❖

1836 The Grand Lodge of Louisiana issued a dispensation for founding the first Masonic lodge in Texas, to be named for J. H. Holland, Grand Master of Louisiana. The lodge was founded in Brazoria, but before long it had to be relocated in haste, as Brazoria was overrun by the army commanded by another Mason named Santa Anna. Senior Deacon Fannin was soon dead at Goliad. After the war, Sam Houston presided over not only the Republic of Texas, but also the creation of the Grand Lodge of Texas. The Masonic Oak, where the first Texas Masons met in secrecy, still stands in Brazoria.

1945 "Plinky" Toepperwein, sharpshooter, died in San Antonio at age sixty-two. In 1900 Elizabeth Servaty was working at a Winchester factory in New England when she met Adolph "Ad" Toepperwein, an exhibition shooter also employed by Winchester. Ad gave his new bride shooting lessons, and they found she was a natural shot. After hitting a tin can, she exclaimed, "I plinked it," mimicking the sound it made; the verb *to plink* entered the language, and "Plinky" became her nickname. She soon joined Ad's touring company, and they performed together for the next four decades. Plinky also set many records for marksmanship. She was the first American woman to hit 100 clay pigeons in a row, and it was no fluke; she did so more than 200 times in her life. Perhaps the greatest testament to her remarkable skills came from Annie Oakley, who told Plinky she was the greatest shot she had ever met.

JANUARY 28

1857 Forced to recognize that the colony of French and Swiss emigrants at La Réunion was doomed to failure, François Jean Cantagrel dissolved the Société de Colonisation Europeo-Americaine au Texas. Two years before, only a tenth of the 2,000 volunteers for the utopian experiment, located near Dallas, had ever arrived, and the number of colonists never exceeded 350. Too few of them were farmers; Cantagrel, the society's agent in America, lamented, "I am sent here to direct an agricultural colony and have no agriculturalists to direct." Today nothing remains of La Réunion except a small cemetery and a historical marker. But the name survives in Reunion Arena.

1891 In Brewster County, east of Fort Davis, a yearling bull became the ghastly symbol of a deadly gunfight. Rancher Henry Harrison Powe, a one-armed Confederate veteran, and Fine Gilliland, agent for the cattle firm Dubois & Wentworth, both claimed the bull, which bore no brand and was separated from its mother. Powe said that the bull came from one of his HHP cows, but Gilliland thought otherwise. Gunfire broke out, Powe fell dead, and Gilliland rode away empty-handed. Some cowboys branded the unlucky animal with "MURDER" on one side and "JAN 28 91" on the other, and for years afterward it wandered the brush as a living *memento mori*.

---- ❖ ----

JANUARY 29

---- ❖ ----

1891 Panic seized much of the Panhandle as reports of a major Indian raid flashed across the region. Settlers barricaded their homes and stockpiled ammunition, and a flurry of telegrams frantically summoned help from Bill McDonald and the Texas Rangers. The spread of the Ghost Dance religion among the tribes of the plains was common knowledge, and the recent massacre at Wounded Knee made it that much easier to believe that they were out for revenge. But it turned out that the "bloodthirsty yells" that had started the rumors came from some cowhands at the Rocking Chair Ranch slaughtering a steer for dinner, and the ominous smoke came not from charred homes but from charred beef. There were no Indians within a hundred miles.

1949 An Army review board cleared Ella Behrens of all accusations, changed her discharge to "honorable," and reimbursed her for lost pay. In 1918 Behrens had been the victim of both anti-German hysteria and the panic brought on by the deadly influenza epidemic. Officers at Camp Bowie, in Fort Worth, arrested the young nurse with the suspicious German-sounding name and accused her of deliberately contaminating soldiers' food with flu germs. She was jailed for eight days, then released, only to be informed that she had been dishonorably discharged from the Army for being absent without leave. It took the next thirty years for Ella to restore her good name.

JANUARY 30

1861 Governor Sam Houston forwarded the ordinance of secession to Lieutenant Governor Edward Clark, to be put before the state Senate. A determined opponent of secession, Houston added an acerbic cover note: "Sir: Enclosed, I have the honor to submit the report of the State Lunatic Asylum, and commend the same to the consideration of your honorable body. Sam Houston."

1925 For the first time in the United States, a state supreme court composed of all women convened, to hear arguments in an appeal of *W. T. Johnson et al v. J. M. Darr et al*, a dispute over a land lien. One party to the suit was the WOW (Woodmen of the World), a fraternal organization to which virtually every male official and attorney in Texas belonged. Thus an all-female court was needed to avoid a conflict of interest. Hortense Sparks Ward was appointed Chief Justice, with Hattie Leah Hennenberg and Ruth Virgina Brazill. On May 23, 1925, they ruled in favor of the WOW. Then, their one case closed, the court dissolved.

JANUARY 31

1927 The state legislature adopted the mockingbird as the Texas state bird, in part because it is "a fighter for the protection of his home, falling, if need be, in its defense, like any true Texan."

FEBRUARY

FEBRUARY 1

1840   Rutersville College, the first college in Texas, opened in the town of the same name. Students could choose from courses in Moral Science and Belles Lettres (*Elocution, Porter's Analysis, Jamieson's Rhetoric, Hedge's Logic, Upham's Intellectual Philosophy, (2d edition), Wayland's Elements of Moral Science, Kame's Elements of Criticism, Paley's Evidences of Christianity, Wayland's Political Economy*), Mathematics, Ancient Languages and Literature, Modern Languages, Natural Science, or the Female Department (any of the above plus *Music on the Piano Forte, Drawing and Painting*).

Fees were advertised as follows:

Elementary Studies, per term,	*$13.00*
Higher branches,	*20.00*
" ", including the languages,	*25.00*
Music on the Piano Forte, per quarter	*15.00*
Board, including washing and fuel, per month,	*12.50*

FEBRUARY 2

1620   Maria Coronel de Agreda, a girl of seventeen from a village near the border between Aragon and Navarre, Spain, took religious vows and adopted the name María de Jesús. She had always been uncommonly pious and had already persuaded her father to convert his castle into a nunnery. On some 500 occasions over the next eleven years, Maria fell into a deep trance in which she dreamed that she was miraculously transported to Texas and New Mexico; there, dressed in the blue cloak of her order, she visited various Indian tribes and introduced them to Christianity. When she described these dreams to her confessor, he forwarded the story to his superiors. They in turn corresponded with the archbishop of Mexico, who inquired of his subordinates whether they knew anything of a mysterious young nun evangelizing in New Spain. Just before his letter reached the superior in New Mexico, a delegation of Jumano Indians came to a convent near Albuquerque and said that a "Lady in Blue" had spoken to them. Missionaries later met other Indians who said that the Lady in Blue had foretold their arrival.

In 1631 Fray Alonso de Benavides traveled from the New World back to Spain to meet Sister Maria in Agreda, and she confirmed that she was in fact the Lady in Blue. Coincidentally, her trances ceased after his visit. She died in 1665, but people in the Southwest occasionally reported meeting a woman dressed in blue on assorted merciful errands as late as the 1940s.

❖

FEBRUARY 3

❖

1848 About seventy followers of Étienne Cabet sailed from Le Havre for New Orleans, hoping to create a utopian communal society in Texas. In his famous 1838 novel *Voyage en Icarie*, after which the Icarian movement was named, Cabet had theorized that human nature was perfectible if given the perfect environment, and his adherents hoped to achieve that perfection in a colony of a million acres in southern Denton County. When they arrived in May, however, they found only a tenth that amount of land allocated for them, in scattered half-sections. Worse, they were informed that they would lose their title if they failed to build a house on each lot by July. Those utopians who were not already dead of malaria returned to New Orleans in despair. Cabet joined them there in December and led them to try again in Nauvoo, Illinois. When that effort also failed, they moved on to St. Louis, but there Cabet died in late 1856.

1889 Near the Canadian River in the Choctaw Nation, someone ambushed Belle Starr with a shotgun, ending the colorful career of the Bandit Queen; the killer was never identified. Much of Starr's notorious life took place in Texas, where in 1866 she married her first husband, Jim Reed, a member of the Younger and James gangs. A deputy sheriff killed Reed in Paris in 1874. In 1880 widow Reed married Sam Starr, another outlaw; she served a year in a federal prison for her part in his horse theft ring and acquired the nickname the Bandit Queen. After Sam Starr was also killed by a lawman in 1886, Belle consoled herself with several lovers until she was murdered. She died only a local celebrity, but an exaggerated two-bit novel entitled *Bella Starr, the Bandit Queen, or, the Female Jesse James* made her a national legend.

FEBRUARY 4

1829 The Mexican government finally recognized the incongruity in the name of the village of La Bahia, situated as it was on the north bank of the San Antonio River, thirty miles inland from the Gulf. La Bahia (the bay) was the abbreviated name of the original presidio and mission established on Matagorda Bay in 1721. They had been relocated inland twice, in 1726 and 1749, but the name had followed them. The new name—an anagram of Hidalgo, the name of a martyr in the struggle for Mexican independence—would be Goliad.

❖

FEBRUARY 5

1837   At seven in the morning, in Camp Independence near Texana, Brigadier Generals Felix Huston and Albert Sidney Johnston dueled for command of the Army of the Republic. President Sam Houston had appointed Johnston to lead the army. But the hot-tempered Huston accused him of treachery and trying to ruin his reputation, and Johnston was not the man to refuse a challenge. At the sixth exchange of pistol shots Johnston fell with a serious wound in his right thigh; it left him an invalid for the time being, and Huston remained in command. Twenty-five years later, Johnston was one of the South's most highly regarded generals. At Shiloh he was shot in the same leg; neither he nor his aides realized the gravity of the wound until it was too late, and the general bled to death.

❖

FEBRUARY 6

1858   The legislature approved the purchase of a monument to the heroes of the Alamo. Since its construction in 1841 by Englishman William B. Nangle, the memorial had been displayed in various cities around Texas, as well as in New Orleans. Built of stones from the Alamo, it took the form of a ten-foot-high pyramid on a square pedestal, with two escutcheons that listed the Alamo dead. After the purchase, it was placed in the vestibule of the old Capitol. But the fire which leveled the Capitol in 1881 also destroyed the monument, although the Daughters of the Republic of Texas collected the fragments.

1971 Astronaut Alan Shephard carefully gripped his specially made six-iron and hit three golf balls, each one bearing the name of Jack Harden, the pro at Houston's River Oaks Country Club. With a flight of 600 yards, Shephard easily set a new record for an iron, or any golf club for that matter, but it still wasn't nearly enough to escape the world's biggest sandtrap—the surface of the Moon.

FEBRUARY 7

1855 Author Charles Angelo Siringo was born in Matagorda County. Siringo worked as a cowboy for fifteen years, on various Texas ranches and on the Chisholm Trail. In 1885 he published his first book, *A Texas Cowboy; or, Fifteen Years on the Hurricane Deck of a Spanish Pony*, now a classic of southwestern literature. His next book, *A Cowboy Detective*, published in 1912, told of his twenty years as a Pinkerton man, where he was involved in some of the agency's most famous cases from Mexico to Alaska. It was originally titled "Pinkerton's Cowboy Detective," but the agency forced him to delete every reference to "Pinkerton" from the book. The furious Siringo wrote another book, *Two Evil Isms, Pinkertonism and Anarchism*, but Pinkerton suppressed it. In 1927, when the aging Siringo was sick and low on money, Houghton Mifflin produced *Riata and Spurs*, a composite of the first two books, but Pinkerton badgered him once again, suing to stop publication. He died the next year.

FEBRUARY 8

1887 Tim "Longhair Jim" Courtright died on the streets of Fort Worth in a gunfight with onetime friend Luke Short. When Courtright was buried, the funeral procession to Oakwood Cemetery was six blocks long. Courtright, with his twin revolvers holstered butt forward, was famed for his quick draw and dead eye, and for a while he earned his living in a Wild West show as a marksman. In 1876, in his early thirties, Courtright was elected marshal of Fort Worth. Defeated for re-election in 1879, he became a freelance detective. He was associated with several suspicious deaths there and in New Mexico but was never convicted of any crime. The reason for his final showdown with Short, one of the rare authentic Hollywood-style gun battles, is now forgotten.

❖

FEBRUARY 9

❖

1914   Country singer Ernest Tubb was born in Crisp. In the early 1940s he was making a meager living as the "Gold Chain Troubadour," selling records as a tie-in with a Fort Worth flour company, when he recorded "Walking the Floor Over You." This million-seller opened doors in Hollywood, and then in Nashville, where he joined the Grand Ole Opry in 1943. Ernest Tubb and his Texas Troubadours were Opry fixtures until he died in 1984; in that time he sold 30 million records. He was a pioneer of the "Texas honky-tonk" style in country music, and was one of the first country artists to add electric guitars to his sound. His fans remember the way he ended each concert by flipping over his guitar to show the message on the back: "Thanks."

1923   Senator Archie Parr, temporarily presiding while Lieutenant Governor T. Whitfield Davidson was away from the chamber, immediately recognized Joe Burkett, a fellow supporter of impeached and deposed governor Jim Ferguson. Burkett introduced a bill to expunge from Senate records all references to the impeachment of "Farmer Jim" and to restore his right to hold office. Parr called for a voice vote, and with a stroke of his gavel summarily ruled that the ayes had it. Before anyone could protest, I. D. Fairchild, also of the Ferguson camp, moved to adjourn, and this was approved in a similar fashion. But two could play at that game. Ferguson opponents rushed to notify Davidson, who promptly reconvened the Senate and accepted a motion that any legislation made in his absence be purged from the record, and this of course passed— by a voice vote. The next morning the *Fort Worth Star-Telegram* described the shenanigans under the headline "Ferguson Citizen for 30 Minutes."

❖

FEBRUARY 10

❖

1901 Five months after the September hurricane that virtually washed away Galveston, the last body officially connected to the disaster was found. The known death toll for the city finished at 4,263. Reliable estimates placed the total closer to 6,000, aside from the 4,000-6,000 killed elsewhere by the same storm.

❖

FEBRUARY 11

❖

1869 Late in the evening, the sternwheeler *Mittie Stephens* approached Jefferson after a trip from Shreveport at the far end of Caddo Lake. A hand on the foredeck, holding a torch to find the shore in the dark, inadvertently lit the hay stacked there, and the fire was soon out of control. The captain made for the shore to beach the vessel and sounded the alarm. To avoid the flames, passengers ran to the stern; ironically, while the inaccessible bow touched land, the water at the other end of the 300-foot ship was ten feet deep. Furthermore, the crew left the paddles turning to keep the boat from drifting away from shore, and as passengers leapt from the stern the wheels drew them in, battering them and forcing them underwater. Forty-three souls survived, sixty-three died, mostly women and children; not one of the children aboard was rescued. Those people who were not drowned were trampled in the crush at the stern. The *Mittie Stephens* was a complete loss, burned to the waterline, but the wreck was visible for decades after.

FEBRUARY 12

1899 A massive arctic front rolled across the state, with paralyzing blizzards and deadly cold. In Tulia, in Swisher County, the temperature reached –23 degrees Fahrenheit, a record that has never been beaten in the history of Texas. At Galveston and Corpus Christi, solid ice brought all water traffic to a halt. Worst of all were the effects on livestock; the wind and snow drove herds of cattle to numbly seek shelter, and later they were found packed in grisly clusters where the barbed wire stopped them and they froze. The "Big Freeze" of 1899 killed 40,000 cattle overnight and brought ruin to many ranchers.

1926 Seventeen years after the nation marked the centennial of Abraham Lincoln's birth, and four years after the dedication of the Lincoln Memorial, Texas officially observed Lincoln's birthday for the first time. In Washington, Congress had just authorized the minting of coins in honor of Confederate war heroes, and now Texas, the last state to be readmitted to the Union, was willing to make this gesture in return.

FEBRUARY 13

1914 Rancher Clemente Vergara crossed the Rio Grande into Mexico, intending to speak to federal authorities about some horses which he believed had been stolen by Mexican soldiers. But as soon as he reached the far side, Mexican troops clubbed him over the head and threw him in jail. The next day his wife and daughter visited him, but on the 15th they were told he had been taken to another jail. Governor Oscar B. Colquitt was ready to send in the Texas Rangers, but U.S. Secretary of State William Jennings Bryan told him that such an invasion was out of the question. By the 25th, American officials had reports that Vergara had been hanged, and indeed, on March 7, his relatives brought back his body. Colquitt announced a $1,000 reward for Vergara's killer, and President Woodrow Wilson assigned additional troops to the border. But in fact there was nothing anyone could do but express helpless outrage at one more brutal death on the Rio Grande.

1991 The Texas legislature established licensing procedures by which members of the Native American Church of North America could legally use peyote in their religious ceremonies. About a quarter million people belong to the church, all of whom must be at least 25 percent Indian by birth to partake. Peyote (*lophophora williamsii*), a small, carrot-shaped cactus, is another uniquely Texan product, for it is grown nowhere else in the United States, and only in Jim Hogg, Starr, Webb, and Zapata Counties.

—————— ❖ ——————
FEBRUARY 14
—————— ❖ ——————

1854 In Marshall, the Texas and Red River Telegraph Company opened the first telegraph office in Texas. From there, lines connected to Shreveport, Natchez, and Alexandria, Louisiana. Before the end of the year Marshall was also tied to Houston, Galveston, and a few smaller towns. There were no telegraph poles in the early days, however; the wires were led across the treetops, and even a moderate breeze, common enough in Texas, could be enough to sever the fragile links.

1882 The Southern Pacific Railroad built a new station in Jeff Davis County and, checking the calendar, named it Valentine. Now every year thousands of romantic spirits in Texas and across the country send their Valentine's Day cards to the post office at Zip Code 79854 to have them stamped with its evocative postmark.

FEBRUARY 15

1969 Artist Frank Albert Jones, about seventy years old, died of cirrhosis of the liver in the Huntsville prison hospital. Born in Clarksville, Jones grew up believing that he was "double-sighted"—able to see spirits—because he was born with a caul over one eye, according to African-American folklore. He first saw the spirits as a boy, and they were with him the rest of his life. When he was about forty, he was imprisoned for rape, and he spent most of the remainder of his life behind bars on a series of charges, all of which he denied. In his later years he began to draw his spirits on scrap paper. Fortuitously, in 1964 the Department of Corrections held its first exhibition of inmate art. Jones's vivid, primitive images of grinning, fire-breathing "haints" looking out from their "devil houses," with titles like "Flying Fish Devil House" and "Creepin' Crawlin' Blue Devil Spider," caught the eye of the director of a Dallas gallery. He arranged to have them appear at shows in Dallas and Fort Worth, and in other states, where they won several awards. After Jones died, several major exhibitions featured his work, much of it signed simply "114591."

FEBRUARY 16

1861 Following orders to return from Fort Mason to Washington, U.S. Army Lieutenant Colonel Robert E. Lee was passing through San Antonio, when he was told by

Confederate officers that he must join the Confederacy, or his baggage would be confiscated. Lee refused and was forced to proceed without his belongings. He never saw them again, even after deciding to serve in the Confederate army after all.

1926   Will Rogers, "age <u>46</u> years and <u>3</u> months, and by occupation a <u>humorist</u>," became a private in the Texas Rangers. He filled out the standard enlistment form, with one modification: The clause regarding salary was crossed out and replaced by "without compensation." Among its other terms, the oath of enlistment required him to certify that he had not "fought a duel with deadly weapons" or acted as a second in one. Certainly Rogers, who never met a man he didn't like, would not have hesitated to attest to that.

FEBRUARY 17

1756   Bernardo de Miranda y Flores, lieutenant governor, set out from San Antonio at the head of two dozen soldiers and civilians, in search of a rumored hill of red, which he and Governor Jacinto de Barrios y Jáuregui presumed meant silver ore. Miranda found the *cerro de almagre*, dug an exploratory shaft, and reported finding enough ore to make every Texan wealthy. Later Captain Diego Parilla of the San Saba mission also collected samples, but Indians destroyed the mission in 1758, and Parilla was never able to return to the site. By the 1770s no one dared approach the area because of attacks by Apaches, but interest in the mine never subsided. Stephen F. Austin sent soldiers to look for it in the 1820s, and the Bowie brothers sought it as well, but by then the location was confused with the San Saba mission, and they found nothing. Finally, in the early twentieth century, Herbert Bolton discovered what was probably the original mine, near Honey Creek in the Riley Mountains; the U.S. Geological Survey examined the ore and declared it worthless. But dreamers continue to hunt for the fabulous silver lode, which they believe is still out there, somewhere.

FEBRUARY 18

1874 Louis Trezevant Wigfall died in Galveston. Elected to the U.S. Senate after the death of J. P. Henderson in June 1858, Wigfall was the most outspoken and vitriolic of the Texan secessionists, a fire-eating anti-abolitionist, and a colorful politician even in an age of colorful politics. He made a point of being present at the beginning of the Civil War, when rebels opened fire on Fort Sumter. Much of his belligerence may have been the result of his alcoholism, or the fact that he believed he was haunted by the ghost of Thomas Bird, the victim of one of Wigfall's numerous duels.

1910 At Houston, famed French aviator Louis Paulhan, license #10 in the Aero Club of France, became the first man to fly above Texas. One gets some idea of the scarcity and excitement of airplanes in those days from the fact that the *Houston Post* and the Western Land Co. paid him $20,000 to fly his Farman biplane as part of a real estate promotion. The first Texan to take to the skies in a heavier-than-air machine seems to have been an L. L. Walker, also of Houston, who flew a Bleriot monoplane eight months later.

FEBRUARY 19

1846 Anson Jones, the last President of the Republic, ended his valedictory speech with the words "The final act in this great drama is now performed; the Republic of Texas is no more," and lowered the Lone Star flag at the annexation cere-

"The Republic of Texas is no more": **Anson Jones** lowers the old flag at the annexation ceremony, in an image more stately than the actual event.

Photo courtesy Texas State Library and Archives Commission

mony in Austin. Before the flag was all the way down, the aged wooden flagpole snapped in two.

FEBRUARY 20

1915 The so-called "Plan of San Diego" was scheduled to commence, in which Mexican Carranzista insurgents would seize control of Texas, New Mexico, Arizona, Colorado, and California, and restore them to Mexico. It was to be a war of extermination, in which all white males sixteen years or older would be executed. The scheme was spoiled in January when Basilio Ramos Jr. was arrested in Brownsville while carrying a copy of the plan. When the great day arrived, violence did not break out, but beginning in the summer, Carranzistas staged a number of border raids which killed twenty-one Americans. The people who suffered the most, however, from the suspicion generated by the Plan of San Diego were Mexicans and Mexican-Americans, some 300 of whom were killed in South Texas simply for looking Hispanic.

FEBRUARY 21

1862   The first major battle in the Confederate campaign to annex the Southwest was a bloody victory for the Rebels. From El Paso, Brigadier General Henry Sibley marched his army of Texans against Fort Craig, a federal outpost in central New Mexico. After a few days of maneuvering, Sibley brought on a battle with the Union garrison, under the command of Colonel Edward Canby, at Val Verde on the Rio Grande. It was a long day of stubborn fighting; two low points for the South were a suicidal charge by a company of Confederate infantry armed only with lances, and Sibley's departure from the field too drunk to command. But in the afternoon they turned Canby's flank and drove the Yankee army back to Fort Craig. Sibley advanced to occupy Albuquerque and Santa Fe and proclaimed Confederate dominion in New Mexico. But before the end of March the tide turned at the Battle of Glorieta, and by May the Texans were back in Texas, having lost a third of their number to wounds, disease, or Union prison camps.

1896   On a sandbar in the middle of the Rio Grande, Judge Roy Bean staged the heavyweight boxing championship between Robert "Ruby Bob" Fitzsimmons and Peter Maher. The bout was originally set to take place in El Paso, but last-minute legislation by opponents of boxing made it illegal to hold it in Texas. The sandbar was in a sort of no-man's land between Texas and Mexico, so the law did not interfere. A ringside seat cost twenty dollars, and Bean sold beer for a dollar a bottle. The fight itself must have been a disappointment, though; Fitzsimmons won after 1 minute and 35 seconds of the first round.

FEBRUARY 22

1817 On Galveston Island, Samuel Bangs and John McLaren used their portable press to create the first document known to have been printed in Texas. The pair were traveling with Francisco Xavier Mina, a twenty-seven-year-old Spanish revolutionary leading an army of fewer than 300 men on an expedition to free Mexico from Spanish rule, and the document was a Manifesto stating Mina's case. The printers and their press landed in Mexico with Mina on April 15, and continued to run off proclamations, patriotic verse, and other propaganda for the cause. But after a few minor successes, Mina was defeated in battle, captured, and executed before the year was out. McLaren had disappeared, but Bangs was taken prisoner; in a rare instance of not killing the messenger, the Royalists let him live and put him to work printing their propaganda instead. When Mexico finally did achieve independence from Spain, the ever-pragmatic Bangs became in turn a printer for the new government.

1819 President John Quincy Adams and Spanish minister Don Luis de Onis signed a treaty giving Florida to the United States and leaving Texas under Spanish control. Many Americans, including Robert Livingston and James Monroe, who negotiated the Louisiana Purchase, and Thomas Jefferson, president at the time of the Purchase in 1803, felt that the territory covered by the agreement had included Texas. In the years since then, a number of "filibustering" expeditions, attempts to seize Texas from Spain, had originated in the United States, although the American government had not sanctioned any of them. The Adams-Onis Treaty failed to bring them to an end; in fact, another one would begin and end before the year was over.

FEBRUARY 23

1888 One of the unforgettable highlights of the first season at Columbus's new Stafford Opera House was a musical troupe known simply as the "Chinese Students." Apparently it was just the wrong fare for a rambunctious Texas town; the audience hissed and booed and wisecracked from beginning to end. Afterwards the manager of the group fired back, calling his hosts "the worst place and the worst people" he'd ever seen. But as the humiliated performers left on the train the next day, the townspeople got in a parting salvo, pelting their helpless victims with a barrage of eggs.

1955 At 7:30 Eastern Time, on a Wednesday night, ABC's *Disneyland* showed "Davy Crockett at the Alamo," the third and final episode of the Frontierland saga "Davy Crockett, King of the Wild Frontier." Fess Parker played Davy, of course, and Buddy Ebsen co-starred as his faithful partner George Russell. The Disney television series itself was only a few months old, but the Crockett serial made it a smash hit, while Crockett merchandise such as coonskin caps and lunch boxes sold like the *Star Wars* junk of another generation. What youngster of those years can ever forget that final image of Davy Crockett standing on the ramparts and swinging Old Betsy?

FEBRUARY 24

1915 E. W. Fry, formerly a judge in Young County, collected a few friends and headed for the courthouse in Graham. A recent audit of county records had found irregularities that led to Fry's indictment, but he couldn't be convicted by evidence that happened to disappear from county files. Deputy Sheriff George Thomas Cherryholmes must have had the same thought, because he and another deputy were guarding the courthouse to prevent just that eventuality. When Fry and his companions, all armed, tried to get in, the sheriff refused, and the result was a gunfight in which Cherryholmes and one of Fry's men were killed. Afterwards, investigators found that the sheriff had fired until he ran out of ammunition. Fry and three other men were tried for murder, but justice was less fastidious in those days, and they were all acquitted.

1967   In Fredericksburg, on what would have been the eighty-second birthday of Chester William Nimitz, his childhood home, the Nimitz Steamboat Hotel, was reopened as the Museum of the Pacific War. Nimitz, a Fleet Admiral of the U.S. Navy and the architect of victory in the Pacific in World War II, had died a year earlier almost to the day. The hotel, which belonged to Nimitz's grandfather and uncle, had a century-long history of its own. It was famous for its distinctive steamboat facade, its comfortable appointments, and the illustrious names that appeared on its guest register, including presidents Hayes and Grant, generals Lee, Sheridan, and Longstreet, and author O. Henry.

FEBRUARY 25

1802   José María Esparza, also known as Gregorio, was born in San Antonio de Béxar. He lived there all his life. When Santa Anna's army reached the city in February 1836, Esparza was a civilian, but he and his family took refuge in the Alamo, since he had served with the rebels who captured San Antonio in the siege of December 1835. They could have left peaceably, but Esparza chose to join the fort's defenders, and he died in the final assault on March 6. Francisco Esparza asked for permission to retrieve his brother's body. This was granted, and so, while all the other Texians were hastily cremated, Gregorio Esparza became the only man from the Alamo to receive a decent burial.

1896   Foster Crawford, bank robber and poet (he often liked to quote Francois Villon), and Elmer "The Slaughter Kid" Lewis held up a bank in Wichita Falls at gunpoint. When cashier Frank Dorsey was too slow opening the vault, one of the two bandits shot him to death. Before they left they wounded another clerk as well. Bill McDonald took after them with a squad of Rangers and caught them in short order, but before they could face trial for murder, they were both lynched from a telegraph pole on the 27th. On hand to watch was George "Tex" Rickard, who had once been a cowhand with Crawford. The pair had invited Rickard to join them in the robbery, but he had declined: "If you boys go and do a damned fool thing like that, the Rangers will ride you down. You're asking me to join you in Boot Hill and I say no to that!" Rickard made the right choice, perhaps more than he knew at that moment, for he had a prosperous life ahead of him, in which he made millions promoting fights and managing boxers, including Jack Dempsey.

❖

FEBRUARY 26

❖

1949   *Lucky Lady II*, a B-50 Superfortress, took off from Carswell Air Force Base in Fort Worth. At the controls was Air Force Captain James Gallagher. The big bomber didn't touch the ground again until March 2, when she landed back at Carswell after her crew of fourteen had completed the first nonstop flight around the world. During their 94 hours in the air they were refueled by B-29s equipped as tankers, and averaged 249 miles per hour in a journey of 23,452 miles.

———————— ❖ ————————

FEBRUARY 27
———————— ❖ ————————

1948 Fort Worth Army Airfield was renamed Carswell Air Force Base, in honor of Major Horace S. Carswell Jr, of Fort Worth. On October 26, 1944, Carswell, a bomber pilot and commander of the 308th Bombardment Group, was flying a B-24 Liberator on a raid against a Japanese convoy when his plane was hit hard by anti-aircraft fire, losing two of its four engines. Most of the crew was able to bail out, but one had his parachute shot up and couldn't jump, so Carswell stayed with the plane and tried to land. The bomber had suffered too much damage; it crashed into a mountainside, killing both men. For sacrificing his own life in a valiant attempt to save that of his crewman, in 1946 Carswell was awarded the Medal of Honor.

———————— ❖ ————————

FEBRUARY 28
———————— ❖ ————————

1948 In San Angelo, twenty-three women met at the San Angelus Hotel to found the Girls Rodeo Association. After decades in which women were expected to contribute nothing to a rodeo but glamor, they had organized the first all-female rodeo in Amarillo in 1947. Now they intended to make women's rodeo a permanent part of the sport, with all-women's events as well as women taking part in Rodeo Cowboys Association (RCA) competitions. Today cowgirls compete in hundreds of rodeos across the country for prizes equal to those awarded to male competitors. When they started the GRA, their total prize money was just $29,000; now it is measured in the millions. Renamed the Women's Professional Rodeo Association in 1982, the WPRA is America's oldest organization for professional female athletes.

FEBRUARY 29

1860 Friederike Recknagel was born on a farm near Round Top, in Fayette County, the daughter of German immigrants. No one knows where Friederike obtained a camera or who taught her to use it, but over a period of about twenty years, beginning in the 1890s, she captured virtually every aspect of life in a small Hill Country town on her glass plates. The buildings, many now lost and unknown save for her images; people in their day-to-day work and play, like hauling logs, knitting, decorating a Christmas tree; special events, such as a Fourth of July parade; the textures of the countryside; she recorded them all in lifelike clarity, without the usual stiff, unnatural poses and sentimentality. After she and her husband left Round Top, Friederike lived another forty years, dying in 1956, but apparently she took no more of her priceless photographs.

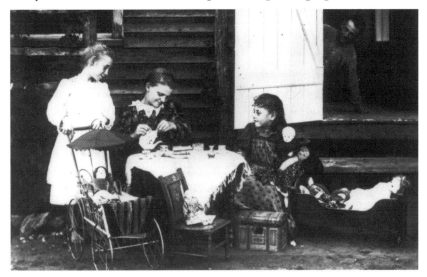

Friederike Recknagel's daughter Louise (right), two friends, and their dolls enjoy tea in 1890s Round Top, while an uninvited guest looks on.

Photo from The UT Institute of Texan Cultures at San Antonio, courtesy of Mr. and Mrs. E. W. Ahlrich

MARCH

✧ MARCH 1 ✧

1939 In Nocona, newspaperman and philanthropist Amon G. Carter fired the starting gun for a Pony Express-style horse race, which would finish at the Golden Gate International Exposition in San Francisco. Enid Justin, the matriarch of the Nocona Boot Company, sponsored the race. Eighteen contestants started off, all but one of them Texans, including one woman. Each rider was allowed to alternate between two horses, the idle one to be trucked ahead to the next switching point. Only eight men finished the race; most simply couldn't make it, but one had to drop out when he and his horse were hit by a car and too badly injured to continue. Shannon Davidson, age twenty-two, of Matador, crossed the line at 2 P.M. on March 24 and claimed his prize: 750 newly minted silver dollars from the San Francisco Mint.

✧ MARCH 2 ✧

1836 At Washington-on-the-Brazos, colonial delegates signed a statement, modeled on Jefferson's Declaration of Independence, proclaiming Texas to be an independent republic. In an irony often overlooked by modern chauvinists, the insurgents would be fighting for the preservation of slavery, which the government of Mexico had abolished seven years before.

1910 At Fort Sam Houston in San Antonio, Lieutenant Benjamin D. Foulois, Army Aviator Number 1, made America's first military air flight in Army Aeroplane Number 1, a Wright brothers biplane with a twenty-five-horsepower pusher engine. He was in the air less than eight minutes, reaching a top speed of 50 miles per hour and an altitude of 100 feet. Foulois, the only designated flyer in the Army Aeronautical Division, took off four times that day; by the end of the fourth flight, a crowd of thousands had gathered to watch. His abrupt fourth landing, which caused $300 in damage (and incidentally prompted an ad hoc innovation, the safety belt), put an end to the day's entertainment. But, although no one could have understood it at the time, the United States Air Force had just been born.

Watched by a growing crowd, Lieutenant Benjamin D. Foulois prepares for takeoff in **Army Aeroplane Number 1** at Fort Sam Houston.

Photo courtesy Texas State Library and Archives Commission

❖

MARCH 3

❖

1906 Attorney and former governor Jim Hogg died in Houston at the age of fifty-five. He had hoped to travel to Battle Creek, Michigan, to treat a throat abscess, but did not set out in time. Among the bequests in Hogg's will, he left his four children the Patton plantation, an estate near Columbia. Hogg had bought the land in 1901, certain that it would eventually produce oil, though he never exploited it himself. In his will he forbade his heirs to sell the land for fifteen years after his death. On January 4, 1918, the West Columbia oilfield came in; overnight, Will, Mike, Tom, and Ima Hogg (there was no Ura) became millionaires.

❖

MARCH 4

❖

1801 Lieutenant M. Muzquiz left Nacogdoches with 100 men to track down and arrest a band of Americans under Philip Nolan, who was reportedly plotting to recruit Indians for a revolt against Spain. Nolan had entered Texas on other occasions for the purpose of capturing mustangs, which he took back to the United States to sell, but some Spanish officials suspected that this expedition had greater, more sinister objectives. On March 21 Muzquiz found Nolan installed in a small wooden fort, at a location which is now uncertain; historians' guesses cover Johnson, Tarrant, McLennan, and Hill Counties. When Nolan refused to surrender, no doubt this confirmed Spanish suspicions of his hostile purposes, and a pitched battle soon followed. Nolan himself was killed when a cannonball struck him, and the men in the fort soon gave themselves up. Two dozen Americans, Spaniards, and black slaves were captured and imprisoned for several years. Nolan's last incursion into Texas may have been just another commercial venture, or it may have been the first of several attempts to create a free Texas. For the next thirty-five years, all such attempts would fail.

MARCH 5

1852 Work began on the new state Capitol building, on Capitol Square in Austin. On July 3 the cornerstone was laid in a grand Masonic ceremony, not surprising since in those days four out of five men of importance in the Texas government were Freemasons. No architectural drawings of the Capitol exist today, but at the time the plans were criticized as sloppy and incomplete. The resulting building was considered structurally unsound, and critics wondered why the result differed from the plans, which described a larger, more ornate structure. Charges of corruption had no effect, however, and the new Capitol building opened in November of 1853.

The old State Capitol building stands in Austin circa 1875,
a few years before a careless clerk burned the place down.

Photo courtesy Texas State Library and Archives Commission

1938 When Gene Howe, editor of the Amarillo *Globe-News*, wanted to atone for offending his mother-in-law, he went about it Texas-style. Howe was the author of a daily column called "The Tactless Texan," signed by "Old Tack," and one day Old Tack was too tactless to suit her. So to make up, Howe proclaimed March 5 to be National Mothers-in-Law Day and organized a parade in which a block-long float carried 650 mothers-in-law. By chance, Eleanor Roosevelt was in Amarillo to deliver a lecture; the First Lady was also a mother-in-law, so Howe invited her to join him on the reviewing stand and presented her with a bouquet of 4,000 roses.

❖

MARCH 6

❖

1836 In the dawn assault by the army under Santa Anna, all the defenders of the Alamo were killed. Among them were Andrés Nava and Damacio Jiménez, both in the company commanded by Juan Seguín. When Texas adopted a new constitution after seceding in early 1861, one of its provisions was the guarantee of free land to the heirs of anyone killed in the service of the revolution. Nava's sister and half-brother applied for a grant, based on the testimony of a San Antonio resident who swore that he had recognized Nava among the dead when they were collected for cremation. The nephew and niece of Jiménez filed a similar claim, based on not only a similar eyewitness to the presence of his corpse among the slain but an affidavit from Seguín, still alive because he had left the Alamo as a messenger shortly before the catastrophe. Both pleas were left pending, however, because the petitioners were too poor to pay the fees necessary to pursue their claims, and neither man's descendants ever obtained due recognition for his sacrifice.

1861   Early aviator Samuel Franklin Cody was born in Birdville. He grew up on a ranch and worked as a cowboy until he was twenty-six, becoming an expert horseman and a crack shot. He then joined a Wild West show, in which he starred as "Captain Cody, King of the Cowboys." His wife, whom he had met in England on a trip to deliver some horses, urged him to start a troupe of his own and perform in London. The Codys, with two of their sons, were an instant hit as "The Great Codys" not just in England but across Europe. By now a resident of England, Cody began seriously experimenting with another boyhood interest, kites. From kites he progressed to dirigibles. He worked on the first British airship, the *Nulli Secondis,* which he flew from Farnborough to London. The inevitable next step was heavier-than-air machines. On October 16, 1908, Cody took off from Farnborough in a craft of his own design and flew a quarter of a mile, the first flight in British history. He went on to build other airplanes, including a seaplane and the *Flying Cathedral*, then the largest plane in the world. But in August 1913 he was killed in the crash of his *Cathedral VI*. His death was a national tragedy, and 50,000 Britons attended his funeral. At Farnborough, a hallowed site in British aviation, his monument is a cast of the tree to which he used to anchor his experimental airplanes. Astonishingly, Cody was virtually illiterate all his life and could barely scrawl his own name.

————— ❖ —————

MARCH 7
————— ❖ —————

1850   Governor Peter H. Bell declared March 7 an annual day of Thanksgiving for Texans. The occasion was actually supposed to be a solemn expression of thanks for the blessings of freedom won by the Revolution of 1836. But Bell wanted to delay it a few days from March 2, the date on which the Texas Declaration of Independence was signed, because Independence Day itself had become the pretext for uninhibited drinking, firing guns into the air, and every other sort of wild behavior.

1901   At the request of the Society of Colonial Dames in Texas, the legislature named the bluebonnet the official state flower. Representative John Nance Garner had advocated the cactus instead, because, unlike the bluebonnet, it was a native plant; his position earned him the nickname "Cactus Jack." But the bluebonnet camp prevailed, and since that day, generations of drivers on the state's highways have been grateful every spring.

—————— ❖ ——————
MARCH 8
—————— ❖ ——————

1942   Dutch forces on the island of Java surrendered to the invading Japanese army. As a consequence the U.S. Army's 2nd Battalion, 131st Field Artillery, 36th Infantry Division, which had only arrived on January 11, was also compelled to surrender. The 36th had been the Texas National Guard until it was mobilized in late 1940, so the battalion was almost entirely composed of Texans. When other American forces on the island were ordered to fall back to Australia, the 2nd was left behind for the good of Allied morale, thereby earning the somber title the "Lost Battalion." The Texans were assigned to a series of harsh POW camps before reaching Burma, where they were forced to work on the infamous "Railroad of Death," including the bridge over the Kwai River. Many of them were among the 70,000 prisoners who died there.

1971   The State Legislature defined the bluebonnet—also known as buffalo clover, wolf flower, and *el conejo* (the rabbit)— to be "*Lupinus Texensis* and any other variety of bluebonnet not heretofore recorded." This was a significant clarification of the original act of 1901, which merely said *Lupinus subcarnosus*.

---❖---

MARCH 9

---❖---

1886 Ida Darden, conservative journalist, was born in Bosque County. In 1916 she began working for the Texas Association Opposed to Woman Suffrage, which viewed votes for women as a feminist fad, a socialist conspiracy, and a threat to white supremacy in that it would encourage black women to vote. Their cause failed in 1920 with the adoption of the Nineteenth Amendment, but Darden continued her work for conservative causes. In January of 1950 she started up a newspaper, the *Southern Conservative*, in Fort Worth. It made her a statewide celebrity—a hero to the Right, and a crank in the eyes of liberals. Every issue in the paper's eleven-year life was dedicated to exposing the subversive movements and degenerate trends that threatened the American Way. Darden's targets included civil rights activism, atheism, taxation of any kind, modern art, the Supreme Court (which she thought should be impeached to a man), and Dwight Eisenhower, whom she considered a Communist doormat.

---❖---

MARCH 10

---❖---

1831 Some two and a half months after colonists had requested it from the provincial government, a bronze six-pound cannon arrived at Gonzales. The townspeople had asked for the gun as protection from Indians, and it was probably mounted on a swivel atop a blockhouse as a conspicuous deterrent against attack. In September 1835, as relations between Mexico and Anglo settlers deteriorated, Colonel Domingo de Ugartechea sent six soldiers from Bexar to take the cannon back. The colonists refused to give it up; they captured the soldiers, buried the gun, and called for help from surrounding settlements. Ugartechea tried again, this time with a force of 100 men. On October 2 their commander, Lieutenant Castañeda, asked for the gun, pointing out that it had been loaned to the town on condition that it be returned to the Mexican military on demand. But the Texian militiamen pointed to the cannon behind their lines, which they had meanwhile dug up and mounted on a carriage, and replied, "There it is—come and take it." Soon they were flying a flag with the same bold words stitched across it. A brief skirmish between the two forces took place, but Castañeda was outnumbered; he also had orders not to start a war. So he withdrew without the cannon. The famous gun eventually found its way to San Antonio, but there it was captured in the fall of the Alamo and melted down.

❖ MARCH 11 ❖

1784   Richard Bache, opponent of Texas annexation, was born in Philadelphia, the son of Benjamin Franklin's daughter Sarah. In 1836, for reasons that are not clear today, Bache left Philadelphia and traveled to Texas, deserting his wife of thirty-one years and their nine children. He rose through a variety of posts in the government of the Republic, and in 1845 he was a delegate to the convention on annexation. George M. Dallas, the brother of the wife he had left in Philadelphia, was now vice president of the United States, and when Bache cast his vote against annexation, the only nay vote of the convention, it was understood that he did so to spite his brother-in-law.

1884   Marshal Ben Thompson of Austin, with his friend John King Fisher, also a lawman and a proficient killer, boldly entered the Vaudeville Theatre in San Antonio. Two years before, Thompson and Jack "Pegleg" Harris, who owned the place, had faced each other in a shootout, and Harris had gone to Boot Hill. Thompson had recently been acquitted in his trial for murder, and now he was back to flaunt his victory by celebrating in his victim's old territory. But for Joe Foster and other friends of Harris, that must have been going too far; Thompson and Fisher both died in a flurry of gunfire.

MARCH 12

1920 In Galveston, 1,600 longshoremen went on strike in unity with dockworkers in other ports on the Gulf and the South Atlantic. The steamship lines used a devious strategy to undermine union loyalties by hiring black scabs to replace white union workers and white scabs to replace black workers. This increased racial tensions on the docks to such a level that Governor Hobby ordered in first Texas Rangers, then a thousand National Guardsmen, to protect the strikebreakers. Finally he declared martial law, suspending the city government and police; suits filed against Hobby and the National Guard, both by the city commissioners and by private parties, were dismissed in court. The longshoremen were back on the job by July of 1921, but they were discouraged by the overt support of open shops by the state. Worse news for them, the legislature, prodded by Hobby, made it illegal to hinder trade within the state, effectively outlawing any strike. An appeals court ruled the law unconstitutional in 1926, but organized labor in Texas was a long time recovering.

MARCH 13

1956 Champion diver David Browning, less than a year out of the naval aviation school at Pensacola, died in the crash of his carrier jet fighter on a training mission in Kansas. Skippy Browning, from 1949 to 1952 the star diver for the University of Texas, was a favorite to win gold in the upcoming Melbourne

Olympics. In 1952, his senior year at UT, he had won the Olympic gold medal in springboard diving in Helsinki, along with his fourth AAU and NCAA championships. He was just about to resume training for Melbourne when he was killed.

MARCH 14

1839   As William Harris Wharton was dismounting from a horse at his brother-in-law's home near Hempstead, his pistol accidentally fired and killed him. Wharton moved to Texas in 1827, and quickly became a prominent agitator for independence. After the revolution, he was Texas's first minister to the United States, with the mission of procuring at least their recognition, and preferably annexation. Wharton succeeded in the first goal, but not the second. He was returning to Texas when his ship was captured by the Mexican navy and he was imprisoned in Matamoros, but he escaped and reached home in time for the 1838 elections, in which he became a state senator. Great things were expected of him, but he died in this perverse accident at the age of only thirty-six.

1964   In the Third Criminal District Court of Dallas County, Judge Joseph Brantley Brown sentenced Jacob L. Rubenstein (Jack Ruby) to death by electrocution for murdering Lee Harvey Oswald. This was the first time in American history that a judge had pronounced a death sentence on national television. Jack Ruby, however, died of cancer before the sentence was carried out.

MARCH 15

1865   Thomas Jefferson Chambers, feisty and egotistical lawyer, land speculator, political aspirant, and murderer, was in the parlor of his Anahuac home with his family when he was killed by a shotgun blast through a window. It is reasonable to presume that the killer was one of Chambers's adversaries in his multitude of contentious land schemes, for, like him, they took their land rights seriously. In 1842 Chambers returned from a trip to the U.S. to find that a John O'Brian had bought one of his tracts for back taxes; he killed O'Brian from ambush and was never indicted. He didn't triumph in the end, however, for O'Brian's widow successfully sued for title to the land in 1855. The year after Chambers was murdered, Charles Willcox, his rival in Anahuac as far back as 1838, bought his land from his widow.

1912 Bluesman Sam "Lightnin'" Hopkins was born in Centerville. He made his first guitar when he was eight years old, from a cigar box and chicken wire. He acquired the nickname "Lightnin'" in the 1940s when he was recording in Los Angeles with piano player Wilson "Thunder" Smith. That session was the first of Hopkins's forty-three records for the Aladdin label, and Aladdin was the first of the nearly twenty labels that put out his records. Like some other black blues players, Hopkins suddenly found himself a hit with the folk music lovers of the 1960s. Instead of small blues clubs, he was playing Carnegie Hall and a command performance in London for the Queen of England. He continued to record, and his albums finally numbered almost ninety, but a 1970 automobile accident slowed him down and curtailed his touring. When he died of cancer in 1982, over 4,000 fans attended his funeral.

❖ MARCH 16

1758 Comanche, Taovaya, and Tonkawa Indians attacked the Mission San Saba de la Santa Cruz, near modern Menard. All but one of the priests were slaughtered; Miguel Molina was wounded but escaped and was rescued after days alone in the wilds. In 1759 Colonel Diego Ortiz Parrilla set out from San Antonio with a retaliatory force of more than 600, including 100 Apaches. On October 7 they reached the area now known as Spanish Fort, where they found the Taovayas in a well-fortified camp over which flew, to their surprise, a French flag. Parrilla attacked, but the Indians fought with a discipline that Parrilla had not counted on. After he had lost fifty men and gained nothing, he could only retreat to San Saba, leaving behind two precious cannon. His mission to chastise the Indians had turned into a humiliating fiasco for himself.

1918   In Fort Worth, the world's first indoor rodeo held its final competitive events, part of the Southwestern Exposition and Fat Stock Show. In the North Side Coliseum, a crowd of more than 20,000 watched as cowboys competed for a purse of $3,000. Staged that year for the first time, the rodeo boosted attendance dramatically, and it instantly became a perennial feature of the Stock Show.

❖ MARCH 17 ❖

1949   In Houston, "Diamond Glenn" McCarthy, King of the Wildcatters, chose Saint Patrick's Day to open his new Shamrock Hotel on Main Street. One hundred seventy-five movie stars and other celebrities were there for the million-dollar blowout. NBC broadcast Dorothy Lamour's radio program live from the Emerald Room, but drunken gate crashers drowned out the performers, then took over the microphone and yelled off-color jokes directly over the uncensored airwaves. NBC cut to another program, and Lamour left in a tearful fury. The hotel itself was not known for tasteful restraint; overpowered by the garish green decor, Frank Lloyd Wright commented, "I always wondered what the inside of a juke box looked like."

❖

MARCH 18

❖

1877 Near what is now Lubbock, about forty buffalo hunters from Rath City attacked the camp of a Comanche party that had killed and scalped one hunter and raided several others. The Indians, led by Black Horse, had a permit from the Fort Sill reservation agent to hunt in Texas, but they were after white men, not buffalo. For several days the hunters, some on horseback and the rest on foot, had trailed the Comanches to Yellow House Canyon, and now, although it was already midday, they decided to strike. The Indians saw that they outnumbered their opponents and stayed to fight instead of running. Both sides tried to charge but were driven back. After a few hours, the hunters recognized that they would have to retreat. They built fires as a decoy and pulled out in the dark, with one man dead and two wounded. A cavalry detachment from Fort Griffin took up the chase, overtook the Comanches in May, and forced them back to the reservation. Like a number of historic sites in Texas, the battleground at Hidden Canyon is now underwater, in Canyon Lake.

1937 Just after 3:00 in the afternoon, shop teacher Lemmie Butler turned on a sander in the basement classroom of the London Consolidated School in New London, Rusk County. No one knew that natural gas had been seeping into the building from a leaky pipeline; the tiny spark from the switch set off a gigantic explosion which seemed to lift the entire building bodily, then the roof and walls collapsed. In a matter of seconds the modern new school had been converted to rubble, with hundreds of students and teachers trapped beneath it. Rusk County was oil country, so heavy equipment was not hard to come by. Medical aid came from all over Texas and neighboring states. Rescuers worked all night to dig out the victims, despite the spring rain. But the death toll was appalling; the exact

Rescue crews work desperately through the night to free students and teachers trapped in the rubble of the New London school.

Photo courtesy Texas State Library and Archives Commission

count could never be known, but it was at least 300. The subsequent inquiry revealed that the school's gas supply came from a "green" gas line which plumbers had tapped to save money, with the approval of the school board. Green gas was odorless, so the leak was never noticed. The legislature passed a law requiring that all gas for commercial use be mixed with a malodorant to aid in the detection of leaks. But for the devastated community of New London, the law came too late.

———————— ❖ ————————
MARCH 19
———————— ❖ ————————

1924 Charles Lindbergh landed his Curtiss Canuck biplane at Brooks Field in San Antonio and reported for army flight school. His month-long trip from Pensacola, Florida, had taken a roundabout route. He and his friend Leon Klink had decided they wanted to fly to California, where Lindbergh could catch a train and make it to San Antonio in time. But at the end of one of the westward legs across Texas, they landed in Camp Wood, using the town square in lieu of a suitable field. This wasn't so unusual in the days of the barnstormers. But the next day, when they wanted to take off again, the wind was in a different direction, and they had to settle for a street that happened to be favorably aligned. Unfortunately, a pair of telegraph poles interfered. Lindbergh measured the space between them and reckoned he had a foot to spare on each side, but his right wing caught one of them and the Canuck spun into the front of a hardware store. The owner figured the publicity was worth more than the damage done, and he told Lindbergh not to worry about paying for repairs. But the trip to California was off; there was barely time to make the plane airworthy again and hurry on to Brooks Field.

❖ MARCH 20 ❖

1903 Olive Ann Fairchild died in Sherman, aged about sixty-five. In her home was a jar of hazelnuts, a reminder of her five years as an Indian captive, when she often lived on nothing else. When she was about thirteen, her family was traveling alone across Arizona when Apaches attacked. They slaughtered all but Olive and her sister Mary and kept the girls as slaves until they sold them to a Mojave chief. After four more years of miserable treatment, during which Mary died, the army ransomed Olive. She then found that her brother Lorenzo had survived the massacre. A biography of the brother and sister published in 1857 was a bestseller and paid for their college education. But Olive was obliged to lecture on tour to help book sales, and she hated appearing in public without the veil that she normally wore to cover the blue tattoo that had marked her as a slave. She spent the last thirty years of her life in Sherman with her husband, a rancher, who burned every copy of *Life Among the Indians* he could find.

MARCH 21

1845 On Good Friday, Prince Karl Zum Solms-Braunfels, Commissioner-General of the Society for the Protection of German Immigrants in Texas, founded a new colony on 1,300 acres bordering the Comal River, naming it New Braunfels. The prince's colorful residence resembled a miniature Bavarian duchy in the Texas wilderness, complete with plumed courtiers. The 200 colonists began a lasting German legacy in the region; their newspaper, the *Neu Braunsfelser Zeitung*, was printed in German for more than a century.

MARCH 22

1894 The freight train carrying Lewis C. Fry and 700 recruits for Coxey's army pulled into El Paso. Social crusader Jacob Coxey had called on unemployed men across the country to converge on Washington and demand public works programs that would create jobs. Fry was the commander of the Los Angeles contingent. In El Paso, they marched to the city hall and camped there overnight. The next day they marched back to the railyards to wait for the next eastbound train, but Southern Pacific management was not interested in subsidizing them and held back every suitable train until the 25th. Fry's men then boarded a freight train, but seventy miles east of town it stopped, and the crew uncoupled the cars and left them sitting in the desert with no food or water. For three days the Southern Pacific ignored protests from El Paso, from Texans across the state, and even Governor Hogg, and the cars did not move until the people of El Paso collected enough money to pay for a special train. Fry and his weary followers reached San Antonio on the 29th and left Texas via Texarkana on April 1. Their numbers dwindled en route. By the time the remnant reached Washington, Coxey was already under arrest for walking on the Capitol lawn and the army had evaporated.

MARCH 23

1892 Painter William Henry Huddle died in Austin of a stroke at the age of forty-five. Huddle specialized in subjects from Texas history and portraits of notable Texans. He portrayed all the presidents of the Republic, followed by the first seventeen governors. He painted Hood's Texas Brigade at the Battle of the Wilderness, and this was received well enough to hang in the old Capitol; ironically this recognition brought about the painting's doom when the building burned down in 1881. Huddle's most famous work by far is *The Surrender of Santa Anna*, which he completed in 1886; five years later the legislature provided $4,000 to buy the painting, and today it still hangs in the Capitol building, easily the most familiar painting of any event in the history of Texas.

MARCH 24

1880 With the rancor of Reconstruction fading, General Phil Sheridan gave a speech at the Tremont Hotel in Galveston, in which he offered a light-hearted apology for the notorious remark that he had made in August of 1866. He explained that at the time it was the peak of summer and he had just endured a long, hard, hot, dusty coach ride from San Antonio when he grumbled, "If I owned Texas and all of Hell, I would rent out Texas and live in Hell."

❖
MARCH 25
❖

1899   After four years of construction, the canal linking Port Arthur to the Gulf of Mexico opened. Arthur Stilwell, the project's guiding hand and Port Arthur's namesake, claimed that his expansive plans for the city were dictated to him by "Brownies" from the spirit world. In 1901, when the nearby Spindletop oil deposits were discovered, the canal proved to be far more valuable than even Arthur Stilwell's ethereal mentors could have predicted.

1918   Fifty Mexican brigands on horseback raided the ranch of Edwin Neville, on the Rio Grande in Presidio County. As Neville and his son Glen ran to a ditch for cover, a rifle bullet hit Glen in the head and killed him. Edwin escaped, but Rosa Castillo, the family housekeeper was also killed; the raiders savaged both bodies. Two troops of U.S. cavalry arrived soon and chased the Mexicans across the river. They caught up with them in the village of Pilares, where a gunfight erupted. The Americans killed thirty-three Mexicans and destroyed the village; one U.S. soldier also died. The raid may have been revenge for another border incident, or it may have been prompted by Pancho Villa, or it may have been mere pillage. Edwin Neville didn't care; for the next thirty years and more, until he died, he waged a private war against the people who killed his son.

❖
MARCH 26
❖

1937   In Crystal City, Zavala County, the "Spinach Capital of the World," the second annual Spinach Festival was enlivened by the dedication of a six-foot concrete statue of Popeye the Sailor Man, complete with painted features and sailor's uniform. According to America's spinach industry experts, between 1931 and 1936 Popeye single-handedly brought about a 33 percent increase in spinach consumption. More than a half century later, Texans are still indebted to Popeye, for Texas is one of America's greatest spinach growing states.

———————— ❖ ————————

MARCH 27

———————— ❖ ————————

1960 Four students from Saint Mary's University in San Antonio, spelunking in the hill country southwest of New Braunfels, discovered the largest cave ever found in Texas. They were not the first people to visit Natural Bridge Caverns, though; 7,000-year-old arrowheads and spearheads have been found near the entrance. Those ancient Indians may have seen the sixty-foot limestone bridge where the cavern opens to the surface, but they never saw the other curious formations inside the cave, like the Hall of the Mountain Kings, 100 feet high and 350 feet long, or the distinctive stalagmites aptly named "fried eggs."

———————— ❖ ————————

MARCH 28

———————— ❖ ————————

1862 Southern hopes of extending the Confederacy across the Southwest to the Pacific came to an end, when an army of Texans was defeated by Union forces at the Battle of Glorieta Pass in New Mexico. The Rebels actually won the main encounter, repeatedly outflanking the Federals and forcing them to retreat. But the Union commander had detached a third of his soldiers to circle around to the enemy's supply train miles to the rear, which was guarded by only a token force. They burned all eighty wagons of ammunition, food, and medicine. The Confederates could claim a tactical victory, but the destruction of their supplies was a strategic calamity. In desolate territory that could never support an army by foraging, they had no choice but to return to Texas.

❖

MARCH 29

❖

1813 In one of the early campaigns to make Texas independent of Spain, a motley army of 800 American adventurers and disgruntled Texans defeated a larger Spanish force near San Antonio. They had originally been recruited by U.S. Army Lieutenant August Magee, but he had died of tuberculosis on February 6, and the filibusters were now under the command of José Bernardo Maximiliano Gutiérrez de Lara. Gutierrez permitted the Royalists to surrender their arms and leave in peace, but he had a score to settle with some of the Spanish officers; he ordered fourteen of them executed, including the provincial governors of Texas and Nuevo León, and their throats were cut. Most of the Americans left his army in disgust when they heard of this atrocity. They didn't know it then, but they saved their own lives as well as their self-respect, for in August the rebel army was crushed at Medina, and hundreds died in Royalist reprisals across Texas.

❖

MARCH 30

❖

1870 President Ulysses S. Grant signed the bill that readmitted Texas to the Union. Under the Reconstruction Acts, Congress ruled that each Confederate state had to ratify the Thirteenth, Fourteenth, and Fifteenth Amendments to the United States Constitution, and adopt a new state constitution which provided suffrage for all adult males regardless of race, before it could be considered for readmission. Naturally, Texas was the last state to fulfill these requirements; with Texas finally rehabilitated, the era of Reconstruction was officially over.

1892 C. P. Huntington, president of the Southern Pacific Railroad, rode the first train to cross the new Pecos High

Bridge, completed in just eighty-seven working days. At 321 feet above the Pecos River, the 2,180-foot span was the highest railroad bridge in North America and the third highest in the world. The bridge no longer stands; it was replaced by a parallel bridge in 1943 and dismantled. But it was still there in 1920, when a young daredevil flyer named Jimmy Doolittle flew his DH-4 under it. The clearance between his wingtips and the spans was so close that he had to check it by first flying his shadow between them. As he was about to fly underneath, he noticed telephone wires directly in his approach path. It was a close call; the wires left nicks in his propeller. Later Doolittle heard that the lineman who had to repair the severed wires did not think his stunt was very funny.

———————— ❖ ————————
MARCH 31
———————— ❖ ————————

1878   Boxer Jack Johnson was born in Galveston. He picked up his boxing skills as a sparring partner and in "battles royal," in which white spectators threw money to the winners of fights between blacks. After being arrested in 1900 for boxing, which was then illegal in Texas, he left the state for good. In 1903 he won the Negro heavyweight championship, but it was five more years before a white boxer would agree to meet him in the ring for the world championship, when he beat Tommy Burns in Sydney, Australia. Only after he knocked out Jim Jeffries, the "Great White Hope," in Reno in 1910, was he officially recognized as the world champion. In 1915 he lost the title in Havana to Jess Willard, a white boxer, by a knockout in the 26th round. He later claimed he had thrown the fight in the hope of re-entering the United States without being prosecuted under the Mann Act; but he eventually served a year for his "crime," a charge concocted by some who resented his boxing prowess almost as much as they did his succession of white wives and mistresses.

APRIL

❖

APRIL 1

1921 Governor Pat Neff vetoed a bill that would have created the West Texas Agricultural and Mechanical College. But Austin's neglect of the western half of the state was a sensitive issue going back to before the turn of the century, and the next day, at a rally in Sweetwater, citizens of several western counties resolved "that we the said citizens here assembled, suggest that if our demands are not complied with by the next special session of the state legislature we will call for the creation of a new state under which we may hope to have equal rights and representation." The legislature may or may not have taken this threat to secede seriously, but a year later the act to found the Texas Technological College did pass. A committee selected Lubbock as the site, and Texas Tech opened its doors in the fall of 1924.

1934 On Easter Sunday, Highway Patrolmen E. D. Wheeler and H. D. Murphy, on motorcycle duty, noticed a car parked at the side of the road a few miles west of Grapevine. As they pulled over and walked toward the vehicle, one of them remarked, "Looks like you folks might have some trouble." A few seconds later they both fell under a blast of gunfire from Bonnie and Clyde. Unaware that she was observed by an old man sitting under a nearby tree, Bonnie calmly walked over and shot one trooper in the face with a sawed-off shotgun, then laughed "look-a-there, his head bounced just like a rubber ball." Then she and Clyde drove off, leaving both officers dead in the road.

APRIL 2

1855 Former Texas Ranger and Indian fighter Nelson Lee, with a party of men driving horses from Brownsville to California, was attacked by Comanches, who took him captive, according to his thrilling account in *Three Years Among the Camanches* [sic]: *The Narrative of Nelson Lee, the Texas Ranger,* published by the Baker Taylor Company in 1859. However, Lee's story was so full of fanciful details that it was hard to know what to believe even among the parts that were not impossible. He escaped death by a hair's-breadth many times, in as many implausible ways. He described his Comanche captors writing in hieroglyphics, planting crops, and building wooden houses on rectilinear streets. It is clear that Lee's book is an example not of early Texas history, but early Texas fiction.

1917 Thomas Terry Connally was seated in the U.S. House of Representatives as a member from Texas. On the same day, President Wilson asked Congress to declare war on Germany. Connally was quickly commissioned as a captain in the army, but at the time of the Armistice he was still in the States. Reflecting on his military career during the Spanish-American War, in which he also volunteered for the Texas Infantry but never reached Cuba, Connally lamented, "I have been in more wars and fought less than any living man."

---❖---
APRIL 3
---❖---

1941 Jeff Hamilton, former slave of Sam Houston, died in Belton, two weeks short of his 101st birthday. In October 1853, at a slave auction in Huntsville, Houston noticed the thirteen-year-old boy crying and bought him from James McKell, who was selling him to pay off a whiskey bill. Hamilton worked in the Houston household as a comparatively pampered slave for the next nine years, until Houston freed all his slaves in 1862. He was the children's playmate and Houston's valet, driver, bodyguard, and office boy. Unlike many slaves, he was permitted to learn the three Rs. After Sam Houston died, Hamilton stayed with the family, although he was free to leave, and was with them until Margaret Lea Houston also died in 1867. For the rest of his life he was an honorary Houston, and in his later years he was a celebrity regarded for his stories of the Houstons and the other important Texans he had met in Sam Houston's service.

1944 By an eight-to-one majority, the United States Supreme Court ruled that the Texas Democratic Party could not bar Lonnie Smith, a black dentist from Houston, from voting in its primary elections on the basis of his race. The Court stated that such discrimination violated the Fifteenth Amendment, because a political party was not a private association. The attorneys who won this final appeal, four years after Smith had first tried to vote in a Harris County primary, included future Supreme Court justice Thurgood Marshall.

---❖---
APRIL 4
---❖---

1969 At Saint Luke's Episcopal Hospital in Houston, Doctor Denton Cooley planted the world's first artificial heart in the chest of Haskell Karp of Skokie, Illinois. The device, now in the Smithsonian, kept Karp alive for sixty-four hours while he waited for a donor, then he received a transplanted human heart. But on April 8, having briefly regained consciousness, he died of pneumonia and kidney failure.

APRIL 5

1869 Fed up with being terrorized by outlaw Benjamin F. Bickerstaff and his gang, the townspeople of Alvarado were waiting in ambush when he and another man rode into town. Accustomed to taking whatever he wanted, Bickerstaff saw them scurrying for cover and sneered, "Rats, to your holes." But he had scarcely dismounted when a fusillade killed his partner and mortally wounded him. As he lay dying, the doctor tending him suggested he should reveal the names of his fellow badmen. Bickerstaff asked, "Doctor, can you keep a secret?" "Yes, I surely can," the doctor replied. The unrepentant killer sighed, "So can I."

1896 Sometime El Paso lawman John Selman, free on bond after a hung jury in his first trial for murdering John Wesley Hardin, got into a late-night altercation with fellow "lawman" George W. Scarborough outside the Wigwam Saloon. Selman was drunk and never went for his pistol, but Scarborough shot him four times. Selman protested to the people who gathered at the scene, "You know I am not afraid of any man, but I never drew my gun." He died the next day. Scarborough was tried for murder, but though his victim had not tried to fire first, the fact that he was armed was enough to bring in a ruling of self-defense.

❖
APRIL 6

❖

1843 Former judge and Lieutenant Governor James W. Robinson arrived at Washington-on-the-Brazos with a proposition from Santa Anna to re-admit Texas as a state of Mexico, but with special privileges. Robinson had been captured in 1842 during the Mexican incursion into Texas and had suggested the offer to Santa Anna from prison, so he may have seen the venture as just a means to get himself out of Mexico. In any case, President Sam Houston dictated a letter to Santa Anna over Robinson's signature, which said, albeit using the elaborate and formal prose of the day, "Go to Hell." But he would allow no official acknowledgment of the insulting suggestion.

1854 Lieutenant Curd Givens and the two companies under his command marched out of Fort Phantom Hill, on the Clear Fork of the Brazos in what is now Jones County. No one in the garrison, probably not even Givens, could have been sorry to hear that the fort was to be closed. It was one of the most detested posts on the Texas frontier, incompetently situated far from water, which soldiers had to haul four miles from a spring, and timber, for which they had to travel as far as forty miles. Perhaps no one wanted to risk being sent back, or perhaps it was just an act of spite, but during the proceedings the fort burned to the ground. Givens was court-martialed twice as a result; the first time he was acquitted, but the second time he received a four-month suspension. Still, he managed to die a captain in 1859.

❖

APRIL 7

1886 A melee in the streets of Laredo between rival political factions became the only known instance in which one side of a Texas feud used a cannon. In Laredo in the 1880s, Raymond Martin led the wealthy Botas (boots), and David Gonzales led the working-class Guaraches (sandals). On the evening of April 6, after a city election that had gone badly for the Guaraches, they dug up an old muzzle-loader that had been planted upright as a hitching post, cleaned it up, mounted it on wheels, loaded it with black powder, and touched it off, to show that they were not discouraged. In response the Botas planned a parade for the next day, to mark the end of "El Club Gonzales-Guarache." Guaraches intercepted the Botas parade, bringing on a massive gun battle that killed at least sixteen men from either side. It took two companies of infantry, one company of cavalry, and a detachment of Texas Rangers to restore the peace.

❖

APRIL 8

1841 James Pinckney Henderson, Saint Augustine lawyer and future first governor of the state of Texas, was acquitted in the shooting death of "a desperado named N. B. Garner, whom I was at last forced to Slay" after Garner repeatedly waylaid Henderson and threatened to kill him. "I regret that the beast forced me to do that which some ruffian ought to have done but I shall never regret that I killed him as I am sure he would have killed me."

❖
APRIL 9
❖

1554 Four ships carrying treasure from New Spain sailed from San Juan de Ulúa under the command of Captain-General Antonio Corzo, with a combined cargo worth two million pesos (more than twenty million dollars today). On the 29th a storm drove three of the vessels ashore on Padre Island; the fourth, the *San Andrés*, limped into Havana fit only to be scrapped after the contents of its holds were transferred to other ships bound for Spain. Most of the roughly three hundred people aboard the three wrecks drowned in the breakers. Of those who reached land, some set off for Mexico in a boat to report the disaster and bring rescuers back; the rest began walking back to Mexico, having badly underestimated the distance. Indians and exposure accounted for all but one man, Fray Marcos de Mena, who staggered into Pánuco weeks later. The ordeal left chips from seven arrowheads painfully embedded in his skin until he died thirty years later.

1965 After three years of construction which cost double the amount originally funded, the Harris County Domed Stadium, acclaimed by the men behind it as "The Eighth Wonder of the World" but generally referred to as the Astrodome, hosted its first event: an exhibition game between the Houston Astros, once the Colt 45s, and the New York Yankees. In the first regular season game in the dome, the Philadelphia Phillies beat the Astros in a two-run shutout. Football didn't come to the dome until 1968, when the Houston Oilers moved in. Players may hate it, but the stadium's other claim to fame is the grass substitute known as Astroturf, first invented for use there because grass couldn't grow in the dim light.

---❖---
APRIL 10
---❖---

1794 Don Pedro de Nava, Commandante General of the Interior Provinces of New Spain, decreed that almost all missions in Texas were to be secularized. The royal government felt that the missions were too great a drain on the treasury and that their missionary function among the Indians had shown too little success. Many in New Spain agreed and thought the decree was long overdue. The proclamation included detailed guidelines for the allocation of personal and community property to those Indians who still lived in and helped maintain the missions, but in the aftermath of secularization, many civil officials predictably exploited the confusion to seize most of that for themselves.

1979 One of the biggest tornadoes on record, and the most destructive in Texas history, ploughed through Wichita Falls. Three thousand homes, or one fifth of all those in the city, were destroyed in a scar across the city a mile wide. Forty-two people died, half of them in automobiles that the twister tossed and smashed like toys, and thousands of others were injured. On the same day, two other North Texas storms struck Vernon and Harrold and killed another twelve people.

---❖---
APRIL 11
---❖---

1836 The two six-pounder cannon known as the Twin Sisters were finally delivered to Sam Houston's army as it continued to retreat from Santa Anna across Texas. The guns had been on a long odyssey since the people of Cincinnati, Ohio, donated the funds for them in November of 1835. They were cast in Cincinnati, shipped to New Orleans labeled "hollow ware" to avoid suspicion, and then sent to Galveston. There they were named the Twin Sisters after the twin daughters of Doctor Charles Rice, although this was also a common name for the Mexican state of Coahuila y Texas. In the hands of Colonel James C. Neill, the Texans's chief artillerist and the same man who had done such fine work fortifying the Alamo, the Sisters played a key role at San Jacinto. After that they continued to serve first the Republic, then, after annexation, the U.S. Army. During the Civil War, although they were long obsolete, Texas retrieved them from an armory in Baton Rouge and put them back into fighting condition. They were in action at the Battle of Galveston in 1863, but after that they disappeared. They may have been buried near Houston to keep them out of Union hands, but none of the many efforts to find them has ever succeeded.

1939 Seito Saibara, Japanese benefactor of rice cultivation in Texas, died in Webster at age seventy-eight. In 1903 the Japanese consul in Houston asked Saibara, a theology student in Hartford, Connecticut, to come to the aid of rice farmers in Texas. Rice was not a new crop here; it dated back half a century or more. But the quality of the Honduran seed was inferior, as was the productivity of Texas farms. Saibara moved to Webster, brought over his family and thirty other countrymen, and founded a minor Japanese colony on a thousand acres. The Emperor donated seed for the first crop, and the rice from that harvest and the next two was used in turn as seed in other parts of Texas. A century after Seito Saibara began his mission, Texas produces billions of pounds of rice every year.

❖ APRIL 12 ❖

1865 The Texas Brigade, "Lee's Grenadiers," surrendered at Appomattox with the rest of the Army of Virginia. In the course of the war, 3,884 men had enlisted. Now, after four years of service in many of the most famous engagements of the Civil War—Second Manassas, Antietam, Gettysburg, Chickamauga, the Wilderness—473 men remained. The rest were killed in action, died of disease, or were wounded and discharged as invalids.

APRIL 13

1832 On the streets of Washington, D.C., Sam Houston caned Ohio Representative William Stanbery, after the congressman had made insinuating remarks about him on the floor of the House. Anything said by a member in the chamber was supposed to be immune from reprisal, and the House tried Houston for violating that privilege. Francis Scott Key, of "Star Spangled Banner" fame, defended him and lost. But after Houston spoke in his own defense, passionately invoking a man's right to defend his honor whatever the consequences, the House gave him an ovation, and he received only a token reprimand. Houston also faced a criminal charge of assault, for which he was fined $500, but President Andrew Jackson saw to it that he never had to pay that either.

1824 Martin De León received permission to bring forty-one families from Mexico and establish the town of Nuestra Señora de Guadalupe de Jesús Victoria on the Guadalupe River. De León was soon involved in a series of confrontations with the Anglo settlers of neighboring colonies, and his aristocratic distaste for Americans did not help matters. Misunderstandings over the boundaries between grants, smuggling by some American colonists, resentment of the government's preferential treatment of Mexicans, all aggravated tensions between De León and the surrounding colonies. In the Revolution of 1836, the De León family was the victim of persecution from both sides. They were Federalists, opposed to Santa

Anna, and paid for their "treason" when Santa Anna's troops occupied the colony. Yet the Texan victory brought them no relief; Americans moving into the area accused them of siding with the Mexicans and drove them out. The Mexican colony of Guadalupe Victoria was gone, and in its place stood Victoria, Texas.

APRIL 14

1788 David Gouverneur Burnet was born in Newark, New Jersey, the son of a delegate to the Continental Congress. Burnet tried a variety of occupations as he wandered from Cincinnati to Natchitoches, Louisiana, including a stint as a volunteer in Venezuela's revolt against Spanish rule. During the Texas Revolution he was briefly president of the Republic and later vice president under Mirabeau B. Lamar. After the Civil War he was elected to the U.S. Senate, but after he had traveled to Washington at his own expense, radical Republicans refused to let him take his seat. Burnet must have doubted such a long and eventful life lay ahead of him when he was in his late twenties and a physician diagnosed him with tuberculosis. But the doctor told him to go to Texas and live with the Indians like an Indian. After a year with the Comanches, Burnet was well, and he lived to the age of eighty-two.

1934 On "Black Sunday," the climactic dust storm of the past few weeks hit Kansas, Oklahoma, and the Texas Panhandle. Enormous black, apocalyptic clouds rolled across the land, moving Woody Guthrie to write the song "So Long, It's Been Good to Know You." After years of drought, with much of the plains farmland either neglected by bankrupt farmers or over plowed by desperate ones, the Dust Bowl had arrived. In 1935 Amarillo experienced 908 hours of dust storms; seven times visibility was officially reduced to zero, up to eleven consecutive hours. Ultimately hundreds, mostly children and the elderly, died of respiratory complications caused by the inescapable grit. Even when the worst was over, the disaster left its mark behind. Around Dalhart, 200,000 acres were buried by sand dunes. But Charles Whitfield of the Soil Conservation Service reasoned that the wind had dropped the sand there, and the wind could be harnessed to take it away. With great metal sheets and sandbag barriers he diverted the airflow, and most of the dunes were erased by 1938.

❖ APRIL 15 ❖

1881 In El Paso, the "Battle of Keating's Saloon" cost four men their lives to no purpose. The Manning brothers, local ranchers, were widely suspected of stealing cattle in Mexico and bringing them back to Texas. Two Mexican lawmen on their trail were murdered near the Manning ranch, and a Mexican posse was in town for an inquest into the deaths of officers Sanchez and Juarique. Afterwards, rancher John Hale and former city marshal George Campbell, both friends of the Mannings and both drunk, accosted Constable Gus Krempkau for siding with the Mexicans. The conversation grew heated, and Hale impulsively shot Krempkau in the chest. Marshal Dallas Stoudenmire, hearing gunplay, rushed to the scene from the nearby Globe Restaurant, saw his friend down, and put a bullet in Hale's forehead. As Krempkau breathed his last, he shot Campbell, who fired back, whereupon he was riddled by Stoudenmire. Some of these shots went wild and killed an innocent bystander. The "Four Dead in Five Seconds" gunfight notwithstanding, the men who killed the two Mexicans were never caught.

1919 The lands previously occupied by the Burning Bush colony were sold at auction at the Smith County Courthouse in Tyler; it was the only way to pay grocer J. L. Vanderver the $12,000 debt the colony had built up. Members of the Society of the Burning Bush, an offshoot of the Free Methodists, gave up all personal possessions, liquor, tobacco, and, for the most part, contact with the rest of the world. Most of the time that they didn't spend working they spent worshiping, an intense and lively business during which they frequently jumped around, rolled on the floor, or turned somersaults. In the end their communal experiment was a failure, and Burning Bush is now a ghost town.

❖

APRIL 16

❖

1831 Johann Friedrich Ernst, a former soldier and postal clerk in Oldenburg, Germany, obtained a land grant in Austin's colony, becoming the first German to settle in Texas with his family. The Ernsts had hurriedly left Oldenburg in September 1829, after he apparently embezzled substantial funds from the post office. As it had and would for countless others, the new land gave him a chance at a fresh start with no past. A letter from Ernst to a friend in Germany, describing his wonderful new life in Texas, influenced other Germans to immigrate. With his kindness and encouragement to those newly arrived from his old home, he became known among them as the "father of the immigrants."

1947 In Texas City, the French freighter *Grandcamp,* formerly the Liberty Ship *Benjamin R. Curtis*, exploded when over 2,000 tons of ammonium nitrate was ignited by a fire on board. Soon the neighboring *High Flyer* was also ablaze, and early the next day her cargo of 900 tons of ammonium nitrate also went off. The blasts destroyed a third vessel, the *Wilson B.*

Keene. Debris covered several square miles, and most of Texas City was leveled or burned; 576 people were killed.

APRIL 17

1897   According to an account in *The Dallas Morning News*, a strange airship appeared over Aurora, then crashed into a windmill and exploded. Townspeople found the remains of the ship marked with indecipherable "hieroglyphics." In the wreckage, they discovered the corpse of a strange little green man, "not an inhabitant of this world"; the alien pilot is supposedly still interred in the Aurora cemetery. Modern investigations indicate that the story was either an elaborate stunt intended to publicize Aurora, or a practical joke on the part of bored radio operators.

APRIL 18

1877   Major John B. Jones began a sweep across Kimble County with three companies of Rangers in five detachments. Kimble had become notoriously overrun with outlaws: With its hills and stands of cedar, a Ranger lieutenant called it "a better hiding place for rascals than any other part of Texas." Now Jones and his men were ready to round up as many rascals as they could catch. In the end the campaign produced forty-one arrests on an encyclopedic list of charges, including forgery, assault, theft, and escape from prison. Twenty-five men were indicted, most notably a sheriff and a county judge charged with malfeasance. But despite the number of lawmen and lawbreakers involved, it was an astonishingly peaceful operation; not one person was killed.

1934   In Fort Worth, J. F. Cantrell opened America's first public laundromat, which he called a "washateria." He offered users their choice of four washing machines, which they could rent by the hour, but they had to bring their own soap.

APRIL 19

1850   In fear of slave uprisings, the Matagorda city government passed an ordinance which forbade blacks, free or not, to walk the city streets after the 9:00 evening bell. The penalty for violating the selective curfew was five to twenty strokes with a lash.

1915   Vernon was the last Texas town to receive an Andrew Carnegie grant to build a public library. The amount of the grants ranged widely, from the $5,000 donated to Pittsburg to the $76,000 that Dallas received; Vernon got $12,500. In almost every instance the library would be the first one ever in the town. In Texas, thirty cities altogether received Carnegie library grants. Ten cities turned the money down, mostly because the one-time grant did not provide for continued upkeep. Fifty years later, less than half the buildings constructed under the program survived as libraries; the rest had been demolished or put to another use.

APRIL 20

1878   At four in the afternoon, soldiers stationed in Laredo finally sortied in response to a raid by marauders from south of the Rio Grande that had started six days before. On Sunday the 14th, about forty Mexicans and Indians crossed into Webb County north of Laredo. They soon killed three men, then split into several groups and began attacking area ranches. A civilian posse followed them, but their call to Fort Ewell for help was ignored. On the 17th the raiders pillaged ranches in La Salle, McMullen, and Duval Counties. On the 18th they entered

Nueces County; another party of ranchers turned out to chase them and asked for help from the military at San Diego, again with no effect. Pleas the next day to San Diego and Laredo were equally futile. Not until the afternoon of the 20th did the troops in Laredo react, and it was too late then; after murdering at least eighteen Americans, the killers had already crossed the river with hundreds of stolen horses.

1948 The battleship USS *Texas* arrived under tow at her new permanent slip in the Houston Ship Channel, next to the San Jacinto battlefield. Obsolete and showing her thirty-some years, she had been slated to be destroyed as a bombing target but was saved by a statewide fund drive, with the support of Admirals Chester Nimitz and Ernest King. She is still there today, the only surviving example of the original dreadnought class and the only remaining ship of the U.S. Navy to have served in both World Wars.

❖ APRIL 21 ❖

1836 In a late afternoon battle that lasted only eighteen minutes, the Texas army under Sam Houston defeated Santa Anna's Mexican army at San Jacinto. Texas lost 9 dead, Mexico 630, as the Texans sought revenge for the Alamo and Goliad in a killing orgy. As Houston's men advanced at the start of the battle, a fifer played a popular and, by the standards of the day, suggestive tune:

> *Will you come to the bower I have shaded for you?*
> *Our bed shall be roses all spangled with dew.*
> *There under the bower of roses you'll lie*
> *With a blush on your cheek, but a smile in your eye.*

1941   During the San Jacinto Day ceremonies at the old battlefield, Governor W. Lee O'Daniel announced that as interim replacement for Senator Morris Sheppard, who had died recently, he would appoint the eighty-six-year-old son of Sam Houston. Andrew Jackson Houston, the oldest man ever to enter the Senate, took his oath in Washington on June 2 but died on June 26 at the Johns Hopkins Hospital in Baltimore. O'Daniel himself campaigned for and won the vacant Senate seat, and cynics believed the governor had selected Houston because he could be trusted not to try to make the appointment permanent.

Governor W. Lee O'Daniel congratulates freshman **Senator Andrew Jackson Houston**, 86 years old.

Photo courtesy Texas State Library and Archives Commission

APRIL 22

1959 Around 900 members of the Davidians, a minority faction within the Seventh-Day Adventists, gathered at New Mount Carmel, their 941-acre farm near Elk, east of Waco. Devotees from as far as Canada came to await a sign of the beginning of God's kingdom. The sign never appeared, however; the Davidians sold most of the land at New Mount Carmel, and the movement dissolved into smaller groups. In the absence of founder Victor Houteff, who had died two years before, Ben Roden claimed what remained of New Mount Carmel and made it the home of the Branch Davidians. In 1985 Ben's son George expelled rival Vernon Howell at gunpoint; Howell and his disciples returned in 1987 and both men were arrested after a gunfight broke out. Roden went to jail, and Howell, who changed his name to David Koresh, took control of the commune. Unlike his pacifist predecessors, his preparations for the end included stockpiling arms, which led to the 1993 confrontation during which nearly a hundred Davidians and Federal agents were killed.

APRIL 23

1936 Roy Orbison, writer and singer of moody rock & roll ballads, was born in Vernon. Orbison's first band was a western group, but at North Texas State College he met Pat Boone and switched the Wink Westerners to the rockabilly Teen Kings. He dropped out to play full time, but the Teen Kings broke up. In 1960, after writing songs for other performers like the Everly Brothers, he had his own first hit with "Only the Lonely." In the next few years, "Crying," "Blue Bayou," "Dream Baby," and "Oh, Pretty Woman" followed, each marked by Orbison's unmistakable clear tenor. Tragedies in his private life interrupted his career: his wife was killed in a traffic accident, then a house fire killed two sons. But at the time of his death of a heart attack in 1988, the music of his youth was receiving renewed respect, he was in the Rock & Roll Hall of Fame, and he was recording again with the likes of George Harrison and Bob Dylan.

APRIL 24

1905 At the Waller County Courthouse in Hempstead, Congressman John McPherson Pinckney and members of the Prohibition League were discussing a petition calling for better enforcement of a recently passed prohibition law. When a fight broke out, Pinckney tried to break it up and was shot for his trouble, though he was unarmed. He, his brother Thomas, and two other men died of bullet wounds from the fracas. Roland Brown was tried on murder charges but acquitted. The incident added Hempstead to the list of Texas towns, like Waco, Harlingen, and Kenedy, branded at one time or another as "Six-Shooter Junction."

APRIL 25

1846 In the first battle of the Mexican War, Captain Seth Norton and his 62 dragoons were overpowered by 1,600 Mexicans under General Anastasio Torrejon, at Carricitos Ranch, just north of the Rio Grande near Brownsville. Sixteen American soldiers were killed, and the rest were captured; the prisoners were exchanged a few days later. On May 11 President James K. Polk addressed Congress, expressing outrage that Mexico had "shed American blood on the American soil," and on May 13 the United States declared war.

1875   Three Black Seminole scouts and one army officer, tracking a band of about thirty Comanches, caught up with them near the Pecos, stealthily approached their position on foot, and opened fire. The four men—Lieutenant John Bullis, Pompey Factor, Isaac Payne, and John Ward—engaged the Indians for nearly an hour and killed three of them, but eventually had to withdraw, only to find that Bullis's horse had run off. Each of the three scouts took a turn carrying Bullis on his horse, while the other two would hold off the pursuing Comanches, who eventually gave up the chase. For refusing to abandon their commander, all three Seminoles were awarded the Medal of Honor.

APRIL 26

1837   On his travels through the Republic, John J. Audubon landed at Galveston, where he paused to observe the birds and beasts before continuing on to Houston. There he was introduced to President Sam Houston and his cabinet. The president's home was "muddy and filthy" and his facial expression "forbidding," but the pioneer ornithologist noted that Houston was as gracious as one could be in such a rugged setting, and "offered us every facility within his power." Audubon also met an army beef contractor living near the San Jacinto battlefield, who promised him some Mexican skulls.

1843   Aboard the sloop of war *Austin* in the Gulf of Mexico, Antonio Landois, William Simpson, Isaac Allen, and James Hudgins were executed for their role in the February 11, 1842 mutiny on the *San Antonio* in New Orleans, in which the men had murdered Lieutenant Charles Fuller because he denied them shore leave. The four sailors were hanged from the foreyard at 12:20 and not lowered until 1:30; during that hour, while four corpses swung in silence, the crew ate lunch.

Whether or not this shack was in truth the original **Executive Mansion**
when Houston became the capital, it does give some idea of the primitive setting
from which the government tried to administer the raw new Republic.

Photo courtesy Texas State Library and Archives Commission

APRIL 27

1839 Memucan Hunt, Texas Minister to the United States,
wrote President Mirabeau B. Lamar of an offer from Samuel F.
B. Morse to grant Texas the rights to his promising invention,
the telegraph. Morse was then struggling to obtain support for
his contraption, and in fact it would be four years before he
received any assistance from the U.S. government. Hunt's letter was put in the "secret archives" of the Republic and then
either lost or ignored. On August 9, 1860, his telegraph now a
solid success, Morse wrote Governor Houston, "I, therefore,
now respectfully withdraw the offer then made in 1838..."

Houston's response is unknown; if the original letter was still misplaced, he may have had no idea what offer Morse was talking about.

1895 William Sydney Porter, later famous as O. Henry, printed the last issue of the Austin *Rolling Stone*, his first publication. The first two issues had come out a year before under the title *Iconoclast*, but when William Cowper Brann decided to revive his magazine of that name in Waco, Porter chose a new name for his weekly. The *Rolling Stone* was not a newspaper per se; it contained mostly humorous or fictional accounts of local events, as well as some short stories later published under Porter's pen name. His difficulties in financing the paper may have been one more reason he was tempted to embezzle money from the First National Bank, for which he eventually went to prison for three years.

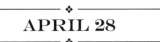

APRIL 28

1933 Actress Carolyn Sue Jones was born in Amarillo. She was one-eighth Indian and believed that the great-grandparent in question was closely related to Geronimo. Jones appeared in more than two dozen films in the fifties and sixties, and received an Oscar nomination for her role as a beatnik in *The Bachelor Party* in 1957. She also had an active television career, for which she is most fondly recalled as Morticia, the gently deranged and unnervingly beautiful mistress of the Addams household.

1988 In Washington, D.C., seventy-five-year-old Lady Bird Johnson was presented with the Congressional Gold Medal, the first given to a former First Lady, in recognition of her decades of work on behalf of humanitarian and environmental causes. On her seventieth birthday, December 22, 1982, one of her most cherished projects was completed when she opened the National Wildflower Research Center in Austin, on sixty acres of land that she had donated.

APRIL 29

1822 Stephen F. Austin, dressed as a beggar to avoid the attention of bandits, arrived in Mexico City from his Brazos colony to deal with the government of the now independent nation of Mexico. First Austin had to negotiate with the new congress, then he had to begin again with Emperor Augustin de Iturbide, then with the congress again after Iturbide's brief reign ended. In April 1823 Mexican officials finally approved the land grant which Stephen's father, Moses, had originally obtained from Spanish authorities in January 1821.

APRIL 30

1598 On the banks of the Rio Grande, near modern El Paso, the expedition led by Juan de Oñate prepared a feast of game and fish to give thanks to God for their safe arrival after a harrowing march across the Chihuahua desert. The Spaniards invited neighboring Indians to join them in what seems to have been the first Thanksgiving in America. One Spanish officer even wrote an impromptu play, which would make it the first drama performed in present-day United States territory.

MAY

❖
MAY 1
❖

1718 Father Antonio de San Buenaventura Olivares founded the Mission of San Antonio de Valero, named for Saint Anthony of Padua and the Duke of Valero, the Spanish viceroy. In time the surrounding stands of cottonwood trees would cause the mission to be renamed the Alamo.

1837 The second session of the First Congress of the Republic of Texas convened in the newest nation's newest capital, Houston City, near the former site of Harrisburg, which Santa Anna had burned to the ground not long before his defeat at San Jacinto. The previous November, the Congress had voted to move from Columbia because the town was too small to accommodate everyone connected with the government, but it was some time before the situation in Houston was any better. The city could offer only a few decent places to stay, and some members had to sleep on blankets on the floor of a tavern (taverns and brothels being the most common business enterprises in early Houston).

❖
MAY 2
❖

1874 Governor Richard Coke commissioned Major John B. Jones of the Rangers, thirty-nine years old, to command the

Rangers' new Frontier Battalion, five companies of seventy-five men formed to protect the remote regions of Texas from Indian raiders and domestic lawbreakers. In his five years in command, Jones and his men compiled a superb record against Indians, rustlers, feuding ranchers, bank robbers, and train robbers. His successes included stopping the Horrell-Higgins feud and killing Sam Bass; his only major failure was the El Paso Salt War, where he intervened too late to prevent several murders by a Mexican mob. In 1879 Governor Oran Roberts appointed Jones as the adjutant general, and he died in that office in 1881.

❖ MAY 3 ❖

1901   After addressing the Daughters of the Republic of Texas in Houston, President William McKinley was introduced to eighty-eight-year-old Mary Smith McCrory Jones, widow of Anson Jones, the last president of the Republic. She presented him with a silk Lone Star flag, mounted on a staff made of wood from the old Capitol building. When McKinley congratulated her on a long and colorful life, she replied that yes, she was "the last leaf on the tree."

1956   Frank Loesser's new musical *The Most Happy Fella* opened on Broadway. The show featured a catchy tune that became a hit across the country: an ode to Dallas entitled "Big D." It was no coincidence that the musical was central to the plot of "Lucy's Night in Town," the March 25, 1957 episode of *I Love Lucy*, with plenty of dialog about how popular it was and how hard it was to get tickets. Lucille Ball and Desi Arnaz had invested heavily in the show and were not reluctant to use their own hit TV program to help it succeed.

❖ MAY 4 ❖

1875 Kicking Bird, a peaceful and pragmatic Kiowa chief, died after drinking poisoned coffee in his lodge at Cache Creek. Some Indians said it was witchcraft, but presumably he was murdered by fellow Kiowas who despised him for collaborating with the U.S. Army. But five years earlier Kicking Bird had shown that his preference for peace did not mean that he was a coward; he led his first and last raid, in which he and a hundred braves soundly whipped the 6th Cavalry under Captain C. B. McClellan at the Battle of the Little Wichita.

❖ MAY 5 ❖

1898 The first volunteers for Teddy Roosevelt's "Rough Riders"—the 1st U.S. Volunteer Cavalry Regiment—arrived in San Antonio. Also known as "Teddy's Terrors" or the "Rocky

Volunteers for **Teddy Roosevelt's "Rough Riders"** pose for a group portrait, unaware that before the end of summer five will likely be dead or wounded.

Photo courtesy Texas State Library and Archives Commission

89

Mountain Rustlers," the recruits were mostly men of the West, with Texas more heavily represented than any other state. Some were the sons of ex-Confederates, bemused to be fighting under the Stars and Stripes. At the end of the month-long training, they left for Tampa. Despite their cavalry designation, they fought on foot because no transport was available to carry their horses to Cuba. By August the "Splendid Little War" was over, and they were back in the U.S. But in that brief adventure, more than one man in three had become a casualty, the highest proportion of any American unit in the war.

1916 Late at night, Mexican bandit chief Rodríguez Ramírez led a raid on the border village of Glenn Spring in Brewster County. Nine soldiers of the 14th Cavalry were stationed there but had no chance against the dozens of attackers. For several hours they fought back, but then the raiders set fire to the adobe building in which they were surrounded, and they had to evacuate; three were killed, as was a young resident of the town. Simultaneously Natividad Álvarez and another band struck Boquillas, twelve miles away. Álvarez was captured, but the bandits took two hostages across the border with them. Three days later the U.S. Army sent eighty troops into Mexico, led by Colonel George T. Langhorne in his personal Cadillac, his chauffeur at the wheel. Langhorne never caught the bandits, but he did retrieve the two hostages unharmed. In the aftermath of the Glenn Spring Raid, President Woodrow Wilson ordered additional National Guard troops to the border, but soon the Rio Grande valley was quiet again, and by 1920 the army posts were empty.

--- ❖ ---
MAY 6
--- ❖ ---

1930 From early in the day until after dark, tornadoes raged all across Texas, north, south, east, and west. To begin, in the morning three storms blew up on a line from Spur, on the verge of the Panhandle, to Austin, in the center of the state. That afternoon, forty-one people were killed in tornadoes that raked Bynum, Irene, Mertens, Frost, and Ennis; in Frost the only building that stood up to the storm was the jail. Hours later thirty-six more died when twisters struck Kenedy, Nordheim, and Runge. The terror continued into the night, as a tornado in Bronson killed two more people. With the three other deaths scattered through the day, the twelve-hour period of back-to-back storms took eighty-two lives.

MAY 7

1860 Julius Real, leader of the 1911 "Whiskey Rebellion," was born on a ranch near Kerrville. During the prohibitionist agitation that led to the passage of the Eighteenth Amendment in 1919, Real personally favored prohibition, but in the State Senate he represented San Antonio, a conspicuously wet district. In 1911 a lame-duck governor and legislature tried to pass a prohibition act for Texas, but Real and ten fellow senators slipped out of Austin into the hills of Bandera County. There they kept hidden, preventing a quorum in the Senate, until the bill was shelved.

MAY 8

1911 Across the Rio Grande from El Paso, the first Battle of Juarez broke out, and reporters, tourists, and locals flocked to the northern bank of the river to watch the spectacle. But for some of the curious observers, the price for seeing the struggle between government troops and Francisco Madero's insurgents was high indeed. Hundreds of stray rounds flew into American territory, killing six and wounding fifteen others.

1973   On a ranch near Knox City, Carl "Bigun" Bradley, the Marlboro Man, died in the saddle. As he tried to free a cow trapped in the mud, his horse reared and fell on him; Bradley and the horse were both killed.

MAY 9

1840   In Marion, Alabama, Margaret Moffette Lea was married to Sam Houston, in spite of her mother's misgivings about an attachment to a man twenty-six years her senior and the subject of scandal regarding his two previous marriages. The first, while Houston was governor of Tennessee, ended after only three months for reasons that were then and still are a complete mystery, upon which he resigned and went to live with Cherokee Indians in Arkansas. The two were not divorced until three years later. His second marriage was recognized under Cherokee law, as was the subsequent divorce. But Margaret may have known something her mother didn't, because she and Sam remained together until his death in 1863.

1957   At the Governor's Mansion in Austin, Price Daniel and his wife were entertaining a group of women. Daniel had just stepped forward to shake a visitor's hand when a 24-pound chunk of plaster fell from the ceiling and hit the floor where he had been standing a second before. That chance move kept Mrs. Daniel in the Governor's Mansion and Lieutenant Governor Ben Ramsey out, as the falling debris would unquestionably have crushed Daniel's skull.

MAY 10

1781   After a siege of two months, Lieutenant Colonel Bernardo de Gálvez and a Spanish force of 7,000 men captured

Fort George, the British bastion in Pensacola, the capital of West Florida. It was the climax of a brilliant Spanish campaign against British possessions in the Gulf, in which Gálvez had significantly aided the cause of the American Revolution, as the Continental Congress acknowledged. It also capped his illustrious military career in the service of Madrid, and four years later Gálvez was appointed to Mexico City as viceroy of New Spain. He was equally well regarded for his accomplishments in that post, and the Texas city of Galveston, originally named Bahia de Galvezton, is his namesake.

1911 Second Lieutenant George Kelly crashed his Curtiss pusher while trying to land at Fort Sam Houston in San Antonio and became the first man to die flying for the U.S. Army. In 1917 the army's new Aviation Camp in San Antonio was renamed Kelly Field in his honor, and today it is Kelly Air Force Base.

❖ MAY 11 ❖

1752 At the mission Nuestra Senora de la Candelaria, near present-day San Gabriel, Fathers Miguel Pinilla and Jose Ganzabal, with parishioner Juan Jose Zevallos, were seated at their evening meal when a blunderbuss was fired through an open door. Zevallos fell dead, and when Ganzabal went to the door an arrow pierced his heart. Within days an Indian named Andres confessed to the murder of Ganzabal, but he insisted that a soldier had fired the shot. The soldiers at the mission were commanded by Captain Felipe de Rábago y Teran, who had an ugly reputation. Zevallos had accused him of seducing his wife, for which Rábago had imprisoned and tortured him. He argued violently with Father Pinilla and others over his licentious behavior and that of his soldiers, as well as his corrupt dealings with Indians. Finally Pinilla had excommunicated Rábago and some thirty of his men, who eventually repented and were absolved. Rábago was tried for the murder of Zevallos but was acquitted in 1760. While he was imprisoned waiting for trial, he apparently reformed. After his release he founded two new missions on the upper Nueces River and spent a fortune of his own money on their defense and upkeep.

MAY 12

1903 In Austin, "The Eyes of Texas" was first performed at the University of Texas varsity minstrel show. University President William L. Prather took his position as a mentor seriously, and he frequently admonished his students, "The eyes of Texas are upon you." For the annual student revue, John Lang Sinclair set Prather's catch phrase to the tune of "I've Been Working on the Railroad." When the glee club quartet sang it, the audience in the Hancock Opera House called for encore after encore, and each time they sang along with greater gusto. "The Eyes of Texas" became UT's anthem, but it has never been the official state song.

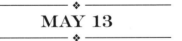

MAY 13

1865 Near Brownsville, Confederate forces won the Battle of Palmito Ranch, the last of the Civil War, more than a month after Appomattox. It is still uncertain whether the commanders on either side knew the war was over, or cared. In an additional ironic touch, near the end of the action some Union soldiers tried to escape capture by swimming to the far bank of the Rio Grande, where they were immediately shot by Mexicans. Whether these were soldiers defending their border or bandits looking for loot is also unclear.

1975 James Robert Wills died of pneumonia in Dallas, eighteen months after a stroke had left him unconscious. Born the son of a talented fiddler in 1905, Bob Wills was playing professionally while still in his teens. In the thirties he formed the band whose name would always be linked with his, the Texas Playboys, and in 1940, in Saginaw, Texas, they recorded the million-seller "New San Antonio Rose," the premier example of the musical form that came to be known as "Texas Swing."

——————— ❖ ———————
MAY 14
——————— ❖ ———————

1942 Sweetwater leased its municipal airport to the War Department for a dollar a year. A local newspaper ran a contest to choose a patriotic name for the new army air field, and in the aftermath of Pearl Harbor "Avenger Field" took the prize. Avenger was used to train hundreds of aviators during the war, but its most noteworthy graduates were the Women's Airforce Service Pilots (WASPs), who trained there from February 1943 to December 1944. Commanded by Jacqueline Cochran, already a famous flyer in her own right, they learned to fly every type of airplane the Army Air Corps had. Their original objective was to ferry aircraft around the country and overseas, in order to free men for combat missions. But they went on to a wide variety of noncombat tasks, including testing damaged and repaired planes, an especially risky form of flying. Of the 25,000 women who applied, 1,074 graduated from the program, and 38 were killed in the line of duty. Yet it was more than thirty years after the war before the U.S. government officially recognized their contribution, granting them honorable discharges and the benefits taken for granted by other veterans.

❖ MAY 15 ❖

1837 Only two weeks after the legislature convened in Houston for the first time, Congressman William Thomas Ward and another legislator, his name now misplaced, met at the edge of town to fight a duel with pistols. In the first round, both men missed. When his adversary's second shot hit Ward's artificial leg, Ward, in the words of an observer, "came to the conclusion that a bullet in a wooden leg was a quite sufficient apology for a slapped cheek and expressed his entire satisfaction."

1916 In a Waco courtroom, a jury found Jesse Washington, a black teenager, guilty of raping and murdering Lucy Fryer, the white fifty-three-year-old wife of a Robinson farmer. Instantly the spectators pushed aside the police, seized Washington, and delivered him to an angry crowd hundreds strong waiting outside. Putting a chain around his neck, they dragged him to City Hall where a bonfire was already prepared, hoisted him by the chain from a tree, then lowered his body, soaked with coal oil, into the fire. After two hours a few of them gathered his charred remains in a cloth sack, drove to Robinson, and hung them from a pole. Newspapers across the country denounced the barbaric lynching, but most papers in Texas made only restrained comments. No one was ever indicted in connection with the "Waco Horror" of 1916.

❖ MAY 16 ❖

1888 The new Capitol in Austin, built of Texas pink granite, was dedicated with great ceremony. Texans were proud to claim the largest state capitol in the nation, with a dome that stood seven feet higher than that of the nation's Capitol in

Washington, D.C. But during the proceedings a spring shower revealed that the roof leaked badly, causing a heated exchange between contractors and legislators over the choice of roofing material. Ultimately the latter admitted they had made the error when insisting on copper instead of slate, but they demanded the roof be replaced at no charge anyway.

1902 Ramón de la Cerda of the Francisco de Asis Ranch was on land of the neighboring King Ranch when Texas Ranger Anderson Baker caught him allegedly rebranding King cattle from a "W" to a "Bar-W." The men exchanged shots, and Ramón was killed. Baker claimed self-defense, but there were signs that the body had been dragged and abused. In September, Baker and two other Rangers were ambushed, and one was killed. Alfredo de la Cerda, Ramón's brother and also a suspected rustler, was arrested with five other men and charged with murder. A prosecution witness was killed, but the trial never took place anyway. Free on bail, de la Cerda swore that he would kill Baker, and at the same time offered $1,000 to anyone else who did the job for him. But Baker didn't wait for Alfredo to come after him; on October 3, he shot him in the back in a Brownsville clothing store. The next year, Baker was acquitted in the deaths of both brothers.

❖

MAY 17

❖

1827 Martha White McWhirter, founder of the Woman's Commonwealth, was born in Gainesboro, Tennessee. In 1855 she and her husband moved to Bell County, near modern Armstrong, and about ten years later they moved to Belton. When her brother and two children died, she saw the tragedies as a chastisement from God. A vision persuaded her that she was filled with the Holy Spirit, and after she shared her epiphany with her prayer group, other women began to feel themselves similarly sanctified. Another vision revealed that she and the others, who were all unhappy in their married lives, should leave home and form a separate community. McWhirter and her followers formed the Woman's Commonwealth and built homes in Belton for themselves, largely with money from Mr. McWhirter, who seems to have been uncommonly understanding and even bequeathed his estate to his estranged wife. McWhirter led the members of the Commonwealth in starting their own businesses, which kept the community solvent through the end of the century. Then the Commonwealth relocated to Washington and Maryland, and there Martha McWhirter died in 1904.

1865 The last of the Union prisoners of war left Camp Ford, a prison camp near Tyler. For about a year after the camp was established, when it held about 1,500 men, the life of the

This bleak sketch of Camp Ford appeared in *Harper's Weekly* two months before the last prisoners were released.

Photo courtesy Texas State Library and Archives Commission

Union prisoners in Camp Ford was tolerable. But in April 1864, 3,000 more prisoners arrived, and the place became almost literally a nightmarish hole. The camp could not shelter them all, and many lived in simple holes in the ground that deflected the wind but offered no protection from the other elements. Other forms of improvised shelter were only marginally better. The Confederacy could provide only a trickle of food and clothing, and most men spent their entire confinement in the clothes they were wearing when they were captured. Of the 6,000 prisoners who passed through Camp Ford, 286 died. Some Confederates were charged with inhumane treatment, but none was ever prosecuted, perhaps because some prisoners reported that the guards at Camp Ford lived in only slightly better conditions.

MAY 18

1837 To discourage General Felix Huston from leading the confident but disorganized and undisciplined Texas army on a hare-brained invasion of Mexico, President Sam Houston issued furloughs to all but 600 men. Huston resigned in disgust and took up his old law practice. But three years later he would get his chance at glory in the Battle of Plum Creek.

1871 A war party of 100 Indians of several tribes from the Fort Sill Reservation, led by chiefs Satanta, Satank, and Maman-ti, attacked Henry Warren's wagon train near Salt Creek. They killed Warren and six teamsters, losing one of their own dead. While the Indians headed back to the reservation, one of the five surviving teamsters hurried to Fort Richardson with the news. At the fort was William Tecumseh Sherman, on a tour of inspection to assess the danger of Indian attack, which he had thought was exaggerated. Sherman proceeded to Fort Sill, where he personally saw to the arrest of the

Indian leaders, but he didn't know how close he had come to losing his own scalp the day before the attack. The war party had seen his entourage, with three other officers and an escort of seventeen troopers, pass the same place, although none of the soldiers spotted the Indians. However, Maman-ti's medicine said they should wait for the next group of white men (who would also happen to be less well armed). Thus Sherman was permitted to die in his bed in New York City twenty years later.

MAY 19

1868 A curiously greenish cloud approached San Antonio from the northwest in the evening, and soon the city was hit by powerful winds. Then enormous hailstones began to fall, some of them weighing as much as two pounds. Crops were smashed, and all sorts of livestock, from chickens to calves and sheep, were beaten to death. Students at Saint Mary's College prayed for their lives, thinking the world was about to end. The barrage of ice pummeled windows, doors, and roofs until there was hardly one intact. The only people who benefitted by the storm were the owners of saloons, who collected a bounty of ice from the two-foot drifts and could briefly offer their customers cold drinks for a change.

1946 In Fort Worth, Ben Hogan won the first Colonial National Invitational Golf Tournament. On the final day he set a new course record of 65 and collected his $3,000 first prize. The Colonial, which is now the oldest PGA tournament still played at the same course where it began, became known as Hogan's Alley after he won it four more times, including his last PGA Tour victory in 1959.

❖ MAY 20 ❖

1875 John Barclay Armstrong, formerly of Tennessee, Missouri, and Arkansas, joined Captain Leander McNelly's company of Texas Rangers. He would go on to become one of the legends of the force. His greatest moment was the capture of the infamous killer John Wesley Hardin in 1877. Armstrong followed him across the Southeast and caught up with him and four gang members in Pensacola, Florida, on a train. When Hardin saw Armstrong's big Colt, he exclaimed, "Texas, by God!" and went for his own gun. While Armstrong wrestled with Hardin, whose pistol was caught in his suspenders, he managed to shoot one of the other four to death. He eventually stunned Hardin with a blow to the head and arrested the other three men. His biggest problem then was extraditing his famous and popular captive back to Texas, but he succeeded, and Hardin was sent to prison for twenty-five years.

1953 The Western Hills Hotel in Fort Worth completed its new 150-foot by 190-foot landing platform and became the first hotel in the United States to open a heliport.

❖ MAY 21 ❖

1906 In an attempt to ensure "an equitable distribution of the waters of the Rio Grande," the United States and Mexico signed a treaty specifying how the water would be shared by American and Mexican farmers. As part of the system, Elephant Butte Dam was built in New Mexico to regulate the flow of water to the border. But in a few years Mexico was diverting more than its fair portion into an irrigation canal just downstream from El Paso known as the Acequia Madre. In 1935 the U.S. trumped Mexico's canal by building the

American Dam on the Rio Grande, just 140 feet north of where the river first coincides with the border. This routes Mexico's fair share to the Acequia Madre and the rest to the American Canal, which serves America's farmers.

MAY 22

1864   Near Velasco, the Union gunboat *Kineo* captured the British schooner *Stingray*, a blockade-runner. The *Kineo*'s captain assigned a prize crew to sail the ship to the Union base at New Orleans, then resumed patrolling. But shortly, to his dismay, he saw his prize change course for the Confederate fort at Velasco. It later transpired that Captain McClosky of the *Stingray* had disabled the prize crew with a plentiful supply of liquor and then retaken the ship.

1953   After seven years of litigation and political turmoil, President Dwight Eisenhower signed the measure restoring to Texas the rights to its offshore property, which the U.S. Supreme Court had first endangered in a 1946 decision, then explicitly revoked in 1949. Senator Price Daniel of Texas had to shepherd the bill through a record-breaking twenty-seven-day filibuster before it finally passed in both houses. The tidelands controversy did not die for good until 1957, after U.S. Attorney General Herbert Brownell sued Texas on the grounds that the offshore boundary was three miles, not three leagues (10.35 miles), from shore. Even though Eisenhower himself denied the premise of the suit, Texas had to defend itself again in the U.S. Supreme Court, where it won on June 1, 1960. In the decades since then, the tidelands thus secured have earned billions of dollars for the public schools of Texas.

❖
MAY 23

❖

1929 Governor Dan Moody signed the bill making "Texas, Our Texas" the official state song. William J. Marsh, an Englishman who had lived in Fort Worth since 1904 and was the organist of the First Presbyterian Church, wrote the song for a contest held in 1924. His entry, with words co-written by Gladys Yoakam Wright, was judged the best of the 286 submitted from around the state. For the rest of his life, Marsh was chagrined by the almost universal misconception that "The Eyes of Texas" was the state song.

1946 The city of Hempstead dedicated its annual Six-Shooter Junction Day to Lillie Drennan, the fifty-year-old queen of the Texas truckers, and held a banquet in her honor. In 1928, with her second husband, Lilllie started the Drennan Truck Line: one second-hand Model T. A year later she was divorced again, and from then until 1952 she ran the company herself, doing as much of the driving as the men who worked for her, sometimes two days at a stretch without sleep. She was proud of the safety record of her drivers, most of them black men, whom she insisted on training herself, sometimes with a kick in the pants and a bellowed dressing-down that a Marine drill instructor could take notes from. In her khaki outfit, work boots, and ten-gallon hat, with a loaded six-gun on the seat next to her, she was known across the nation as one of those colorful characters that only Texas could produce.

❖
MAY 24

❖

1865 The sidewheeler *Lark* became the last ship to run the Union blockade and enter Galveston Harbor. But the city, like much of the Confederacy following Appomattox, was in a lawless state. Several hundred people boarded the ship in a mob and ransacked her cargo.

1953 The CBS history program *You Are There* broadcast an episode entitled "The Defense of the Alamo." A revival of the same series in the 1970s showed "Siege of the Alamo," a retelling of the same story, starring Fred Gwynne as Davy Crockett.

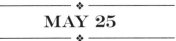

MAY 25

1934 Two days after being ambushed by lawmen in Louisiana, Clyde Barrow was buried in the West Dallas Cemetery next to his brother Buck, killed in one of the gang's earlier encounters with police. Clyde's epitaph: *Gone but not forgotten.* Bonnie Parker was buried in Fishtrap Cemetery the next day but was moved to Crown Hill in the northwest part of the city a few years later. Her headstone read, *As the flowers are made sweeter by the sunshine and dew, so this old world is made brighter by the likes of you.*

1953 In Houston, the first noncommercial educational television station in the United States went on the air. KUHT, on Channel 8, was operated by the University of Houston; its initial broadcast schedule was just four hours a day, Monday through Friday.

MAY 26

1942 Plagued by poor circulation that had recently cost him an amputated leg, "Doctor" John R. Brinkley died of a heart attack in San Antonio at the age of sixty. Forbidden to practice medicine in Kansas, in 1933 Brinkley moved to Del Rio, where he could use a high-powered radio transmitter at Villa Acuña, just across the river, to advertise his goat gland implants for virility and Mercurochrome injections for the restoration of youth, the same frauds that had made him rich in Kansas before he was thrown out. The money from deluded patients continued to pour in, on the order of twelve million dollars in five years. But malpractice suits and the IRS forced him to sell the mansion, the exotic automobiles, the yachts, and the rest, and when he died, Brinkley was bankrupt.

MAY 27

1882 An inebriated and belligerent Marshal Dallas Stoudenmire, sitting in on a meeting of the El Paso City Council, offered his opinion of the motion to dismiss him from office: "I can straddle every goddamned alderman here." To make his meaning clear to the less penetrating among the councilmen, he drew his six-shooter and twirled it on his trigger finger. The meeting was adjourned without voting on the issue. But two days later Stoudenmire, now sober, chose to resign.

MAY 28

1971 On a foggy Memorial Day weekend, the private plane carrying Texas native Audie Murphy crashed in the mountains near Roanoke, Virginia, killing Murphy, four other passengers, and the pilot. Born in Kingston in 1924, Audie Leon Murphy served with the 3rd Infantry Division in Europe during World War II. He became a national hero and the most decorated American soldier of the war, his thirty-three awards including the Congressional Medal of Honor. Invited to Hollywood by James Cagney after the war, Murphy at first struggled through years of bit parts but eventually starred in dozens of movies. The 1955 film of his best-selling autobiography *To Hell and Back*, in which he portrayed himself, grossed more than any other Universal picture until *Jaws* finally overtook it twenty years later. Murphy is buried in Arlington Cemetery; the number of visitors to his grave site each year is second only to that of President John F. Kennedy.

MAY 29

1541 After more than a month of wandering across the barren plains of northern New Mexico and Texas, the expedition of Francisco Vázquez de Coronado stumbled into Palo Duro Canyon, whose fruit and water saved the hundreds of parched explorers. "El Turco" (the Turk), a Pawnee guide Coronado had acquired in New Mexico, had promised to lead Coronado to the golden city of Quivira. Coronado had listened, despite the warning of another Indian named Ysopete, who said that El Turco was lying about Quivira, that nothing was there but grass and buffalo, and that the guide had deliberately led them on a pointless trek across the desert. Coronado set off north with thirty men in one last effort to find the city of gold; when he found nothing, he had El Turco garroted and began the disheartening march back to Mexico.

1898 *The Dallas Morning News* published "The News March," the latest composition by promising Texas composer Rose Myrtle Jones, dedicated *to the Leading Newspapers of Texas, "The Galveston News" and "The Dallas News," By Rose M. Jones, Composer, Denison, Texas, March, 1898.* Jones dedicated another march to the empress of Germany, who responded with an appreciative letter. The twenty-year-old was predicted to "rank with the foremost composers of the south, if not of America." But today Grove's dictionary, the ultimate reference on music, has never heard of her.

❖
MAY 30

❖

1871 Restaurateur Adelaida Cuellar was born near Matehuala, in Nuevo León, Mexico. In 1926, now living in Texas, she opened a homemade tamale stand at the Kaufman County Fair. Encouraged by the response, she and her family opened a restaurant in Kaufman, but the Depression ended that, as it did the attempts by her sons to open similar businesses in several East Texas towns. But in 1940 they tried again in the Dallas suburb of Oak Lawn. Mama Cuellar's home recipes had found their proper clientele at last. Within a few years the Cuellars opened other El Chico restaurants in Fort Worth, Houston, and Waco, and by the time of Adelaida's death in 1969 at the age of ninety-seven, they were everywhere in the Southwest.

1890 In Fort Worth, the two-year-old Spring Palace burned to the ground in minutes. Of the thousands of people in the building for a dance that evening, only one, an Englishman named Al Hayne, was killed, as he helped women and children escape the fire. The Spring Palace, with its fantastically ornate exterior and its dome second in size only to the U.S. Capitol, was built to house an annual fair showcasing everything Texan, from agricultural and mining products to science, art, history, dance, and sports. Today there are two relics of the Spring Palace in Fort Worth: The Stock Show is the indirect result of an unsuccessful movement to revive the annual fair; and at Lancaster and Main, where the building stood, a monument recalls the heroic death of Al Hayne.

❖
MAY 31
❖

1901   The body of Emma Seelye, Union soldier and spy, was moved from La Porte to Houston's Washington Cemetery. In May of 1861, Seelye enlisted in a Michigan volunteer regiment disguised as Private "Frank Thompson." After serving as a male nurse, she was recruited for espionage duties, in which she often "masqueraded" as a woman pie vendor behind Confederate lines. When she caught malaria in 1863, she deserted rather than be examined. After the war her memoir *Nurse and Spy in the Union Army* was a best-seller; in the 1880s her story finally moved Congress to clear her of the desertion charge and grant her a pension. She died in 1898, the only female ever to belong to the Grand Army of the Republic, and it was at their request that she was moved to a plot reserved for GAR veterans.

1919   In a twin-engine Handley-Paige bomber circling 2,000 feet above Ellington Field, southeast of Houston, Chaplain Lieutenant J. E. Reese performed the first known airborne wedding ceremony. While Lieutenant E. W. Kilgore piloted the chapel on wings, Reese pronounced Lieutenant R. W. Meade and Miss Marjorie Dumont man and wife. The unorthodox rites were part of the Flying Frolic air show and were "witnessed" by 10,000 spectators.

JUNE

❖
JUNE 1
❖

1836 At Velasco, General Santa Anna boarded the schooner *Invincible* of the Texas navy, which would carry him to Vera Cruz per the treaty signed after San Jacinto. He took a moment to write to his Texan hosts:

> *My Friends:*
> *I have been a witness of your courage on the field of battle, and know you to be generous. Rely with confidence on my sincerity, and you shall never have cause to regret the kindness shown me. In returning to my native land I beg you to receive the thanks of your grateful friend,*
> *Antonio Lopez de Santa Anna*

A storm delayed the *Invincible*'s departure, however. After two days, at the insistence of disgruntled soldiers and civilians, Santa Anna was brought back ashore. General Burnet had him protected by armed guards, and tempers eventually cooled. But meanwhile, political unrest in Mexico in Santa Anna's absence was making it increasingly unlikely that any treaty negotiated with him would have any value. Santa Anna did not leave Texas until November 20, when President Houston had him escorted not to Mexico but to Washington, D.C., to lobby President Andrew Jackson to recognize Texan independence. On December 26, having accomplished nothing of value to Texas, Santa Anna finally left Washington for home.

JUNE 2

1821 Moses Austin died of pneumonia at his daughter's home in Hazel Run, Missouri. Only weeks before, he had learned that, with the help of his new ally Baron de Bastrop, he had finally obtained the consent of Governor Antonio Martínez to build the port of Austina on the Texas coast, with a colony of 300 American families. With his dying request, dictated to his wife Mary, he urged his son, Stephen F. Austin, not to forsake the "Texas Venture."

JUNE 3

1836 Near Copano Bay, Major Isaac Burton and thirty cavalrymen captured the ship *Watchman* by decoying a few of the crew ashore in a small boat, then returning on the same boat and seizing the ship. They then used that ship to lure two others, the *Comanche* and the *Fanny Butler*, which they also captured. All three vessels were eventually returned to their American owners, but their valuable cargo of supplies intended for Santa Anna's army went to Sam Houston's men instead. For their amphibious exploit, the cavalry became known as the "Texas Horse Marines."

1908 On a tract north of Austin, the Confederate Woman's Home was opened, with the mission of caring for indigent widows of Confederate soldiers, as well as other women who had served the Confederate cause. Three women were admitted the first day; in a year the number grew to sixteen. As the number of applicants increased, the original two-story, fifteen-room facility was enlarged, and the population peaked at a little over a hundred in the 1920s and early 1930s. By 1963 there were only three women left of the 3,400 who had lived there. They were moved to other nursing homes, and the Confederate Woman's Home was closed after fifty-five years.

JUNE 4

1836 General Andrade of the Mexican army, withdrawing from Texas by Santa Anna's order after San Jacinto, halted his forces in the vicinity of Goliad. Only the day before, Texas troops under General Rusk had buried with military honors the victims of the Goliad massacre, and Rusk advised Andrade that he might not be able to control his men if they saw Mexican soldiers. Andrade must have concurred; he had his men cut a rough road through seven miles of dense brush to detour around the town.

JUNE 5

1837 To avoid the prospect of legal chaos, Congress passed a bill which made binding the hundreds of unconventional or informal marriages that had taken place in the absence of available ministers and judges in the remote parts of Texas, and assured the legitimacy of their offspring.

JUNE 6

1849 Major Ripley Arnold raised the Stars and Stripes over a new army post, where the Clear Fork of the Trinity River merged with the West Fork. He named the fort after a hero of the recent war with Mexico, who had recently died in San Antonio of cholera: General William Jenkins Worth.

1936 After 150,000 people watched a parade through the streets of Dallas, complete with floats depicting the Alamo, a gusher, conquistadors, and other images of Texas history,

Governor James Allred opened the Texas Centennial Exposition at Fair Park. He unlocked the gates with a $50,000 key, fashioned for the occasion from over a pound of gold and platinum, which a few years later was stolen and never seen again. Towns all over Texas celebrated the hundredth anniversary of the Revolution of 1836, but the 25-million-dollar fair in Dallas overshadowed all the others, including Fort Worth's Frontier Centennial, which opened the following month. Six million people paid to see the exhibits and shows in some fifty buildings, including the Cavalcade of Texas, the Hall of State, the Crystal Maze, Ripley's Odotorium, and the Streets of Paris (notable for its shocking nude dancers, who were regrettably instructed to cover up).

JUNE 7

1879 Nearly a year after he betrayed Sam Bass and his gang to Texas Rangers, Jim "Judas" Murphy died of poisoning—an accident or a suicide, depending on whose opinion one asked. There was, and is, some speculation that Murphy died not at his own hand but at that of Frank Jackson, the only survivor of the shootout at Round Rock. But there is simply no reliable record of Jackson's whereabouts after the 1878 gun battle.

1952 Radio announcer José Cantú died when his car hit a tree near Brownsville. For six years, Cantú's weekly "Programa Popular" on KBOR mixed Tejano music, political humor, and exposés of corrupt local officials. It made him a local hero to Hispanics and the nemesis of valley bigots, as well as drawing big ratings for the station. There were rumors that his enemies had tampered with his brakes, but nothing was ever proven.

❖
JUNE 8

❖

1837 Mrs. Pamelia Mann bought Houston's only hotel from Colonel Benjamin Fort Smith, who had built the place only months before at the northeast corner of Franklin and Travis. Soon she renamed it the Mansion House. It was regarded as the top hotel in town and had the further advantage of its own brothel. For both purposes it was conveniently close to the Capitol building and the Executive Mansion. Despite city ordinances against lewd female behavior, Mrs. Mann and her establishment prospered for many years.

1871 At the Fort Sill Reservation, Chief Satank (Sitting Bear), a member of the elite Kiowa warrior caste, was thrown into a wagon in chains, to be carried to Fort Richardson and tried as a murderer for his part in a raid on a wagon train. Satank, determined to die rather than submit to this disgrace, patiently worked the handcuffs from his wrists, ignoring the tears in his skin. When his hands were free, he jumped a guard and seized his rifle, singing the Kiowa death song. But before he could fire, the other guards shot him several times. They dumped him out of the wagon, still alive, and left him to die in the road.

❖
JUNE 9

❖

1844 From his vantage point in a tree, Ranger Noah Cheery called down to Captain John Coffee Hays, "Jerusalem, captain, yonder comes a thousand Indians!" The fifteen Rangers hastily broke camp, mounted up, and prepared to deal with the Comanche raiding party led by Yellow Wolf, less than a thousand but probably a hundred anyway.

The Comanches tried to lure the Texans into a trap, but Hays was too wary for that and led his men around the Indian lines to attack them from the rear. Nonetheless the charge brought on a perilous, hand-to-hand struggle. Finally the Indians retreated. The Rangers followed them closely for three miles, taking advantage of the firepower of their Colt revolvers. Yellow Wolf was among the dozens of dead Comanches, while one Ranger was killed. The fight near Walker's Creek was the first in which the Colt proved itself in combat; a Comanche lamented that a man with a revolver "had a shot for every finger on his hand." To commemorate this triumph of his powerful new sidearm, Samuel Colt engraved the scene on the cylinder of the 1847 Walker Dragoon.

JUNE 10

1957 Former FBI agent and county attorney Jim Simpson led a sweep of Galveston's gambling and prostitution joints. Texas Rangers and eleven assistant attorneys general confiscated thousands of slot machines, roulette wheels, and gaming tables. Simpson didn't smash the illicit equipment; hoping to get some impressive footage of the operation, he had the contraband loaded aboard a barge, towed out into the Gulf of Mexico, and dumped into the water. To his surprise it floated, drawing complaints from the Coast Guard about a navigational hazard. But aside from that small hitch, the raid was a great success. It marked the beginning of the end for the Maceo mob family and the "Free State of Galveston."

JUNE 11

1838 In Houston, Henri Corri and his company advertised the opening of the first professional theater in Texas: *The Public are respectfully informed that the Scenery, which was materially injured in the voyage from the United States, having been repaired by Messrs. Chambers & Jackson, the Company will have the honor of* *making their appearance on Monday Evening, June 11, 1838; When will be presented Sheridan Knowles' celebrated Comedy of The Hunchback. Previous to the Comedy, Mr. Carlos will recite an Opening Address. After which the whole Company will sing A New National Texian Anthem, Written expressly for the occasion by Mr. Corri. The Whole to conclude with the popular farce of The Dumb Belle, or I'm Perfection. The members of the Orchestra having not yet arrived from Mobile, the Managers request the kind indulgence of their patrons for a few days.*

1865 Fletcher Stockdale began the shortest tenure of any governor of Texas, succeeding Pendleton Murrah, who had fled to Mexico. Stockdale would be out of office just six weeks later, as a Reconstruction government took control of the state. Perhaps Murrah did not regret leaving the Governor's Mansion as much as another man would have, for a fire there had uncovered his most private secret. On the night of his wedding in Marshall, his bride Sue Ellen had waited upstairs for him to come to her, and he had sat downstairs all night, expecting her to come for him. Mortified, he was cool to her from that time forward, and the marriage was never consummated. When fire broke out in the Governor's Mansion, he called her "my dear" as he led her to safety. She was overcome by this first sign of tenderness in fourteen years, and she confided the reason to a friend. The friend could not resist repeating the story, and soon it was all over Austin.

❖
JUNE 12
❖

1901 An error by an interpreter may have led to a violent tragedy in Karnes County. Sheriff W. T. Morris and two deputies interviewed Gregorio Cortez and his brother Romaldo abo.ut a recent horse theft, and Deputy Boone Choate translated. Choate asked Cortez if he had just traded a "caballo"

Killer and rustler **Gregorio Cortez** does not look particularly bloodthirsty in this portrait by the Bolton & Mitchell studio of Laredo.

Photo courtesy Texas State Library and Archives Commission

(horse); Cortez, having traded a "yegua" (mare), said no, which sounded to Morris like a lie. Then Cortez said, "No me puede arrestar por nada" (You can't arrest me for nothing.), which Choate translated to "No white man can arrest me." The misunderstandings escalated into a gunfight; first Morris wounded Romaldo, then Gregorio killed Morris. Cortez got away and began an epic flight from the law. A posse caught up with him on a ranch near Belmont, but he escaped again, after killing another deputy sheriff, and headed toward the Rio Grande. He was finally captured in Laredo on the 22nd. Meanwhile nine other Hispanics had been killed on suspicion of being in league with the "sheriff killer." Cortez was tried for murder four times, the first three convictions being reversed on appeal, and served nine years in prison before being pardoned. He died of pneumonia three years later, the hero of numerous folk ballads.

JUNE 13

1691 Don Domingo Teran de Los Rios founded a mission on a fertile plain at the headwaters of a picturesque river. As that date on the Catholic calendar was sacred to Saint Anthony of Padua, he named both the river and the new town San Antonio.

JUNE 14

1852 In the ballot to choose between Hallettsville and the incumbent Petersburg as the Lavaca County seat, Hallettsville won 210 to 179. Petersburg boosters alleged that the votes had been tampered with. On July 6 some of them burst into Chief Justice John Livergood's office and destroyed the ballots; Livergood shortly resigned. Commissioners voided the election and declared Petersburg the winner, but then two of the commissioners resigned after receiving threatening letters. Another election was held, and Hallettsville won again. To safeguard the ballots this time, a delegation from Hallettsville came to Petersburg to collect the evidence, but aroused Petersburgers took them prisoner, then sent them home empty-handed. Two hundred armed men from Hallettsville came back and carried the records away by *force majeure*.

Ultimately the matter went to the courts, and Hallettsville was not confirmed as the county seat until 1860.

1875 Governor Richard Coke offered the presidency of the Texas Agricultural and Mining College to Jefferson Davis, former president of the Confederate States of America. Coke promised him the substantial salary of four thousand dollars a year, and wrote, "...come and live with and be one of us, and make your home and resting place, after a long and eventful public service, among a people who will never cease to love and honor you." But Davis replied that Coke had overestimated his abilities, and that he was not the right man for the position.

JUNE 15

1836 The Arkansas Territory was admitted as the twenty-fifth state of the Union. Some of the settlers on the south bank of the Red River expected to become United States citizens in Miller County, Arkansas, but others considered the land part of the Republic of Texas. The dispute over jurisdiction lasted throughout the life of the Republic; delegates were elected to both the Texas and Arkansas legislatures. Not until the annexation of Texas in 1845 was the border clarified for good.

1943 In Beaumont, roughly 3,000 white men, most of them from the shipyards, went berserk after hearing that a black man had raped a white woman. Racial tensions were already high: A black man accused of raping a shipyard worker's daughter had recently been shot and killed by police, the Ku

During the race riot of 1943, the mob breaks into the Beaumont City Jail to seize a black prisoner.

Photo courtesy Texas State Library and Archives Commission

Klux Klan was planning a big rally on the 29th, and the Juneteenth celebration was only four days away. The rioters spread out across the black section of the city, beating black people, torching buildings, and ransacking stores and homes. Four people, three black and one white, were killed outright or fatally injured. The governor declared martial law, but by the time the National Guard, Texas Rangers, and State Police arrived, the riot had already dissipated. Of the more than two hundred men taken into custody, almost all were released for lack of evidence.

❖
JUNE 16
❖

1838 In the U.S. House of Representatives, John Quincy Adams began a three-week filibuster against annexation of Texas, which eventually foiled the efforts of southerners who wished to add another slave state to the union. When new ambassador Anson Jones arrived in Washington in October, he announced that Texas had withdrawn its petition of annexation, to preserve the dignity of the Republic.

1965 The last disputed land claim from the aftermath of the Mexican War was resolved by the legislature, in favor of the holder of the original Mexican land grant. This ended more than a century of litigation that began when Anglo newcomers to Texas began contesting the land titles of Mexican occupants, despite guarantees provided by the Treaty of Guadalupe Hidalgo. In the 1850s a commission headed by William H. Bourland began the task of arbitrating the conflicting claims, for which they were to submit recommendations to the legislature. In the more than 300 claims presented to the commissioners, they found in favor of the original Spanish or Mexican titles in 234 cases and rejected only a handful. But they did not rule on some 70 of them before the commission was dissolved. The remainder were left to the courts, and although it took several generations to do so, all but two of the Mexican claimants succeeded in gaining uncontested title to their lands. The legislature settled the few suits that lingered into the 1920s and 1930s, and the one that lasted 115 years.

JUNE 17

1899 Eleven days of uninterrupted rainfall began in the Brazos valley and its tributaries, eventually dumping close to nine inches of rain on an area of more than 66,000 square miles. As the water collected in the Brazos, the river surged over its banks and flooded 12,000 square miles. It was impossible to say how deep the water was at its peak, because it literally submerged so many flood gauges. The one certain statistic to emerge from the deluge: 284 people were known to have drowned.

JUNE 18

1953 The *Houston Chronicle* reported that a Brownsville family had sighted a six-foot-tall "mothman" perched in a pecan tree in their front yard, with wings, a glowing aura, skin-tight dark clothing, and boots. After a moment the apparition took off, swooped over the houses across the street, and disappeared into the night.

1990 The Lutheran Church of Saint Servatius, in the German town of Quedlinburg, filed suit in the U.S. District Court in Dallas against the heirs of Joe T. Meador of Whitewright, once an American serviceman in Germany during the Second World War. In 1945 Meador's battalion guarded the mine in which the church's art treasures were stored and from which some of them disappeared. Church officials were unable to find them until a thousand-year-old gospel in a jeweled binding was sold in Europe in 1990. The trail eventually led to the vault of the First National Bank of Whitewright, which held the rest of the missing objects. The Texas statute of limitations, two years, had obviously elapsed, so the Germans agreed to buy the stolen treasures back for $2.75 million, including the amount already paid for the gospel in 1990. Before the precious works went back to Germany, the Dallas Museum of Art was permitted to exhibit them for a month, and other Texans could see at last what had lain concealed in their midst for half a century.

JUNE 19

1865   As the Civil War dragged to a close, Major General Gordon Granger occupied Galveston with his Union forces and issued General Order Number 3: "The people of Texas are informed that in accordance with a proclamation from the Executive of the United States 'all slaves are free.'" This event would be the origin of the annual "Juneteenth" celebration.

1936   At the Texas Centennial Exposition in Dallas, the Hall of Negro Life was dedicated on Juneteenth. The exhibits were organized into six themes: education, medicine, agriculture, mechanical arts, industry, and fine arts. Over 400,000 visitors, more than half of them white, viewed the objects contributed by thirty-two states, took in the daily plays and musical performances, and dined in "Little Harlem." Like most of the buildings in the Exposition, the Hall, built in only three months, has since disappeared.

❖
JUNE 20
❖

1857   William Goyens died at the age of sixty-three on his land near Nacogdoches. Goyens was a son of a former slave in North Carolina, freed in recognition of his service in the American Revolution. William was seized by slavers several times but was always able to pay the ransom and free himself. At his death Goyens owned 12,000 acres—and five slaves.

1930   Near San Antonio, Governor Dan Moody officiated at the dedication of the new army air base, Randolph Field. After the widow of Captain William Randolph, an army flyer from Texas killed in a recent crash, raised the American flag over the base for the first time, 15,000 people watched as 233 military aircraft flew overhead in tribute. It was billed as the world's biggest gathering of aircraft. But for some, especially the younger among those present, the most exciting moment came when Governor Moody's car caught fire, then exploded, though no one was hurt.

❖
JUNE 21
❖

1857   Charles Courtice Alderton was born to English immigrant parents in Brooklyn, New York. He would study medicine at the University of Texas in Galveston, then practice pharmacy at W. B. Morrison's Old Corner Drug Store in Waco. There, in 1885, he would concoct a peculiar carbonated beverage which quickly became a favorite all over town, then throughout Texas. Morrison would later explain that the drink was named after a doctor whose daughter he had admired as a youth in Rural Retreat, Virginia. The doctor's name: Charles Pepper.

❖
JUNE 22
❖

1872 E. M. Smith won the court suit in which he claimed title to the land on which the Capitol building stood. The land had previously belonged to Samuel Goucher, who had the title as of 1838. Goucher and his family were thought wiped out by an Indian raid, but in fact his children William, James, and Jane were kidnapped, and later they were found and ransomed. James and Jane had since died, but Smith fast-talked William into selling him the 1,500 acres for $500. In 1874 Smith finally got his money from the legislature.

1949 After a lifetime of fighting fires at oil and gas wells, Ward "Tex" Thornton was murdered at the age of fifty-seven. Thornton was known throughout the Southwest as the "king of the oil-well firefighters"; he invented an asbestos-wrapped nitroglycerin torpedo to be lowered onto a well and detonated to blow out the flames and also designed the asbestos suit worn by firefighters. Having survived the hazards of countless oil and gas fires, including one explosion that left a crater 200 feet wide, he met his death at the hands of two hitchhikers he had given a ride.

❖
JUNE 23
❖

1819 At the Old Stone Fort of Nacogdoches, General or Doctor James Long, with a filibuster expedition of 300 men from Mississippi and Louisiana, proclaimed the independence of Texas from Spain. The Supreme Council of the short-lived entity hoped to enlist Jean Laffite of Galveston and went so far as to name him governor of the island. But a shortage of provisions forced Long's men to scatter across East Texas to forage. By the end of October they had fled back across the Sabine

River, after Governor Antonio Martínez sent an army of 500 soldiers to drive them out. Long tried again in 1820 but was no more successful. This time he was captured and later shot and killed by a guard.

JUNE 24

1878   The day after he was arrested and jailed in Albany, rustler, bushwhacker, and former sheriff John M. Larn was killed by a party of masked vigilantes who broke into the jail and shot him in his cell. It must have seemed like a familiar scene to Larn, who, in the nine years since he arrived in Texas, had ridden with many a vigilance committee himself, most notoriously the Tin Hat Brigade of Fort Griffin, which summarily hanged its share of horse thieves. In 1878 Larn and John Selman, another man with a history of killing with or without a badge, had a contract to deliver cattle to the army. Other ranchers grew suspicious when rustlers struck their herds but never Larn's. A posse found hides with the wrong brand on Larn's premises, and he himself suffered the same swift justice for which he was feared.

1932   The Odessa Rodeo hosted the first jackrabbit roping contest in Texas. Grace Hendricks beat all her male opponents by roping a hare from horseback in only five seconds flat. In 1977 Odessa revived the event, but times had changed. Defenders of animal rights maintained that the contest was cruel to the rabbits and set them free; they were thwarted when the animals wandered back at feeding time. This time the contestants were on foot, and Jack Torian won with a time of six seconds. But an injunction in 1978 ensured that there would be no more jackrabbit rodeos in Odessa.

❖
JUNE 25
❖

1874 Judge Wilson Hey of Mason County wrote to Governor Richard Coke, asking him to send troops to help suppress the rampant cattle rustling in the county. His request was timely, but the response was not. In February 1875 the Mason County War, or Hoodoo War, broke out, in which vigilantes, feuding families, and opportunists looking to settle scores of their own took the lives of perhaps twenty men: some of them rustlers, some of them murderers, some just friends of the wrong people. In August the governor ordered Major John B. Jones and thirty Texas Rangers to restore the peace, but Jones accomplished little, partly because most residents were tight-lipped, partly because some of his men turned out to be old friends of some of the suspected killers. No one was ever brought to justice for any of the Mason County deaths, but the feuds died down toward the end of 1876. On January 21, 1877, the courthouse in Mason burned down, with all its records of the Mason County War.

1947 Former U.S. Army sergeant Macario García of Sugar Land, born in Mexico, became an American citizen. At the time, García was a Texas celebrity on two accounts. First, in November 1944, in Germany, he won the Medal of Honor when he single-handedly knocked out two enemy machine gun nests, killing or capturing ten men despite wounds in his shoulder and his foot. Second, in September 1945, not long after his return from Europe, the owner of a restaurant in Richmond refused to seat him because he was Hispanic. García was incensed at this treatment and said as much. The two men got into a fistfight, and police arrested García . But with the aid of LULAC, other groups, and scores of citizens who resented this shabby homecoming for a serviceman decorated with the

125

nation's highest honor, at his trial he was acquitted of all charges.

JUNE 26

1832 About 100 armed Texans transporting a cannon from Brazoria to Anahuac engaged a similar number of Mexican soldiers, the garrison at Velasco, who tried to confiscate the gun. When the Mexican force ran out of ammunition, they had to surrender; the terms allowed them to return to Mexico unmolested. The Texans lost about ten dead, the Mexicans five. Of the numerous incidents and confrontations leading to the Texas Revolution, this battle was the first in which Texans and Mexicans actually killed each other.

1914 Mildred "Babe" Didrikson, one of America's supreme athletes, was born in Port Arthur. As a one-woman team she competed in the 1932 AAU Championships, where she won five events and set four new world records, scoring more points than the second-place team. In the 1932 Olympics, she won gold medals in the high hurdle and javelin throw, setting world records in both events. After a few years making a living on tour as an exhibition performer, she took on golf. As an amateur she won the 1946 U.S. Women's Tournament, then in 1947 she won seventeen matches in a row. After she turned professional, she won the U.S. Women's Open twice. In 1950 the Associated Press named her Woman Athlete of the First Half-Century. But in 1955 she entered a hospital in Galveston for cancer treatment; she died little more than a year later. She is buried in Beaumont, where a museum is dedicated to her memory.

❖
JUNE 27
❖

1874 Over a hundred Indians of several tribes, led by Comanche chief Quanah Parker, ambushed a party of twenty-eight buffalo hunters at Adobe Walls. Holed up in a few mud buildings, the hunters used their big rifles to kill some thirty or forty attackers, losing three of their own. The Indians settled in for a siege. But on the third day, Billy Dixon, judged the best marksman of the group, decided he would try just one shot with his .50 caliber Sharps at a handful of chiefs on horseback, watching from a hilltop nearly a mile away. To his surprise, and no doubt that of everyone in both camps, one of the riders toppled to the ground. This must have been the final blow for the warriors, who were already stung to find that they were not invulnerable, as Comanche chief Isa-tai had promised they would be. Soon they withdrew; later a few of the Cheyenne in the party thrashed Isa-tai.

❖
JUNE 28
❖

1892 The USS *Texas*, a second-class battleship, was launched at the Norfolk Navy Yard. By the standards of the European navies of the day she was unimpressive, with armor too weak in relation to her twelve-inch guns. But her prowess was never tested by a serious opponent; her only engagement took place six years later in the Spanish-American War, when she was part of the American fleet that annihilated a vastly outgunned Spanish force at Santiago.

1994 Monahans, in eternally sunny Ward County, recorded a temperature of 120 degrees Fahrenheit, tying the state record set on August 12, 1938 in Seymour.

JUNE 29

1893 Ranger Captain Frank Jones and five other Rangers tried to arrest suspected rustlers Jesus Olguin and his son Severio at their ranch called Tres Jacales (Three Huts) on Pirate Island. The island was a no-man's-land between the old and new beds of the Rio Grande, created in 1854 by one of the channel's periodic shifts. From their adobe hut, the Olguins opened fire on the Rangers, hitting Jones several times and killing him. The Rangers had to retreat to Texas without their quarry. Mexican authorities arrested the two men and took them to Juarez, but there is no sign that they were ever prosecuted.

1895 Deputy Marshal George W. Scarborough lured cattle rustler Martin Mroz and his gang onto the bridge from Ciudad Juarez to El Paso. When the outlaws reached the Texas end of the bridge, Scarborough, former chief of police Jeff Milton, and Texas Ranger Frank McMahon opened fire, killing them to a man. The ambush was probably set up by Mroz's attorney, John Wesley Hardin, who was having an affair with his wife, Helen Beulah Mroz.

JUNE 30

1965 James Lyon, a Houston banker, opened Galveston's Flagship Hotel, the first hotel in the country built over a pier. The Flagship still stands on the 340-foot-wide 25th Street "Pleasure Pier," which projects 1,500 feet into the Gulf of Mexico.

JULY

❖
JULY 1
❖

1901 Veteran rancher Anna Martin founded the Commercial Bank of Mason and became the only female head of a bank in the country. She remained president of the bank for the last twenty-four years of her life. In 1864 Anna was forced to take over the family store in Hedwig's Hill, Mason County, when her husband Karl was made an invalid by an illness that killed him fifteen years later. She made the store prosper and began to plow the added income into cattle and land: Eventually she owned 50,000 acres in three counties. A comment she once made would have served as a perfect epitaph when she died at eighty-two: "I heard men say, 'oh, she is only a woman,' but I showed them what a woman could do."

1925 Deeming helium to be vital for military use as a safe alternative to the hydrogen used in dirigibles and blimps, the Bureau of Mines assumed control of all helium production in the United States. In essence, this meant the Panhandle gas fields around Amarillo, which were then, and are still, the greatest known concentration of helium on earth. The Defense Department doesn't operate many blimps today, but helium is still in demand for medical and industrial purposes. In 1968, the one hundredth anniversary of the discovery of the element helium in the spectrum of the star Helios (our sun), Amarillo erected the Helium Time Column, a stainless steel time capsule in the shape of a helium atom six stories tall.

JULY 2

1936 Sixteen-year-old Keith Rumbel fired several rockets from McAllen to Reynosa and vice versa, the first and only time that international mail has been carried by rocket power. The object of Rumbel's pyrotechnical exercise was to raise money for his father's American Legion Post by selling exclusive covers to philatelists. His first missile exploded over the Rio Grande, and its cargo fluttered down into the river, half of it never to be recovered. His next shot hit the U.S. Bar in downtown Reynosa. But the rest landed intact and at least close enough to the target to be accessible, at ranges from 1,000 feet to almost a mile.

JULY 3

1907 Pedro Jaramillo, the Folk Saint of Falfurrias, died at about seventy years old. In his home was over $5,000 in fifty-cent coins. Don Pedrito became a healer, or *curandero,* as a young man when he woke to a voice that told him that God had granted him the gift of healing. Despite his obvious lack of medical training, many people resorted to him because the nearest doctor was fifty miles away. In his ordinary peasant dress, he became a familiar figure over much of the southern tip of Texas at the turn of the century. He charged nothing for his treatments and prescriptions (which consisted of the first thing that occurred to him at the moment), but he received thousands of donations of a dollar or half-dollar, which he spent on food for visiting patients and donations to area churches. Some of his remedies became legends, like the woman who sent a servant to get a cure for a chronic headache:

Pedrito recommended she cut her head off, and when the servant relayed this advice the woman threw such a tantrum that she forgot her headache. His grave in Falfurrias is now a shrine, where every year hundreds still go to be healed.

1931 The "Red River War" began, as the Red River Bridge Company filed in a Houston court for an injunction against the Texas Highway Commission. Texas and Oklahoma had just built a new bridge across the river at Denison, and the company wanted it kept closed until the Highway Commission fulfilled its agreement to buy their old toll bridge, which the new free bridge would naturally make obsolete. The court issued the injunction on the 10th, and Texas governor Ross S. Sterling ordered the new bridge barricaded at the Texas end. Governor William Murray of Oklahoma had no intention of letting Texas close his new bridge, however, and sent a highway crew on the 16th to demolish the barrier. When Sterling sent Texas Rangers to put it back up, Alfalfa Bill ordered his men to block the toll bridge, leaving both bridges unusable. On the 23rd the Texas legislature met in special session to appease the Red River Bridge Company, which then acquiesced in canceling the injunction. The new bridge reopened on the 25th. But meanwhile Murray had declared martial law at the Oklahoma end of the toll bridge and ordered a guard unit to occupy it; he himself showed up with an old six-shooter. When the original injunction was officially closed on August 6, the guard was recalled and the war ended, its only casualty a guardsman who tripped and stabbed himself in the leg with his bayonet and was treated at the nearest hospital—in Denison.

------------ ❖ ------------
JULY 4
------------ ❖ ------------

1865 At Eagle Pass, General Joseph Shelby, CSA, commander of the Iron Cavalry Brigade from Missouri, solemnly let his Confederate battle flag sink beneath the Rio Grande. His unit, which crossed the border into Mexico as the war ended, was the last Confederate force to surrender, leading some to call the site the "Grave of the Confederacy."

1909 In northwest Howard County, the fledgling town of Soash, named for land promoter William P. Soash of Iowa, held a big shindig, with a barbecue dinner, a rodeo, a baseball game, a vaudeville show, and even a dance under electric lights. Twenty-five hundred prospective residents attended, conveyed by a special excursion train, and it looked like W. P. would make a killing in land sales. But the drought that began that summer lasted three years; all prospects of further development literally dried up. The Soash Land Company, which had once operated in eight states, went bankrupt, and the community of Soash was soon a ghost town.

——————— ❖ ———————
JULY 5
——————— ❖ ———————

1956 Pioneer of Texas aviation Floyd H. "Slats" Rodgers died in McAllen. He started work with the Gulf, Colorado, and Santa Fe Railroad and even qualified as a locomotive engineer. But in his late twenties, his boyhood interest in kites developed into a passion for aviation. In 1912 Rodgers designed and built his first airplane in Texas, which he named *Old Soggy Number 1* because of a stubbornly droopy wing. After that he lived the classic life of aviation's early days: barnstormer, stunt pilot, Prohibition-era bootlegger (for which he paid with a six-month jail term), and crop duster. He was issued the first pilot's license in the state and was also the first pilot to have his license revoked.

❖
JULY 6

❖

1870 The Senate confirmed the nomination of Second Lieutenant James Davidson as adjutant general of Texas, with a promotion to the rank of colonel. This put Davidson in charge of the newly organized State Police. He executed his office diligently and aggressively, although the force itself was the subject of controversy in a Texas where Reconstruction had ended mere months before. In December of 1872, Davidson left Texas on state business, and in his absence it surfaced that he had drawn funds from the Treasury to pay the State Police but had kept the money for himself. Governor Edmund J. Davis offered a reward for his capture and put the State Police on his trail, but Davidson had vanished. He and the $37,000 were never found.

❖
JULY 7

❖

1838 Peter Grayson, the Republic's naval agent to the United States and Sam Houston's choice to succeed him as president, committed suicide in Bean's Station, Tennessee, possibly in despair because the woman he loved had rejected his proposal of marriage, but more likely because of the mental illness that had plagued him for a decade or more. Houston's next choice, Chief Justice James Collinsworth, promptly drowned after falling, probably drunk, from a boat into Galveston Bay. Houston himself could not run because the constitution did not allow consecutive terms for a president, and the loss of the two best candidates among his supporters ensured that his rival Mirabeau B. Lamar would be elected in September.

1911   Alphonso Steele, age ninety-four, the last living veteran of Sam Houston's army at San Jacinto, died in Mexia. Steele was badly wounded early in the battle, but lived another seventy-five years. In 1906 he and six other veterans visited the battleground for the seventieth anniversary, but since then his other comrades had all passed on. Now all the men who charged to shouts of "Remember the Alamo," and radically changed history in twenty minutes, were gone.

JULY 8

1860   The "Texas Troubles" began with a rash of fires in several North Texas towns, the worst damage occurring in Dallas and Denton. In an atmosphere already filled with distrust and fear, vigilante committees appeared quickly. Editorials in newspapers across the state warned that a bloody slave revolt was imminent, but over the next three months the only blood shed was that of some thirty abolitionists and slaves, hanged despite a lack of clear evidence that any plot existed. It is more likely, as some people even thought at the time, that the fires started when unusually hot weather triggered spontaneous combustion of newfangled phosphorus matches.

JULY 9

1857   The first overland mail coach left San Antonio, headed for San Diego, California, via El Paso and Santa Fe, New Mexico. The service, founded by San Antonio merchant George H. Giddings and New Englander James Birch, continued semimonthly until the Civil War. Typical time for the 1,500-mile ordeal was three to four weeks, for which a hardy passenger paid the substantial sum of $200.

❖
JULY 10
❖

1939   Wilford Bascom Smith, editor of *The Pitchfork*, died in Dallas. Pitchfork Smith began publishing his muckraking magazine in Kansas City in 1907, but his radical opinions moved more people to burn their copies than to read them. He moved to Dallas in 1908, and there he published *The Pitchfork* for the next thirty-one years. His fiery oratory made him a popular speaker as well as journalist, and he fought oppression, injustice, fraud, and hypocrisy from the podium as well as in print. One gets some idea of his tenacity in debate from the headline of his obituary in *The Dallas Morning News*: "Death Wins Argument With Pitchfork Smith."

❖
JULY 11
❖

1919   The day after the *Chicago Defender* described the death of Lemuel Walters, a young black man from Longview murdered by a white mob for wanting to marry a white woman from Kilgore, two men, supposedly the woman's brothers, beat Samuel Jones of Longview, the author of the article. Word of the attack spread among residents of both races, and Jones's neighborhood became the scene of first a gunfight, then a general riot as a white mob burned Jones's home and several others. Before the National Guard could gain control, one black man was killed. Forty-seven men, white and black, were arrested on charges of attempted murder, arson, or assault, but none was ever prosecuted.

❖
JULY 12
❖

1844   William Sumter Murphy, United States minister to the Republic of Texas, died in Galveston of yellow fever. He was on his way back to Washington, having been recalled when negotiations for annexation broke down, despite the support of both Murphy and President Sam Houston. Given that it was a purely diplomatic position, being U.S. minister to Texas was a surprisingly dangerous assignment; Murphy was the third man to die at his post in four years.

1912 Twenty-one-year-old Katherine Stinson became the fourth woman in America to earn her pilot's license. She needed money to study music in Europe and thought being a stunt pilot would be a good way to earn it. But she soon forgot music, and flying became her chosen career. In 1913 she and her family established the Stinson School of Flying in San Antonio, where the U.S. Army permitted her to use the parade ground of Fort Sam Houston as a runway. Stinson was recognized as the most advanced female pilot in the country: the first of her sex to loop-the-loop (and only the fourth pilot in America to do so), the first to fly at night, the first to skywrite in the dark, the first to fly the U.S. Mail. She even built her own aircraft. When the U.S. entered the war in Europe, the "world's greatest woman pilot" applied for military aviation but was rejected because of her gender, so she served as an ambulance driver. She came home with tuberculosis, which ended her flying career. She spent the rest of her life as an architect and died in 1977.

❖ JULY 13 ❖

1883 Six drunken cowboys, having painted the little town of Pecos red, caught the Texas & Pacific to Toyah, fifteen miles to the west. They started a repeat performance, but soon found themselves cornered by three Texas Rangers and a posse of locals. No doubt to their surprise and dismay, a serious gun battle erupted, and when the smoke cleared, one of the cowpokes was dead, along with an unlucky bystander, and four of the remaining five were badly wounded.

1944 A training flight of B-24 Liberator bombers from Biggs Army Air Field in El Paso mistook the town of Sierra Blanca for their practice range and dumped their payload on the Hudspeth County seat. They dropped ten bombs, but fortunately they were only carrying dummies, which contained mostly sand plus a small charge to make the impact visible from the air. Five of them landed on railroad tracks, and one hit the driveway of a service station, but no one was injured and no buildings were damaged.

JULY 14

1918 At the height of anti-German hysteria in America, when even the words "hamburger" and "sauerkraut" sounded too foreign and were replaced with "liberty burger" and "liberty cabbage," and the nation's orchestras boycotted composers with Germanic names like Bach or Beethoven, the sizable German immigrant population of Texas looked for ways to demonstrate its loyalty. The farmers of New Brandenburg in Stonewall County, concerned that the name of their town had an overly Teutonic ring, wanted to change it to something more patriotic. They decided Old Glory was just the thing, and Old Glory, Texas, population around one hundred, is still there today.

JULY 15

1930 Robert Ernest House, the obstetrician who discovered "truth serum," died of a stroke at the age of fifty-four. In 1924, in his practice in the Ellis County town of Ferris, House was experimenting with the sedative scopolamine hydrobromide when he noticed that patients entered a state in which they could respond to questions but could not rationalize their answers. That is to say, they could not avoid telling the truth. His discovery brought him national attention, and for the rest of his life he worked with law enforcement agencies in studying the application of the drug to the interrogation of suspects.

JULY 16

1839 The two-day Battle of the Neches, which started on the 15th after Cherokee chief Bowles refused to sign a one-sided treaty with the Republic, ended with Sam Houston's friend Bowles dead and the Cherokee routed. The Texas army of 500 men was commanded by a galaxy of the Republic's early leaders: Vice President David G. Burnet, Secretary of War Albert Sidney Johnston, future chief justice Thomas Jefferson Rusk, and future vice president Edward Burleson were all there. Some 700 Indians fought behind Bowles, a red-haired, freckled half-Scot who proudly wore a sword and sash that had been a gift from Houston; he was shot down when he refused to retreat. Houston was enraged by what he called the "murder" of his old companion, no less so when Burleson sent him Bowles's hat as a trophy. But no matter what Houston might say, the day of the Cherokee in Texas was over.

Son of a Scottish immigrant and a Cherokee squaw, **Chief Bowles** died wearing Sam Houston's sword.

Photo courtesy Texas State Library and Archives Commission

❖
JULY 17
❖

1882 Cattleman George Reynolds of Fort Griffin visited a Kansas City hospital to have an arrowhead removed, fifteen years after he was shot in a fight with Indians on a horse-stealing raid near his West Texas ranch in April 1867. The stone chip had pained him all those years, as it slowly worked from front to back. But now Reynolds could feel a bump near his spine, and the arrowhead was readily extracted at last.

1938 Douglas Corrigan, born in Galveston, left New York's Roosevelt Field in his rickety Curtiss OX5 Robin monoplane, nicknamed *Lizzy*, ostensibly headed back to Los Angeles, whence he had arrived a few days before. Corrigan, who helped build Charles Lindbergh's *Spirit of Saint Louis* in 1927, had asked for clearance to fly nonstop from New York to Ireland, but the Bureau of Air Commerce had refused, saying that his aircraft was unfit for such a long and dangerous flight. To the surprise of those watching from the ground, *Lizzy* headed not west but east; twenty-three hours later she landed at Baldonnel Airport in Dublin. Corrigan claimed that his compass had let him down and was instantly dubbed "Wrong Way Corrigan." When he and *Lizzy* returned to America (by ship), air officials levied a token penalty, and Corrigan was given a ticker tape parade down Broadway.

❖
JULY 18
❖

1926 J. Frank Norris, controversial and nationally famous fundamentalist, shot and killed lumberman D. C. Chipps, a friend of Mayor Henry C. Meacham of Fort Worth, in the office of the First Baptist Church, where Norris had been pastor for seventeen years. Norris was tried for murder, but he claimed he had acted in self-defense and was acquitted. Although his opinions were so extreme that he and the First Baptist Church were excluded from the annual meeting of the Baptist General Convention for two years, he remained pastor of the church until he died twenty-six years later.

JULY 19

1876 The first steam locomotive, operated by the Texas and Pacific Railroad, pulled into Fort Worth. All the businesses in the city had loaned every man they could spare to work on grading the roadbed into town, in a desperate effort to beat the deadline set by the T&P. It was a triumph for the "Panther City," so named after a recent letter had appeared in the *Dallas Herald* claiming that the town was so dead that a panther could be observed sleeping undisturbed on the main thoroughfare.

1878 In Round Rock, Sam Bass and two accomplices were scouting the town in preparation for a bank robbery the next day, when two deputy sheriffs challenged them and were shot down. Several Texas Rangers, tipped off by a gang member, were waiting in town but were taken by surprise, knowing that the robbery was planned for the following day. Still they killed one man and fatally wounded Bass; the other robber escaped. Bass died two days later, on his twenty-seventh birthday. With the exception of his first train robbery at Big Spring, Nebraska, which yielded 3,000 twenty-dollar gold pieces, all of Bass's robberies had earned him little more than drinking money.

JULY 20

1969 The first word transmitted to Earth from the surface of the Moon was the name of the largest city in Texas. Astronaut Neil Armstrong, in command of *Apollo XI*, notified the Manned Spacecraft Center, a quarter million miles away, that the Lunar Module had touched down safely: "Houston, Tranquility Base here. The Eagle has landed."

1979 The 101-year-old three-masted barque *Elissa* arrived at her new permanent home in Galveston. Nine years earlier Peter Throckmorton, a curator of the National Maritime Historical Society, had noticed her at a dock in Piraeus and mortgaged his home to purchase her from Greek smugglers. From the time of her launching on Scotland's Clyde River in 1877, the *Elissa* led a varied career under a variety of names, rigs, and flags, visiting ports around the world, including Galveston. Now, once more under her original name, she belonged to the Galveston Historical Foundation, which spent the next three years restoring her hull, deck, masts, yards, rigging, and sails, before opening her to the public. The *Elissa* still sails on occasion and takes part in gatherings of square-riggers from around the world.

JULY 21

1925 Frontier woman doctor Sofie Dalia Herzog died in Houston, at age seventy-nine. She was buried with her necklace of twenty-four lead bullets. Born and schooled in Vienna, she was living in New Jersey when she visited her daughter in Brazoria in the late 1890s and decided to stay. She overcame the inevitable resistance to a female physician and was eventually welcomed as "Doctor Sofie." The Saint Louis, Brownsville, and Mexico Railway ran through the region, and for years she frequently treated injured rail workers. Just after the turn of the century she took on the post of chief surgeon, and she worked for the railroad almost until her death. Gunshot wounds were an everyday occurrence in that time and place; when she had accumulated twenty-four slugs plucked from her patients, she had a Houston jeweler string them between gold links as a good luck charm, which she wore to her grave.

JULY 22

1861 Even among the general celebrations following the previous day's Confederate victory at First Bull Run, sugar planter Benjamin F. Terry of Fort Bend County, a volunteer aide to General Longstreet, attracted attention with an exploit of his own. He reconnoitered the Fairfax Courthouse and audaciously replaced the Union flag with a rebel banner. This dashing gesture may have helped Terry overcome the Confederate War Department's lack of interest in troops from Texas, for he returned home with authority to raise a cavalry regiment. Terry's Texas Rangers would be one of the most famous cavalry units of the war on either side, but Terry would not enjoy that acclaim, for he was killed in their first engagement.

JULY 23

1798 Jane Wilkinson was born in Charles County, Maryland. As the wife of Doctor James Long, in 1819 and 1821 she waited out his two misguided attempts to make Texas independent of Mexico. During the second abortive uprising, Long left her in his fort at Bolivar Point, where she was stranded through the winter of 1821-1822, alone except for her six-year-old daughter, a twelve-year-old servant girl, and a mongrel dog. Furthermore, she was pregnant and delivered a daughter on December 21, 1821, for which she is often called the "Mother of Texas" (although hers was not in fact the first Anglo child born here). When Karankawa Indians threatened, she frightened them away with a cannon and a flag made from a red flannel petticoat. Meanwhile Long had been captured, and in April he was killed in Mexico City. But Jane lived another fifty-eight years. She later ran boardinghouses, first in Brazoria, then in Richmond, where according to tradition she caught the eyes of some of the leaders of the 1836 Revolution, like Sam Houston and Mirabeau B. Lamar (who wrote her love poems). But she was still unmarried at her death in 1880.

1861 Near modern Deming, New Mexico, a band of Apaches led by Mangas Coloradas attacked the last stage to leave El Paso for the West Coast. On board were seven Union sympathizers from Texas seeking asylum in California; the Indians killed them all.

JULY 24

1917 In the rush to arm after America entered the First World War, construction of Camp Logan, a new training center, began just west of Houston. The 3rd Battalion of the 24th Infantry, a black unit, was assigned there, and immediately became the object of racial slurs and harassment in the city. On August 23 two Houston policemen arrested a black woman for gambling; a black private and a black MP who confronted the police were also taken in. At the camp, a rumor that police had killed a black soldier grew into hysteria. When someone shouted that a white mob was coming for them, Sergeant Vida Henry led 100 armed men to the neighborhood where the trouble had started. In the rampage that followed, they killed five policemen and fifteen other white men. Three of the soldiers were also killed, and after the mutineers headed back to camp, Henry shot himself in the head. Martial law, a curfew, and troops from Galveston and San Antonio brought calm back to Houston. At Fort Sam Houston in San Antonio, a series of courts martial found 110 men of the 3rd Battalion guilty of mutiny; 19 were hanged and 63 imprisoned for life.

The next year, after the Armistice, the Hogg brothers bought the land, and it is now the site of Memorial Park.

JULY 25

1943 The destroyer escort USS *Harmon* (DE-678) was launched at Quincy, Massachusetts, the first ship in the U.S. Navy to be named after a black American. Leonard Roy Harmon, born in Cuero, enlisted in Houston in 1939. After training he reported aboard the heavy cruiser *San Francisco* as a Mess Attendant 1st Class. At the Battle of Guadalcanal, on the night of November 13, 1942, Harmon's ship was part of a force of cruisers and destroyers that barged into a Japanese fleet led by two battleships. The *San Francisco* was badly mauled in the confused fighting, and Harmon gave his life by placing his body over a wounded shipmate exposed to machine gun fire. For his sacrifice, he was awarded a posthumous Navy Cross.

JULY 26

1887 With a vision of exploiting the railroads to make Fort Worth the cattle capital of Texas, a group of Fort Worth businessmen chartered the Union Stockyards. Ten years later the Fort Worth Stockyards hosted the first Southwestern Exposition and Livestock Show, which is still one of the nation's greatest. By the turn of the century the sprawling complex of pens and packing plants, headlined by the Armour and Swift companies, was the largest livestock market in the Southwest, and remained one of the three or four biggest in the nation until the 1950s. In the latter fifties and sixties rail freight traffic declined, and local auctions decentralized much of the cattle business; the Swift and Armour plants closed. Though the Fort Worth Stockyards are no longer active in their original purpose, they are still preserved as a monument to the days when Fort Worth was known around the country as "Cowtown."

JULY 27

1861 Lieutenant Colonel John R. Baylor, with the fewer than 300 troops of the 2nd Texas Mounted Rifles, captured Fort Fillmore and its garrison of 500 Union soldiers, in New Mexico north of El Paso. He declared the creation of the Confederate Territory of Arizona, comprising the southern half of New Mexico and Arizona, with himself as military governor. But the following March, the Union victory at Glorieta Pass ended Confederate dreams of a Western empire.

JULY 28

1898 In Corsicana, a peg-legged itinerant tightrope walker, with a cast-iron stove strapped to his back, attempted to traverse a rope stretched between the roofs of two buildings on either side of Beaton Street. But despite the notch in the end of his wooden leg that fit the rope, he lost his balance and fell to earth. In his last extremity the stranger, who claimed to be sixty-nine years old, called for a rabbi, but there was none in town. No one caught his name before he expired, and his headstone in the Hebrew Cemetery reads simply "Rope Walker."

1933 William E. Morris of Nueces County received the country's first payment under the cotton acreage reduction program, intended to boost low cotton prices which had wiped out farmers in Texas and across the South. For plowing under his 47 acres of cotton, President Franklin Delano Roosevelt sent Morris a check for $517.

JULY 29

1860   In Jacksboro, fire destroyed the offices of the weekly newspaper *The White Man*. The paper was founded earlier that year as a mouthpiece for virulent advocates of the removal, if not outright extermination, of all Indians in Texas. Governor Sam Houston's conciliatory policies were naturally a favorite target. With its convenient location on the Butterfield Overland Mail route, *The White Man* reached probably a thousand readers in North Texas. In time it expanded its mission to preaching secession and supporting the institution of slavery, so it was not surprising that the editors blamed the fire on abolitionists. They started the paper up again in Weatherford, but it shut down in late 1861.

1947   On "Boot Hill," on the outskirts of Nocona, second-generation bootmaker Miss Enid Justin broke ground for a big new Nocona Boot factory. Enid's brothers had moved the family business to Fort Worth after their father's death, but Enid felt that he would have wished to remain in Nocona, so she continued operations there under the Nocona name, and prospered. Not until 1981 would Nocona Boots merge with Justin Industries and the two branches of the family tradition be reunited.

JULY 30

1923   Roy Mitchell, convicted of murdering four white men and two white women, calmly stepped onto the gallows platform behind the McLennan County courthouse in Waco, and said, "Goodbye, everybody." Just before the trap fell, he muttered, "Take me home," and the Phantom Killer of the Brazos was dead. Mitchell is commonly thought to have been the last man publicly hanged in Texas. But Nathan Lee, another black man, executed in the Brazoria County seat of Angleton on August 31, 1923, for killing his white employer with a shotgun, was actually the last.

1956 A fire at the Shamrock-McKee Oil tank farm, between Dumas and Sunray in Moore County, suddenly turned into a horrifying catastrophe. Firemen from both towns were called to fight the blaze, which initially involved only one of the tanks. But 50-foot flames touched off three other tanks, igniting a total of 50,000 barrels. The fireball was visible in Amarillo, forty miles away. Ten firemen and nine Shamrock employees were killed, and thirty-two others badly burned. Even spectators a quarter mile from the scene suffered serious burns.

❖

JULY 31

❖

1964 James Travis Reeves, born in Galloway and raised in Carthage, died at the age of forty in a plane crash near Nashville, along with his piano player Dean Manuel. In the late 1940s, after a stint as a disc jockey in Henderson, Jim Reeves started singing and recording, using the name Sonny Day. By 1953 he was appearing on the "Louisiana Hayride," and in 1955 he joined the Grand Ole Opry. Three years after his funeral in Carthage, he was inducted into the Country Music Hall of Fame.

AUGUST

❖ AUGUST 1 ❖

1918 Sheriff John Banister of Coleman County died in Coleman. To fill the term until elections in November, the county commissioners appointed his wife of twenty-four years, Emma, to succeed him as sheriff. Emma Banister, who for years had helped her husband run the sheriff's office and the county jail, thus became the first female sheriff in United States history. The appointment made headlines across the country, particularly since women still could not vote. But although she handled her duties so well that the commissioners invited her to run for office, she turned in her badge and went back to the family farm in Santa Anna, where she lived another thirty-eight years.

1973 In La Grange, Fayette County, the "Best Little Whorehouse in Texas" was closed down after more than a century and a quarter of uninterrupted service. Every night of the previous week, newsman Marvin Zindler of Houston television station KTRK had run an exposé of the famous brothel the Chicken Ranch, alleging that it was connected with organized crime and corrupt law officials. Although Edna Milton ran the nation's oldest cathouse with impeccable standards and even cooperated with Sheriff T. J. Flournoy in screening employees for criminal records, the publicity was more than

Governor Dolph Briscoe could ignore, and he ordered Flournoy to shut the place down. The name, incidentally, dates from the Depression, when money was scarce but poultry wasn't, and the price for one moment of ecstasy was one chicken.

AUGUST 2

1946 A visitor from space splashed down in Brewster County, as the Peña Blanca Spring meteorite landed in a swimming pool on the Gage ranch. In fact, Texas is a leader in collecting meteorites, both in the United States and in the world as a whole. Meteorites in Texas history date back at least to 1772, when explorer Athanase de Mézières learned of a gigantic rock venerated for its supernatural properties by Indians around the upper Brazos, who called it Medicine Rock. White traders eventually acquired the "Texas Iron" and brought it down the Red River to Louisiana. In 1835 Yale University's Peabody Museum of Natural History became its home, and there the 1,635-pound lump of iron and nickel can be found today. Odessa's crater goes back much farther than that, of course; it was formed 20,000 years ago when a meteorite struck the limestone bedrock and exploded, leaving nothing but a hole 500 feet across.

AUGUST 3

1970 The coastal towns of Aransas Pass and Robstown logged record gusts of 180 miles per hour during Hurricane Celia, a storm characterized by lower than average rainfall but extremely high winds. Celia left thirteen people dead and seven counties declared disaster areas.

❖ AUGUST 4 ❖

1838 In Nacogdoches, the Córdova Rebellion came to light. For months Texans had heard rumors of an alliance between the Mexican government and the Indians in Texas, mostly Cherokee, in which the Indians were promised the return of their lands if they would help Mexico retake Texas. When a Nacogdoches posse looking for horse thieves met a group of about one hundred Mexicans, who opened fire on them, the Texas government sent the militia to deal with them. Meanwhile the insurrectionists, led by Vicente Córdova, an eminent man of Nacogdoches, had recruited about three hundred Indians, but faced with serious armed resistance most of them dispersed. Córdova and a fragment of his army were retreating to Mexico when another Texas volunteer force overtook them on the Guadalupe River near Seguin; Córdova made it across the border barely alive. Back in Nacogdoches, thirty-three Hispanic suspects were arrested for treason, but only one was convicted; four days before he would have been executed, he was pardoned. But the link between Mexico and the uprising was far from imaginary. Papers found on two Mexicans killed in separate incidents clearly implicated the Mexican government in secretly inciting the Cherokee, including Sam Houston's friend Chief Bowles. In July 1839 Bowles was killed in the Battle of the Neches, and the Cherokee were driven out of the Republic.

❖ AUGUST 5 ❖

1961 Six Flags Over Texas, one of America's first theme parks, opened in Arlington. The vast amusement park is named for the six countries whose flags have flown over Texas: Spain, France, Mexico, the Republic of Texas, the Confederacy, and the United States. More than a million people visit Six Flags every year, among them the roller coaster afficionados who want to experience the Texas Giant, one of the highest old-fashioned wooden roller coasters in the world.

1973 Trapeze artist and female impersonator Vander Clyde died at his sister's home in Round Rock, where he was born in 1904. At the age of fourteen, in San Antonio, he joined the circus act of the "World Famous Aerial Queens" the Alfaretta Sisters, who insisted that he wear a girl's costume. Soon he was working on a solo routine in which he performed in female dress, then revealed his secret at the end of the act. As "Barbette," he toured the United States and then Europe, where he became a darling of Paris society and the literati. He remained enormously popular through the 1930s, and his career ended only when he caught pneumonia in 1938 while appearing in New York. The disease crippled him, and it was more than a year before he could walk again. But he continued to inspire Continental poets like Jean Cocteau, who were enthralled by the combination of feminine grace and masculine strength, enacted at heights where perfection became a matter not just of artistry but of life and death.

———— ❖ ————
AUGUST 6
———— ❖ ————

1880 At Rattlesnake Springs, five companies of the black Tenth U.S. Cavalry ambushed a raiding party of 150 Apaches led by Victorio. For the past year, Victorio and his warriors had pillaged both sides of the Rio Grande along the Chihuahua-New Mexico border, and recently they had entered the mountains of West Texas. Colonel Benjamin Grierson estimated that the best place to intercept Victorio would be the waterholes where the Indians were likely to stop, and after a prodigious ride of 65 miles in 21 hours, his men were in position when the raiders approached Rattlesnake Springs in the afternoon. After a three-hour battle, Victorio could only retreat southwest toward Mexico. There, in October, Colonel Joaquín Terrazas and the Chihuahua state militia cornered him and killed every last warrior, sparing only squaws and children.

AUGUST 7

1867   In Jefferson, U.S. Revenue collector David B. Bonfoey confronted a deputy collector named W. H. Fowler, and accused him of conniving with area cotton dealers to embezzle taxes. Fowler drew a pistol, and threatened to kill Bonfoey unless he signed a receipt that would absolve him of any misdeed. When Bonfoey agreed, Fowler naively put down his gun to prepare the receipt, and Bonfoey pulled his own pistol and shot him dead. He was jailed pending an inquiry into the affair. Late in that same month, Bonfoey's wife was attacked at their home in Marshall, where a safe held $34,000 in tax money plus $13,000 of their personal savings. The robbers failed to break into the safe, but they left her in a coma with her skull split open, and she died without ever awakening. The detail of federal guards assigned to the house was accused of the crime, but this was Reconstruction Texas; the military government sent the men out of town, and they soon disappeared. When Bonfoey came home to Marshall, he visited his wife's grave, collapsed there in grief, and died the next day.

AUGUST 8

1840   Two days after attacking nearby Victoria, Chief Buffalo Hump led a thousand Comanches and Kiowas, including five hundred warriors, in an assault on the little port of Linnville, where they again took the residents by surprise. Most of the townspeople managed to evacuate to boats and ships in the harbor, but from that refuge they could only watch as the Indians spent the day looting and burning their town. In the afternoon they moved on with thousands of horses, a few captives, and as much plunder as they could carry. In the attacks on the two towns and outlying farms, Buffalo Hump's warriors killed about twenty-three people. But four days later, two hundred volunteers and Texas Rangers led by General Felix Huston caught them at Plum Creek. Despite the imbalance in numbers, the Texans charged; in the resulting melee, they killed about one hundred of the Indians and drove off the rest. Modern Lockhart, the site of the battle, commemorates the settlers' victory in an annual re-enactment.

❖ AUGUST 9 ❖

1923 Reverend Burrell Cannon, reputed aviation pioneer, died in Marshall. Twenty-one years earlier, in Pittsburg, the Reverend supposedly built a flying machine based on a description in the Book of Ezekiel, in which "a wheel in the middle of a wheel" figured prominently. His design was driven by a "wind wheel," a device somewhat reminiscent of an autogyro, which Cannon patented on May 31, 1901. If it is true he actually flew the craft, then he beat the Wright Brothers by more than two years. In any case, in 1901 Cannon chartered the Ezekiel Airship Manufacturing Company, and sold $20,000 worth of shares to assorted citizens of Pittsburg. In 1903 he put his invention on a train, meaning to show it to potential backers in Saint Louis. But in Texarkana strong winds threw the frail contraption from its railroad car, irreparably damaging it, and that was the end of the mysterious Ezekiel Airship.

1946 In Hays County, near Driftwood, the last of the Confederate reunions at Camp Ben McCulloch convened. No members of the camp were present, however, as the last two veterans had died in the previous year, so the final reunion was principally a memorial to them. Exactly fifty years had elapsed since the camp was founded as the site for an annual three days of nostalgia and tall tales for ex-soldiers of the Confederacy. At its peak, more than 5,000 people attended every year. Today residents of Hays County still like to picnic there.

AUGUST 10

1862 Sixty-eight Union loyalists from Comfort, mostly German immigrants, were on their way to Mexico after the Texas government had proclaimed that anyone who would not swear allegiance to the Confederacy must leave the state. They were camped on the banks of the Nueces River when a larger force of Confederates attacked. In a battle that lasted an hour, twenty-seven of them were killed or wounded, then the rest escaped. The Confederate commander ordered the nine wounded prisoners killed. After the war, the men's remains were returned to Comfort; their monument, the only Northern memorial in a Confederate state, reads *"Treue der Union"* (True to the Union).

1909 Howard R. Hughes of Beaumont was granted two patents for his rotary drill bit, which revolutionized the oil industry. Previous rock drills had worked by scraping the surface away, and much of the rock above promising oil sites was just too hard for such drills to penetrate. But Hughes designed a bit that used conical cutters with hardened steel teeth to grind the rock into powder. When he tested his new bit for the first time at Goose Creek, a site where he had previously been unable to make even a dent, the drill penetrated fourteen feet in eleven hours. Within a few years the Hughes bit was the standard around the world. Hughes's third famous product, besides his drill bit and the Hughes Tool Company, was his aviator son Howard Jr.

AUGUST 11

1861 A detachment of ten Confederate soldiers and two Mexican scouts from Fort Davis, led by Lieutenant Reuben Mays, commander of the garrison, found themselves trapped by Mescalero Apaches in a canyon south of the fort. Mays had pursued the Indians into the ravine despite the advice of a civilian in the party, a seasoned frontiersman named Jack Woodland, and when it was too late for them to back out, the Apaches opened fire and hit every man, killing several outright. Woodland was hit twice before he and one of the Mexicans could find cover together. When night fell, Woodland gave his rifle to his companion, saying he was as good as dead but would fight on, saving his last round for himself to avoid capture and torture. He told the man to escape if he could, which in the darkness he managed to do. Several days later he led rescuers back to the site, but the Indians had vanished, leaving only one body and a few fragments of clothing.

AUGUST 12

1896 In Nogales, Arizona, several dozen Indians attacked the Mexican customs house. Exiles from Mexico, they identified themselves as *Teresitas*, or followers of Teresa Urrea, a twenty-two-year-old Mexican-born *curandera* (faith healer) who then lived in El Paso. Before she came to the United States, Urrea was involved, perhaps involuntarily, in several uprisings by the downtrodden of Sonora who were moved by her example of a simple and just life. For that she was deported; now the same government that had expelled her demanded she be extradited back to Mexico. In a statement printed in the *El*

Paso Herald, she insisted she was not connected to the episode in Arizona, but after three attempts on her life, she decided to leave El Paso. She moved to Arizona, but well away from the border and Nogales. Teresa continued her career of miraculous healing, but on at least one occasion her powers apparently were of no use: In 1900 she married a Yaqui Indian, and the next day he went insane and had to be committed.

AUGUST 13

1966　The East Texas town of Longview joined the nation-wide reaction to a careless remark by Beatle John Lennon. After the *New York Times* reprinted an interview by Maureen Cleave of the *Evening Standard*, in which Lennon said that the Beatles were "more popular than Christ," radio station KLUE sponsored a public bonfire of Beatles albums. All over the Bible Belt, offended Christians burned effigies of the Fab Four, and a priest in Cleveland, Ohio, threatened to excommunicate any-one who attended their upcoming concert in his city. Manager Brian Epstein almost canceled the rest of the tour, but Lennon issued a retraction and all the shows went on without incident.

AUGUST 14

1719　The ship *Maréchal d'Estrée* of the French West Indies Company set sail for Louisiana. Among her officers was twenty-four-year-old François Simars de Bellisle. After the ship lost her way in the Gulf of Mexico and overshot the Mississippi River, she went aground in the vicinity of Galveston Bay. Bellisle and four other men went ashore to reconnoiter, but the *d'Estrée* worked free again and sailed off, leaving the five Frenchmen behind. They started out to walk back to French territory, but when winter arrived they perished one after another, until only Bellisle remained. The following year he met some Atákapan Indians who took everything he had but kept him alive as a slave. When they met some Bidai Indians, he slipped them a letter to be handed to any white man. The letter passed through many Indian hands, but at last reached the French at Natchitoches. Bellisle finally arrived there in February 1721. Later that year he was part of another expedition that landed in Galveston Bay (again by accident). At least the miscue gave Bellisle the opportunity to get back some of his own. The Atákapan were surprised to see their slave free, and even more surprised when he captured nine of his former masters and carried them to Biloxi.

❖ AUGUST 15 ❖

1844 An exasperated President Sam Houston finally dispatched a force of militia to Shelbyville under the command of General Travis Broocks, with orders to quell a months-old conflict which had cost several lives. The two parties to the dispute were the "Regulators," an armed body originally formed to suppress bandits and rustlers, and the "Moderators," another armed force constituted to control the excesses of the Regulators. Houston himself eventually arrived to reconcile the two factions, lecturing them in a paternal tone as if scolding some rambunctious schoolboys.

1905 Temple Lea Houston died at the age of forty-five in Woodward, Oklahoma, where he was buried. Temple was the youngest child of Sam and Margaret Lea Houston and the first child born in the Governor's Mansion. He grew up to be a lawyer, famous for his flamboyant dress, his superb oratory, and his brace of pistols, with which he was a top-notch marksman. As an attorney in Woodward, a small, wild frontier town, he took part in some memorable cases. He once fired blanks at a jury to show the state of mind of his client in a murder case, in which the victim was an expert gunman against whom the defendant would have had no chance in a "fair" fight. Another time he killed one brother of his opponent in a case and wounded another, both of them sons of the presiding judge; the shooting was ruled self-defense. Some time after the gunfight, two of the brothers, Al and Frank Jennings, turned to the life of the outlaw but showed themselves completely inept at their new trade. Their gang stole about $200 per man before they were captured and sent to prison.

AUGUST 16

1862 Federal gunboats shelled Corpus Christi after their demand for surrender was refused. According to legend, Union sailors had removed the charges from several shells to hide some pilfered bourbon and couldn't switch them back without revealing the theft. The resulting "whiskey bombs" made the siege more tolerable for many residents.

1931 In Jeff Davis County, near the little town of Valentine, the strongest earthquake ever recorded in Texas shook the earth, with a reading of around 6.0 on the Richter Scale. Most Texas quakes are caused by a few known fault lines, but some of the smaller ones are actually a side effect of human intervention in the form of oil and gas wells. Historically Texas experiences a quake every year or two on average, most of them minor, although about one in four causes some damage. Paradoxically, the only person ever killed by a Texas earthquake was not killed in Texas. On March 7, 1923, a tremor whose epicenter was in El Paso flattened an adobe house across the river in Ciudad Juárez, and a man inside died of suffocation.

❖
AUGUST 17
❖

1973 NASA's Manned Spacecraft Center was renamed the Lyndon B. Johnson Space Center, in honor of the thirty-sixth president, who had died in January. When NASA Administrator James E. Webb announced the location of the new complex in 1961—southeast of Houston on land acquired from Rice University—politicians from other states complained that then Vice President Johnson and Houston Congressman Albert Thomas of the House Appropriations Committee had used excessive pressure to win the economic plum for their state. But NASA denied that the decision had been influenced by politics, and their choice stood.

❖
AUGUST 18
❖

1886 In the Haynes Saloon in Trail City, Colorado, the gun of one Joe Sparrow ended the violent career of Prentice "Print" Olive. In the 1860s Olive and his three brothers built up one of the biggest cattle ranches in Williamson County, but their surviving neighbors didn't approve of their methods; and one Olive or another was frequently on trial for murder. Their most grisly deed was inflicting the "death of the skins" on two rustlers; the Olives wrapped them, still alive, in green cowhides (bearing the Olive brand) and let the sun gradually shrink the skins around them. Although none of the Olives was ever convicted of murder, one died in a gunfight, and things generally got too hot for Print. He moved to Colorado, then to Nebraska, and brutal incidents occurred wherever he went. After a Nebraska court acquitted the men who killed his brother Bob, he led the mob that lynched them and burned their bodies; again he went unpunished. But his trial broke him financially, and he headed back to Colorado and destiny in the Haynes Saloon.

AUGUST 19

1895 In the Acme Saloon in El Paso, John Wesley Hardin, the reputed killer of more than thirty men, was rolling dice when Old John Selman shot him in the back of the head. With a view to the three wounds in Hardin's body, all fired from behind, Constable Selman was tried for murder. But he claimed his action was justified by Hardin's threats to him and his son Young John over a "lady," and the trial ended with a hung jury. Selman himself died in a gunfight before he could be tried again.

AUGUST 20

1813 General Joaquín de Arredondo marched into San Antonio with a Royalist army of 1,800 men. He was fresh from his victory two days before at Medina, the bloodiest battle ever fought in Texas, in which 1,300 of the 1,400 republican rebels either died fighting or were captured and executed. Now Arredondo rounded up 800 prisoners on the plaza facing the Alamo. Anyone carrying a weapon, he had executed without further inquiry. At the end of the day he ordered some 300 people crowded into a granary, where many perished overnight. It hardly mattered, as most of those still alive on the 21st were also shot.

AUGUST 21

1844 After returning to Galveston from his naval campaign off the Yucatán coast and receiving a hero's welcome and a twenty-one-gun salute, Commodore Edwin W. Moore was court-martialed at his own request, on charges of embezzlement, disobedience of orders, treason, and murder. The court found him guilty only of disobedience. President Sam Houston, who had declared Moore a pirate when he refused to bring his fleet back to Texas as ordered, was furious and vetoed the verdict, but it didn't matter; Congress refused to punish him. Moore remained an officer of the Texas navy until it ceased to exist at annexation.

AUGUST 22

1841 William P. Aubrey and Henry L. Kinney, merchants of Corpus Christi, were acquitted of treason in the capture of Philip Dimmitt, hero of the Texas Revolution and author of the Goliad Declaration of Independence. Aubrey and Kinney ran a trading post which sold contraband across the border, and they were suspected of collusion with the Mexican forces who seized Dimmitt, their business rival, in July, particularly as the soldiers raided Dimmitt's place but bypassed theirs. While Dimmitt languished in a Matamoros cell, Texans clamored for his release. President Mirabeau B. Lamar sent Kinney, of all people, to Mexico to negotiate, but it was no use; the Mexicans had charged Dimmitt with treason for his part in the Revolution. As he and other Texans were marching in chains to Mexico City and prison, Dimmitt killed himself with an overdose of morphine, saying that he preferred a "Roman's death" to a lifetime in captivity.

AUGUST 23

1911 Having heard the old soldier's tale that cannon fire could stimulate rainfall, Charles W. Post, the breakfast cereal millionaire, hoped that this fact could be useful in ending a drought on his Panhandle ranch. He attached dynamite to kites and floated it up into the air, then exploded it, experimenting to find the ideal interval between bursts. After setting off about two hundred fifty rounds, he was rewarded with a drenching cloudburst, followed by a week of intermittent rain. He tried the same trick the following year and reported that it worked about half the time.

❖
AUGUST 24
❖

1917 William P. Hobby became interim governor, as the state legislature impeached Governor Jim Ferguson on twenty-one articles. Congress might have overlooked many of Ferguson's infractions, but his fatal mistake may have been his veto of a bill appropriating funds for the University of Texas, a bill which passed shortly after he was removed. A certain degree of rascality was expected of any Texas governor, but the UT alumni were a powerful body, and in their eyes his neglect of their alma mater was a cardinal sin, accompanied as it was by comments like "This high toned stuff at the university is not doing the people any good."

Miriam A. "Ma" Ferguson was twice elected governor after her husband "Farmer Jim" was impeached and made ineligible for office; her campaign offered Texans "two governors for the price of one."

Photo courtesy Texas State Library and Archives Commission

1944 Japanese destroyers depth-charged the submarine USS *Harder* and sent her to the bottom of the Philippine Sea, ending her sixth patrol. Her first and only skipper was Lieutenant Commander Samuel David Dealey of Dallas. Dealey and his crew had already made their mark in the Pacific by sinking sixteen Japanese ships, most notably the five destroyers on which he used the dangerous but effective maneuver of meeting them head on, launching torpedoes, and diving. His boat won two presidential unit citations, and he was recognized with the Medal of Honor, the Navy Cross, the Silver Star, and the army's Distinguished Service Cross, which General Douglas MacArthur pinned on him personally. Dealey Plaza in Dallas is dedicated to his memory.

AUGUST 25

1843 English adventurer, explorer, soldier-of-fortune, and travel writer William Bollaert visited Austin. He found the city virtually empty, for President Sam Houston had moved the capital to Washington-on-the-Brazos during the recent invasion by a Mexican army. "The President's House is falling to pieces," he wrote in his journal, "and now the residence of bats. The Capitol is the abode of bats, lizards, and stray cattle...If these buildings and others in the city are not repaired in a short time Austin will be a heap of ruins." Austin was saved by the annexation of Texas in 1845; it became the seat of government of the new state, and within a few years was more prosperous than ever.

AUGUST 26

1837 After appearing for three months, the advertisement of a fifty-dollar reward for the return of a slave named Joe was discontinued from the Houston *Telegraph and Texas Register*. Joe was a slave of William B. Travis and one of the few men to leave the Alamo alive after Travis and his command were annihilated on March 6, 1836. A few weeks after the battle he was back at Travis's plantation near Columbia, and he remained there until April of the following year. Then, on the first anniversary of San Jacinto, he escaped; given that no one had collected the reward after three months, he probably was never recaptured.

1856 Following a suggestion by Secretary of War Jefferson Davis, a shipment of thirty-three Egyptian camels arrived in Camp Verde to be evaluated by the Army as a possible alternative to horses and mules in desert terrain. The animals were accompanied by four Egyptian handlers (one, named Hadji Ali, was nicknamed Hi-Jolly and was the inspiration for the 1960s folk song of the same name). All the camels enlisted in the Army of the Confederacy in 1861 and were reconstructed in 1865; by then they were 100 in number. They had demonstrated their superiority in endurance and carrying ability, but funds for the experiment were discontinued. Some of the camels were sold to a circus, others wandered into the wild, where for years they could still occasionally be seen.

—————— ❖ ——————
AUGUST 27
—————— ❖ ——————

1897 Eleven years after her fourth husband, Sophia Suttenfield Aughinbaugh Coffee Butt Porter, age eighty-one, died at Glen Eden, her Red River home of more than fifty years. In the Civil War, Mrs. Butt earned the title of the "Confederate Paul Revere" when she supposedly rode to notify Colonel James G. Bourland and his Border Regiment that Union troops had stopped at her plantation. The story is suspect, if only because there are so many different versions of it. In one she lulled the enemy soldiers with wine to make her getaway; in another she locked them in the cellar. Based on her warning, Bourland either arrived in time to capture the Union soldiers or was able to escape their trap. After her death, Sophia's home was valued highly in Grayson County. In the 1940s, with Lake Texoma due to cover the site, the building was carefully taken apart to be rebuilt on higher ground, but someone misunderstood and burned all the lumber.

AUGUST 28

1902 Even in the twentieth century, some cattlemen still expressed their hostility to homesteaders the old-fashioned way. Near an isolated windmill on the Panhandle prairie, lawyer and small landowner James William Jarrott, once a member of the state legislature, was shot dead by a person or persons unknown. At the time his wife Mollie was sick in bed in a Lubbock hotel, but she refused to give up their claim; she came home to the Swastika Ranch and ran it herself. In time she expanded it and built up a fine herd of Herefords. She invested in Lubbock real estate and came to be regarded as the city's premiere businesswoman. She died there in 1960, fifty-eight years after a bushwhacker had tried to drive her family off the land.

AUGUST 29

1915 Two months after escaping house arrest at Fort Bliss for violating U.S. neutrality, Mexican counterrevolutionary Pascual Orozco Jr. rode onto the Love ranch near Sierra Blanca, twenty miles from the border. He and his four compatriots stole fresh horses and galloped away, with Love and some of his men on their trail, joined shortly by fifteen lawmen and cavalry troops, who later claimed they did not recognize the fugitives and assumed that they were chasing just another gang of banditos or rustlers. The next day, in a canyon of the Van Horn Mountains, the posse overtook them and killed every man. To his many sympathizers in Texas, Orozco's death looked like murder, and the posse members were indicted but quickly acquitted. Thousands of Orozquistas attended his funeral in El Paso, but the fears of reprisals against Anglos in South Texas proved unfounded.

AUGUST 30

1836   Four days after buying half a league of malarial lowlands at the head of Buffalo Bayou for $5,000, brothers Augustus C. and John K. Allen advertised the myriad virtues of the new town which they proposed to call Houston. The lengthy paean in Columbia's *Telegraph and Texas Register* was one of the most successful, and brazen, strokes in the history of real estate promotion: "There is no place in Texas more healthy, having an abundance of excellent spring water and enjoying the sea breeze in all its freshness. No place in Texas possesses so many advantages... handsome and beautifully elevated, salubrious and well-watered..." In November, at Sam Houston's urging, the legislature selected Houston as the new capital of the Republic.

1856   Charles Edward Travis, son of William B. Travis of the Alamo and until recently a captain in the U.S. Cavalry, felt himself vindicated when the state legislature resolved that the court-martial that had just dismissed him from the service had erred, and that President Franklin Pierce should intervene. Travis, who was disliked by most of his fellow officers, had been convicted of "conduct unbecoming an officer and a gentleman," namely slander, cheating at cards, and absence without leave. Pierce deferred to the court-martial, and Travis's heavy-handed efforts to make several witnesses recant their testimony backfired on him. He retreated to his sister's home in Washington County, and there he died four years later of tuberculosis.

AUGUST 31

1934 Asa "Ace" Borger walked into the post office of the Panhandle boomtown which he had founded and which bore his name. While he was collecting his mail, county treasurer and financial rival Arthur Huey entered, carrying a .45 caliber Colt. Huey had previously made threats against Borger's life, and now he carried them out, shooting at him five times with his Colt, then firing four more rounds with Borger's own pistol. When Huey finally stopped, Borger was dead and another man was fatally wounded. But when he was tried for murder, Huey claimed that Borger was in fact after him, and he was only defending himself when he shot first. The jury found him innocent, but within three years the county treasurer was in prison for embezzling county funds.

SEPTEMBER

❖ SEPTEMBER 1 ❖

1835 The Texas navy won its first laurels with the capture of a Mexican warship. The schooner *San Felipe*, towed in the light winds by the steamer *Laura*, engaged the Mexican schooner *Correo de México* near the mouth of the Brazos. Damaged and with many of her crew wounded, the *Correo* tried to escape, but the next morning the *San Felipe* overtook her, again with the aid of the *Laura*, and she had to surrender. The *Correo*'s commander, Lieutenant Thomas Thompson, had no papers proving his commission in the Mexican navy, so the Texans took him to New Orleans to be charged as a pirate. After a tumultuous trial, in which both the prosecutor and the defense attorney were jailed for creating a disturbance in court, the charges were dismissed.

❖ SEPTEMBER 2 ❖

1856 Joseph Harrell, a prominent citizen of Austin, who lived on Lavaca Street close behind the new Governor's Mansion, sent an irate letter to the state legislature. He wrote to protest the placement of the Mansion's privy directly across from his front door. He had never seen the plans for the grounds, and he returned home from a trip out of the city to find the outhouse already built. It offended him so greatly that he had personally paid the contractor $125 to dismantle it and rebuild it elsewhere, and now he demanded reimbursement. Eventually Congress relented and paid him.

This image of the Governor's Mansion dates from about 1880, when the outhouse that so mortified neighbor Joseph Harrell was long gone.

Photo courtesy Texas State Library and Archives Commission

1870 Cattleman and landowner Samuel Augustus Maverick died in San Antonio, age sixty-seven. Maverick was also a prominent Texas politician: a delegate to the Washington convention on independence in 1836, mayor of San Antonio, a state legislator, and a judge. But his name is famous principally because he left a small herd of cattle wandering freely for several years on Matagorda Peninsula, and any unbranded calf became known as a "maverick."

SEPTEMBER 3

1844 The first thirty or so French colonists from Alsace arrived at the land grant of Henri Castro, the Republic's consul general to France and himself a native of Bayonne on the Bay of Biscay. In its early years the Castroville colony, on the Medina River west of San Antonio, struggled with drought, locusts, cholera, and Comanches, but eventually they overcame these trials. They built their homes and businesses in a distinctive European style for which the town became known as "Little Alsace." Castro himself did not fare as well, however; he invested $200,000 of his own funds, a huge sum in those days, to transport the colonists and provide supplies, but he gained almost none of the expected profits from land sales. Like virtually every land speculator who brought European immigrants to Texas, he found himself financially ruined.

SEPTEMBER 4

1913 Lieutenant Moss L. Love was killed during a training flight at San Diego. In 1914 the Army named a new airfield on the outskirts of Dallas after Lieutenant Love. In August 1927 the city of Dallas, needing a site for a commercial airport, bought 167 acres of Love Field, and passenger service to Houston and San Antonio commenced on a small scale the next year. Decades passed and Love Field grew; by 1973 it was America's sixth largest terminal, with seven million passengers annually. But that year it was nearly shut down at the insistence of the backers of the newly opened DFW International Airport. Only a hard-fought suit by Southwest Airlines, the only carrier left at Love, kept the beleaguered airport open, and now Southwest alone serves three million passengers a year at Love Field.

SEPTEMBER 5

1856 At Columbus, three "ringleaders" of a rumored slave uprising were hanged after a unanimous vote—not a trial—by some concerned Colorado County citizens. Two hundred other slaves were punished severely, and at least one was whipped to death. The "plan," which they revealed under torture, was to murder all the white men in the area, then run to Mexico with their wives and valuables. They also confessed that Mexicans had conspired with them.

1867 Joseph McCoy shipped the first trainload of Texas cattle from Abilene, Kansas. Abilene quickly became the northern terminus of the Chisholm Trail, named for trader and wagoneer Jesse Chisholm, who hauled trade goods on the same route. In 1867 McCoy shipped 35,000 head in 1,000 cattle cars for which he was paid five dollars per car. The next year the number more than doubled to 75,000 head. In 1871 the volume peaked at 700,000 head of cattle. But in the 1870s barbed wire began to spread across the plains, impeding the passage of the herds. Fort Worth opened its own stockyards, with the ambition of becoming the collection point for Texas cattle. By the mid-eighties, after five million cattle had alternately ambled and stampeded to market, the Chisholm Trail was a memory.

SEPTEMBER 6

1961 Former Army Air Corps flight instructor Lloyd Nolen and a few of his friends received a Texas charter for a nonprofit corporation dedicated to restoring and preserving specimens of the great combat aircraft of World War II. According to legend, the name Confederate Air Force was anonymously scrawled on their first acquisition, a P-51 Mustang; they liked it so much they adopted it as the name of their new organization. With the influx of donations from other aviation buffs, they quickly outgrew the original facilities in Mercedes and moved to Harlingen in 1968, then to Midland in 1991, having amassed over a hundred aircraft, most of which they maintain in flying condition.

SEPTEMBER 7

1936   Charles Hardin Holley was born in Lubbock. With the support of his parents, he developed his musical talents and was performing in local clubs when he was thirteen years old. In 1957 his song "That'll Be the Day," recorded with his band The Crickets, instantly made Buddy Holly famous. Several more hits followed, including "Peggy Sue" and "Oh Boy!" But he was killed, along with Ritchie Valens and J. P. "Big Bopper" Richardson, in an airplane crash while on tour the next year.

SEPTEMBER 8

1900   Hurricane winds of at least 120 miles per hour struck Galveston; the storm produced a freak high tide which actually submerged the entire island for several hours. Estimates of the number of Galvestonians killed ranged from 6,000 to 8,000, most of them drowned in the waters that first surrounded then crushed their homes; but some people were literally decapitated by slate tiles which the wind ripped from rooftops and flung at lethal speeds. When the storm was over, most of the city looked like a fantastic pile of driftwood. The Galveston hurricane of 1900 is still the worst natural disaster ever to strike the United States.

SEPTEMBER 9

1921 As a hurricane moved northeast from Mexico, Thrall in Williamson County recorded 38.20 inches of rain in 24 hours, the greatest one-day rainfall in United States history. To the south, San Antonio was inundated under nine feet of water. All told, floods in five counties killed 215 people. The deluge led directly to the construction of San Antonio's famous Paseo del Rio or Riverwalk; the project originated as a flood control measure which would have roofed over the San Antonio River with concrete. But conservation and beautification groups argued that the area should be converted to a scenic walkway with shops and restaurants. Construction finally began in 1939, and the riverwalk opened in 1941. It didn't catch on with the public until the late 1960s, but now it is a major source of tourist revenue. Sadly, the original architect's vision of "a gentle breeze carrying the delightful aroma of honeysuckle and sweet olive" has succumbed to the noise and fumes from the outboard engines of barges that carry visitors up and down the river.

SEPTEMBER 10

1853 Symptomatic of the upsurge in the temperance movement, Bastrop, southeast of Austin, voted to outlaw the sale of alcohol, becoming the first dry community in the state. Prohibition had its ups and downs in early Texas. The Republic never went as far as banning liquor, but the legislature did make it a local option in 1843. Within months of annexation, a new state law passed which ostensibly closed all saloons, but it was repealed in 1856, having never been taken seriously by the citizenry or by law enforcement.

1874 Colonel Nelson A. Miles, on a campaign against Indians along the Red River, sent a patrol of two scouts and four enlisted men to find out what was delaying his supply train (which happened to be under siege by seventy Indians). Two days later, near the Washita River in Hemphill County, the six men ran into over a hundred Comanche and Kiowa warriors. A firefight instantly broke out, and five of them were hit before they could reach the slight cover of a buffalo wallow, which they frantically improved by scooping the earth into a flimsy parapet. They held the Indians off with accurate rifle fire, but their wounds combined with the elements to torment them: first heat and thirst, then raw cold as a blue norther rumbled through. After a night of suffering, during which one soldier died of his chest wound, they found the Indians gone at sunrise. This was explained when four companies of cavalry rode up. After the five survivors reached medical attention, one of the scouts, with a bullet in his knee, had the leg amputated, but the others recovered. All six received the Medal of Honor, although Congress later revoked the scouts' medals because they were civilians.

— ❖ —

SEPTEMBER 11
— ❖ —

1842 In a San Antonio court, the case of *Shields Booker v. the City of San Antonio* opened, with Judge Anderson Hutchinson presiding. But while Doctor Booker was presenting his claim that the city owed him fifty pesos, a Mexican army commanded by General Adrian Woll was marching into San Antonio. After taking possession of the city, Woll ordered everyone in the courtroom—judge, plaintiff, attorneys, and spectators—conducted to a prison in Mexico. The following

March, while they were still held there in chains, a drunken guard shot Booker; the ball may have been meant for a Mexican officer sitting next to Booker, but all the same he died two days later. His lawsuit remained pending on the court docket for two more years, then it was finally dismissed because "the plaintiff had failed to appear."

1961 Hurricane Carla delivered the highest sustained wind speeds in Texas history, as Matagorda and Port Lavaca caught readings of 145 miles per hour; the gusts were estimated to peak at 175 miles per hour. The storm tide at Port Lavaca, which crested at 18.5 feet, destroyed the causeway that carried State Highway 35 across Lavaca Bay (later the Texas Parks and Wildlife Department converted it into a fishing pier more than half a mile long). The eye of Carla came ashore at Port O'Connor, and flattened the town. Anything that had not already blown away was demolished by the tidal surge, which washed ten miles inland. Close to half a million people evacuated the Gulf Coast, but still thirty-four people were killed, and damage reached $300 million; the U.S. Navy responded by rushing the aircraft carrier USS *Antietam* from Pensacola to the Texas coast with supplies and emergency medical aid. Two curious notes from the story of Carla: the Rocket Chemical Company shipped its entire inventory of WD-40® to hurricane victims desperately trying to free rusted and seized machinery; a local television reporter named Dan Rather from Houston's CBS affiliate KHOU gained his first nationwide exposure covering the storm.

❖

SEPTEMBER 12

❖

1845 Twenty-three-year-old Lieutenant Ulysses S. Grant just missed an early and agonizing death when at the last second he decided not to board the sidewheeler *Dayton* at Corpus

Christi. She was carrying officers and soldiers of Zachary Taylor's army from the mainland to the depot on Saint Joseph Island when, at about noon, one of her boilers exploded. The explosion ruptured her hull and, as she sank, the second boiler also burst. Two army lieutenants and six officers and men of the *Dayton*'s crew were killed; rescuers in a small boat picked up the rest. Ironically, this was to have been the *Dayton*'s last run for the army. One of the officers aboard was carrying a final payment for her owners, with a letter terminating their contract.

1962 At Rice University, a perennial cellar-dweller in the Southwest Conference, President John F. Kennedy spoke of America's destiny in outer space and of the great adventure which, as a world leader, the nation was bound to undertake: namely, landing a man on the Moon. He also spoke of the enormous challenges involved and compared them to the great obstacles that man had overcome in the past: *But why, some say, the moon? Why choose this as our goal? And they may well ask why climb the highest mountain? Why, 35 years ago, fly the Atlantic? Why does Rice play Texas?*

SEPTEMBER 13

1860 A posse of anti-abolitionists from Texas brought Methodist minister Anthony Bewley back to Fort Worth, ten days after capturing him in Missouri as he fled amid suspicions of helping to plot a slave revolt. Bewley was singled out after the publication of an incriminating letter, probably forged, addressed to Reverend *William* Bewley. The luckless abolitionist must have suspected that he had only a few hours to live. That night a group of vigilantes took him from the custody of the law and turned him over to a lynch mob. The next day they cut him down and buried him, but not too deep; after a few weeks someone dug him up, flayed the bones, and left them in the sun atop a storehouse, where children found the gruesome relics and made toys of them.

SEPTEMBER 14

1950   In the little East Texas town of Kountze, veteran journalist Archer Jesse Fullingim printed the first edition of the weekly *Kountze News*. In his satirical column, "The Printer Fires Both Barrels," he took on the John Birchers, the Klan, and a variety of politicians, whether of local, state, or national prominence. Despite the *News*'s tiny circulation, his editorials were reprinted in major Texas papers and read nationwide. The two permanent legacies of the quarter century in which Fullingim ran the *News* are the Big Thicket National Preserve, which he passionately endorsed despite the hostility of local logging interests, and the nickname by which he first referred to Senator Richard M. Nixon: "Tricky Dicky."

1964   President Lyndon Johnson presented J. Frank Dobie with the Medal of Freedom, America's highest award for civilian achievement. Four days later, Dobie was dead at the age of seventy-five. From 1922, when he became the secretary of the Texas Folklore Society in Austin, Dobie was recognized, first statewide and then nationally, as the state's most notable literary figure. Books like *Coronado's Children*, *On the Open Range*, and *Tales of Old Time Texas* brought him numerous honors, including a Literary Guild Award, a professorship at the University of Texas despite his lack of a Ph.D., and, finally, interment in the State Cemetery.

❖
SEPTEMBER 15

❖

1896 In an era when railroad accidents in America were a gruesome commonplace that killed thousands each year, 40,000 people swarmed to the ephemeral town of "Crush," Texas, to see two locomotives deliberately ram each other head-on. In 1895 George Crush, of the Missouri, Kansas, and Texas Railroad, dreamed up the stunt. He advertised the event for months and sent the two doomed engines, Old Numbers 999 and 1001, on tour around the state. In September, just north of Waco, the MK&T laid four miles of track and put up a grandstand, tents, and other facilities that made the scene look like a fairground. By 5:00 in the afternoon, twice the expected 20,000 people had arrived at the depot erected for just this one day, having paid two dollars for a round-trip from anywhere in Texas. The two brightly painted locomotives started rolling from opposite ends of the track; directly in front of the crowd, they met at top speed with a satisfying crash and roar. But the next instant, despite engineers' assurances to George Crush that it wouldn't happen, both their boilers exploded. Shrapnel whizzed in all directions and into the packed mass of spectators; three people were killed and others badly injured. That evening, after the transitory population of Crush had gone home and the town had been dismantled, its namesake was fired by the MK&T, but they gave him back his job the next day. A few years later, the great Scott Joplin wrote a march to commemorate the "Crash at Crush."

1949 At 7:30 on a Thursday night, ABC presented a new television series, based on a popular radio program; *The Lone Ranger* was soon the straggling network's biggest hit and remained so for years. The first three episodes were a miniserial that told the story of Texas Ranger John Reid and his five fellow Rangers, who were tracking Butch Cavendish and his outlaw gang when they were caught in an ambush and all were killed except Reid. Badly wounded and left for dead, he crawled to a water hole, where an Indian named Tonto found him and helped him to recover, thereby repaying an old debt, for Reid had once saved his life. After a reckoning with Cavendish, the Ranger, now presumed dead, vowed to dedicate his life to righting wrongs on the frontier, concealed by a black mask and aided by Tonto, who swore allegiance to his *kemo sabe* (trusty scout). They would live on the revenue from a silver mine that Reid and his brother (one of the dead Rangers) had owned, and the mine would also provide the bullets for the Lone Ranger's six-guns. Clayton Moore and Jay Silverheels (who was in fact a Mohawk) rode the West in prime time for eight years and then on Saturday mornings for decades. Yet few people realize that Britt Reid, the Green Hornet, was the son of John Reid's nephew Dan.

❖ SEPTEMBER 16 ❖

1810 Father Miguel Hidalgo y Costilla, already suspect in the eyes of the Royalist government and expecting to be arrested soon anyway, led hundreds of his flock in seizing the prison at Dolores, 150 miles northwest of Mexico City. Hidalgo's *grito de Dolores* (cry of Dolores), in which he called for a free Mexico, was the beginning of the battle for independence from Spain, but he did not live to see his country achieve its freedom. Within months he was taken prisoner, and in July 1811 he was executed by a firing squad. In 1825 the four-year-old Republic of Mexico designated September 16 as Independence Day, and the patriotic holiday was celebrated in Texas as it was throughout the country. Although Texas is no longer part of Mexico, Tejanos still celebrate the anniversary as a *fiesta patria*, carrying on a cultural tradition that has endured for generations.

---❖---
SEPTEMBER 17
---❖---

1862 The battle known in the North as Antietam Creek, and in the South as Sharpsburg, was the bloodiest day of the Civil War, and the soldiers of Texas fared the worst of all. General John Bell Hood, asked by Lee what had become of his division, replied, "They are lying on the field, where you sent them, sir. My division has been almost wiped out!" Rushed into action to prop up the Confederate's sagging left flank, the Texas Brigade's 854 men lost 560 killed or wounded, and one regiment, the 1st Texas, suffered 186 casualties among 226 men, or 82 percent—the highest in any regiment on either side during the entire war.

1875 A hurricane struck Indianola, a major port on the Gulf Coast, killing more than nine hundred people and destroying three buildings in four. Indianolans doggedly rebuilt, but on August 19, 1886, an even more violent storm completely obliterated the town. The Calhoun County seat was relocated to Port Lavaca, but this was a move only in the abstract, as the courthouse and all records stored there had disappeared. Indianola remains a ghost town, nothing more than a few foundations and a historical marker.

---❖---
SEPTEMBER 18
---❖---

1850 Four months after leaving New York, the California-bound expedition led by a twenty-four-year-old swindler named Parker French reached El Paso. French had enticed 180 Easterners into paying $250 each ($100 for those who worked their way) to travel in safety and comfort across Texas to the gold rush; they were to be refunded five dollars for each day beyond the sixty days projected for the journey. After sailing to

Port Lavaca via Cuba and New Orleans, they set out on foot for San Antonio. There French obtained fresh supplies from the army by fraud. In mid-July they began the El Paso leg, during which they were robbed by Indians. By the time they reached El Paso, French already owed his victims a substantial refund. When they turned on him and discovered he was broke, he fled across the Rio Grande. Half of the pilgrims pressed on overland, the rest headed southwest across Mexico hoping to catch a ship on the western shore. French actually tried to hold up some of the latter, but he suffered a gunshot wound in his arm, which had to be amputated. He was last seen in Washington in 1877, and no one knows how or when the scalawag died.

❖ SEPTEMBER 19 ❖

1863   At the Battle of Chickamauga Creek in northwest Georgia, the Texas Brigade of Hood's Division prepared to attack the Union lines after a Tennessee regiment had been bloodily repulsed. "Rise up, Tennesseans, and see the Texans go in!" one of them swaggered. But his unit received the same treatment, and as the survivors came staggering back, one of the recuperating Tennesseans found the strength to call out, "Rise up, Tennesseans, and see the Texans come out!"

1967   Of course, Texas is known as one of the most tornado-prone states in the country. But this day saw the beginning of something wild even by Texas standards. Over the next five days, 115 tornadoes touched down across the state, spawned by Hurricane Beulah, which came ashore near Brownsville. Of the thirteen people killed by Beulah, five died in tornadoes. On the 20th, a record 67 twisters struck, and by the end of the month 124 had occurred, another Texas record. With a month like that September, it was not surprising that 1967 was also a record year, with 232 Texas tornadoes.

❖

SEPTEMBER 20

❖

1973 In the tennis match billed as the "Battle of the Sexes," 30,742 ticket holders and fifty million television viewers watched Billie Jean King, twenty-nine, beat Bobby Riggs, fifty-five, in the Houston Astrodome. Riggs, in his prime an undeniably great player, constantly denigrated women tennis players, challenging the best of them to try to outplay a man. When Margaret Court took up the gauntlet in May 1973, he humiliated her with a defeat in straight sets on national television. When King did the same to him, she became not simply $100,000 richer, but a hero to advocates of women's rights around the world.

❖

SEPTEMBER 21

❖

1971 The American League approved the relocation of the Washington Senators baseball team to Arlington, where they would be known as the Texas Rangers. The 1972 season, the first for the Rangers, started off wrong and then got worse. A strike by professional baseball players delayed their opening game two weeks, and even though it was played on San Jacinto Day, barely 20,000 fans showed up. Only one game drew more people than that one, which was not difficult to understand when the team finished the year with 54 wins and 100 losses. By the end of 1973, with another dismal record of 57-105, the team's fourth manager had come and gone. Since then the team has spent more time in the valleys than on the peaks, even with the addition of stars like Nolan Ryan and Juan Gonzales, and it was not until 1996, their 25th season, that the Rangers broke through into the unfamiliar world of post-season play.

SEPTEMBER 22

1745 Five long months after he sailed from Veracruz bound for New Orleans in his merchant ship *Superbe*, Chevalier Grenier finally reached the Mississippi River. Grenier was yet another of the shipwrecked Europeans who dot the history of the Gulf Coast with their narratives of endless, nightmarish journeys on foot, beset by Indians and the elements. A victim of his own errant navigation and a careless lookout, three weeks out of Veracruz he ran the *Superbe* aground near Matagorda Bay. Grossly misjudging his position, Grenier led his crew west, supposedly toward Pensacola. When the coast-line started to curve south, he recognized his error, but continued southwest, his goal now Tampico. On July 5, after walking 500 miles in 43 days, Grenier staggered into Tampico with a third of the men he had started with. There he bought the ship in which he completed his much-prolonged voyage.

SEPTEMBER 23

1900 Houston millionaire William Marsh Rice was fatally poisoned with mercury pills by his valet, Charlie Jones. Together with corrupt lawyer Albert Patrick, Jones hoped to claim Rice's estate by means of a forged will. But Rice's attorney, Captain James A. Baker, ordered an autopsy, which revealed that Rice had been murdered. In return for immunity, Jones turned state's evidence against Patrick, who was convicted of murder and spent eleven years in Sing Sing before receiving a pardon. Rice's bequest to the city where he had made his fortune was the endowment of the William Marsh Rice Institute for the Advancement of Letters, Science, and Art, better known as Rice University.

---◆---
SEPTEMBER 24
---◆---

1962 The first Van Cliburn International Piano Competition began in Fort Worth. When it was over, the winner was Ralph Votapek of Milwaukee, Wisconsin. His prize included $10,000 in cash (nearly half of it contributed by Cliburn himself) and a debut performance at Carnegie Hall. Like Votapek, most of the Cliburn medalists have gone on to successful but unspectacular musical careers; the one dramatic exception is Romanian Radu Lupu, a great star on the concert stage and in the recording studio. Nonetheless, the quadrennial Van Cliburn Competition is one of the most prestigious competitive musical events in the world.

---◆---
SEPTEMBER 25
---◆---

1839 In Paris, diplomats of Texas and France signed a Treaty of Amity, Navigation, and Commerce, making France the second nation to recognize the Republic and the first in Europe to do so. Commissioner James Hamilton had struggled to make the treaty possible, hoping to sell France, or any other European government, five million dollars in bonds, on which he would make a ten percent commission. The French showed some interest but declined in the end, and Hamilton was ruined, unable to recover the $200,000 he had personally invested in the effort. In late 1857 he was sailing from Washington back to Texas, hoping that the state was at last willing to reimburse him for his loss, when his ship collided with another in the Gulf of Mexico and sank; James Hamilton drowned in the act of saving the lives of another passenger and her child.

SEPTEMBER 26

1843   Viticulturalist Thomas Munson was born in Astoria, Illinois. In April 1876, with degrees in horticulture from the University of Kentucky, he opened a nursery business in Denison. Struck by the abundance of wild grapes in the area, Munson began a lifetime study of native North American grape varieties, eventually traveling to forty states and territories. By the 1880s his many scholarly articles had earned him recognition as the top authority on the subject, and the French sought his help in combating the *phylloxera* louse that was ravaging Europe's vineyards. Munson shipped them *phylloxera*-resistant mustang grapevine roots from Bell County, and these were grafted to French vines. For his role in saving the French wine industry, in 1888 the French government sent a delegation to Denison to present him with the Legion of Honor, making him the second American to receive that distinction (Thomas Edison was the first).

SEPTEMBER 27

1848   West Texas pioneer and diarist Susan Emily Bartholomew was born on a cotton farm in Shelby County. With her first and second husbands she lived at Fort Davis, Stone Ranch, Albany, and other parts of Stephens, Eastland, and Shackelford Counties. The diaries Susan kept during the years between 1865 and 1896 are a priceless record of life in the remote reaches of Texas in the latter nineteenth century. *The Fort Griffin Fandangle*, a musical pageant of West Texas history held outdoors at Albany every year, is largely based on her account of the hardships and rewards of daily life on the fringes of civilization.

---------- ❖ ----------
SEPTEMBER 28
---------- ❖ ----------

1874 One of the most influential battles between the U.S. Army and the Indians in Texas was comparatively bloodless, at least in human terms. Colonel Ranald MacKenzie and the 4th Cavalry trailed a large body of Comanches, Kiowas, and other tribes to a camp hidden in Palo Duro Canyon, in the Panhandle. The soldiers managed to approach down the steep slopes to the floor of the canyon before Indian sentries raised the alarm. The warriors fought to pin down MacKenzie's troops while the Indian families broke camp and escaped. Tactically the battle was a draw, as MacKenzie destroyed what he could and withdrew, but with him he took 1,400 of the Indians' precious horses, most of which he later had shot. The army lost only one man killed, the Indians perhaps four. But without their horses and their winter food, the Indians were powerless to continue their foray and were forced to return to the reservations in the Indian Territory.

---------- ❖ ----------
SEPTEMBER 29
---------- ❖ ----------

1898 The town of Karnack opened its new post office. Karnack derived its name from the curious fact that the distance from Caddo Lake to Karnack, Texas, was the same as the distance from the Nile River to Karnack, Egypt, in the time of the Pharaohs. The Texan's sense of humor, or the Texan's taste for the quirky, shows in the names of dozens of towns across the state, as this sample will make clear: Alum, Baby Head, Bare Butte, Buck Naked, Bug Tussle, Cut and Shoot, Ding Dong, Dull, Energy, Fairy, Grit, Happy ("the town without a frown"), Hog Eye, Jot 'Em Down, Loco, Looneyville, Pancake, Pep, Shake Rag, Tarzan, Uncertain, Wink, X-Ray, and Zigzag.

1907 Orvon Gene Autry was born in Tioga. After a string of hit records in the thirties, Republic Pictures signed Autry, and he eventually appeared in over ninety films. During the Second World War he flew for the Army Air Corps in Africa and the Far East. In the fifties he capped his musical career with perennial favorites like "Frosty the Snowman," and in 1969 he was admitted to the Country Music Hall of Fame. From 1950 to 1956 he starred in *The Gene Autry Show* on CBS, in which he rode his trick horse Champion from one adventure to the next, accompanied by comical sidekick Pat Buttram. Autry once proposed to buy the whole town of Tioga and rename it "Autry Spring" or "Gene Autry," but the town declined his offer. There is, however, a Gene Autry, Oklahoma, renamed from Berwyn in 1941.

SEPTEMBER 30

1859 From his family's ranch a few miles west of Brownsville, Juan Cortina—landowner, rustler, and hero to oppressed Tejanos—issued the first of his manifestos, proclaiming the equal rights of Hispanic Texans and demanding that those who violated their rights be punished according to law. The first "Cortina War" started on July 13, when Cortina shot a Brownsville marshal and got out of town. On September 28 he returned with fifty or so armed men; they rode the streets shouting "Death to the Americans," shot five men to emphasize the point, and terrorized the town for a day before withdrawing. Cortina easily drove off an attack by a Matamoros militia company and a small impromptu force who called themselves the Brownsville Tigers. In November a company of Texas Rangers also moved against Cortina, and they were also repulsed. On November 23 Cortina issued his second manifesto, urging Governor Sam Houston to stand up for the rights of Tejanos. But in December a second company of Rangers and a U.S. Army contingent arrived, and on the 27th they drove Cortina across the border, with the loss of sixty of his men. Cortina was far from finished, however. In May 1861 the second "War" began when he led an invasion of Zapata County, but once more he was defeated and driven south of the Rio Grande. In the 1870s ranchers again accused him of rustling and, under pressure from the United States, Mexico arrested him and confined him to Mexico City. In his remaining twenty years he never disturbed the peace on the border again.

Juan Cortina's jaunty carriage helps explain how he became a hero to dispossessed Tejanos in the Rio Grande valley.

Photo courtesy Texas State Library and Archives Commission

OCTOBER

❖
OCTOBER 1

❖

1590 Explorer Gaspar Castaño de Sosa broke his camp on the banks of the Rio Grande, near modern Del Rio, and headed northwest. He was thus the first Jew known to enter Texas, although externally he had converted to Catholicism. Unfortunately, before beginning his trek in search of a rumored silver mine, he had not received the viceroy's permission. On his return to Mexico in 1591, he was arrested and exiled and later murdered despite a reprieve issued in the meantime. New Spain was not a good place to be Jewish. On December 8, 1596, Luis de Carvajal the Younger, son of a friend of Castaño's, was burned at the stake with his mother and three sisters, for "relapsing," and this connection probably prejudiced the court against Castaño.

1849 Sentenced to three years for horse theft, William Samson of Fayette County became the first prisoner of the new Huntsville Penitentiary, before the brick structure was even finished. Samson was one of only three prisoners in Huntsville that year; they were held in a temporary facility of logs and iron bars with room for twelve.

❖ OCTOBER 2 ❖

1846 Soldier and former Ranger Samuel H. Walker left Texas for Washington D.C. on a recruiting trip. While he was in the East he visited Samuel Colt, who made the revolvers that he and the rest of John C. Hays's Ranger company had used to such effect at Walker's Creek in 1844. Walker recommended some important enhancements to the five-shot .36 caliber Paterson design; the result—a massive .44 caliber six-gun with plenty of stopping power—was named the Walker Colt. Designed to be holstered on the saddle, not on the hip, the gun was a favorite of Rangers and mounted soldiers in Texas and made the Colt the standard of handguns. Samuel Colt sent a pair of presentation models to Walker at the front in the Mexican War, but shortly afterwards, in October 1847, Walker was killed.

1918 Mollie Kirkland Bailey, "The Circus Queen of the Southwest," died in Houston at the age of seventy-three, after breaking her hip in a fall. Mollie Kirkland grew up on an opulent plantation near Mobile, Alabama. When a circus came to Mobile in the summer of 1857, she fell in love with the owner's son, bandleader James Augustus "Gus" Bailey, and despite her parents' objections, the fourteen-year-old was married in March 1858. The couple toured with their own musical show, and after the Civil War they worked aboard a showboat. In the 1880s they assembled the state's first circus, which toured for the next forty years, billed as "A Texas Show for Texas People."

❖ OCTOBER 3 ❖

1981 Governor Bill Clements declared the nine-banded armadillo the official mascot of Texas. His proclamation hasn't improved the lot of armadillos here, however. Their flattened husks still dot the state's highways, and *Dasypus novemcinctus* is still a popular ingredient in chili and barbecue recipes. The Texas tradition of eating armadillo goes back a long way. In the 1930s the nickname "Hoover hogs" simultaneously blamed Herbert Hoover for the Depression, likened the taste of armadillo to pork, and celebrated the fact that, when you could get it, armadillo meat was free.

OCTOBER 4

1869 After dark, seventy or more hooded Knights of the Rising Sun broke into the Jefferson city jail, forced their way into the cell where Reconstruction activist George Washington Smith was held, shot him to death, and then continued to shoot into his dead body. They also killed two black associates of Smith who were in the jail that night. Smith should never have been there. The day before, he had been in an armed skirmish with several political antagonists and had sought the protection of the nearby army post. But civil authorities charged him with assault, and the major in command of the fort was confident that their assurances, augmented by the military guard that he assigned, would ensure Smith's safety. The mob quickly pushed past the handful of soldiers; when they could not immediately get at Smith's cell, they shot him down through the window. Not trusting the trial of the accused to the same civil system that had allowed Smith's murder, the army commander in Texas insisted on a military tribunal, but it made little difference. They arrested thirty-five men and prosecuted twenty-four of them. After a trial of more than two months, the court convicted only three men of murder; these were given life sentences, but there is no proof that they ever served a day.

1876 The state's first publicly funded institution for higher education, the Agricultural and Mechanical College of Texas, opened in Bryan. The location in the hinterlands had its hazards, not the least of which were the prowling wolves, which attacked one student on campus in broad daylight. In 1963 the college was renamed Texas A&M University; officially, the initials "A" and "M" no longer represent any specific words. The Corps of Cadets has been an Aggie fixture since the origins of the school, and although membership is no longer mandatory, the Corps is still the largest uniformed student organization outside of the nation's military academies.

❖ OCTOBER 5 ❖

1837   After battering the coast of Mexico for three days, a hurricane drifted north to Brownsville. It then paralleled the coastline on its path across Corpus Christi, Galveston, and Sabine Pass, before continuing on to Louisiana on the 6th. Buildings were leveled along the entire Gulf Coast, and at least two people were killed. Several ships, including two schooners of the Texas navy, were either sunk or driven ashore, sometimes a distance of miles. This, the first hurricane known to traverse the entire Texas coast, was named Racer's Storm, after a British warship also caught in the gale before it came ashore.

1899   Railroad king Edward Henry "Ned" Green drove his two-cylinder Saint Louis, possibly the state's first automobile, from Terrell to Dallas. On roads designed for horses to the extent they could be said to have been designed at all, the thirty-mile jaunt took five hours. En route the outlandish vehicle frightened pets and small children, and later Green found himself being sued by farmers whose cows had run dry or whose horses had bolted in fright. But at this time of his life, Ned Green was entitled to a little harmless entertainment. He was in Texas and his eccentric mother was in New York, so he enjoyed himself, reveling in the society of presidents and loose women. Hetty Green, although a millionaire herself, raised him in a miserly atmosphere of affected poverty, and at the age of eighteen his leg was amputated after a minor injury because she was too cheap to take him to a doctor until it was too late.

———————— ❖ ————————

OCTOBER 6

———————— ❖ ————————

1839 In a field near Gonzales, Reuben Ross and Ben McCulloch faced each other in an illegal duel, although neither felt the least animosity toward the other. There was only one reason they were about to exchange rifle shots at a hundred feet: the terms of the *code duello*. Ross had been Alonzo Sweitzer's second when he challenged McCulloch the day before, and McCulloch declined on the grounds that Sweitzer had previously refused to accept his challenge, which made him a coward not worthy to fight a gentleman on the field of honor. But according to the intricate rules of the duel, an insult to the principal could be construed as an insult to his second, so Ross felt obligated to challenge McCulloch on his own part, despite McCulloch's assurances that he intended no such reflection. Ross fired first, and the ball struck McCulloch's right arm, leaving it permanently impaired. Both men considered the matter settled and shook hands. Ross sent his own doctor to treat the wound and told McCulloch he regretted the necessity of challenging a man he so respected. McCulloch was actually indicted for accepting Ross's challenge, but the prosecutor, another gentleman who understood affairs of honor, chose to have the case dismissed. On the following Christmas Eve, McCulloch's brother Henry killed Reuben Ross in a duel with pistols.

1897 William Cowper Brann, editor and founder of the Waco magazine the *Iconoclast* and a fervent crusader against hypocrisy and corruption, was beaten by three men, one of them a judge, in response to his irreverent criticism of Baylor

University. On November 19, Brann's friend Judge George Gerald shot and killed the editor of the *Waco Times-Herald*, J. W. Harris, in a related dispute. Finally, on the afternoon of April 1, 1898, the feud ended when Brann and Captain Tom Davis shot each other in front of Davis's office on Fourth Street. Although Davis hit Brann in the back "where his suspenders crossed," Brann was able to draw his pistol and put several slugs in Davis; both men died the next day.

❖ OCTOBER 7 ❖

1876   Camped near Deep Creek, ten miles northwest of present-day Snyder, professional buffalo hunter J. Wright Mooar was astonished to see an all-white buffalo in the midst of a small herd. He rushed to his camp to fetch partner Dan Down, then hurried back in the dimming evening light. Mooar fired and the white buffalo fell, but the herd stampeded and he had to shoot three more to divert them from trampling Down and himself. For the rest of his life, Mooar proudly displayed the hide, one of only seven ever recorded, and it can still be seen at a ranch near Snyder.

1883   Susanna Dickinson—the widow of Alamo defender Almaron Dickinson and the woman who brought news of the defeat to Sam Houston—died in Austin, about seventy years old. John W. Hannig, her husband from her fifth and only prosperous marriage, wrote her epitaph:

> *We only know that thou hast gone*
> *And that the same relentless tide*
> *Which bore thee from us still glides on*
> *And we who mourn thee with it glide.*

The Battle of the Alamo was not the only hard experience in **Susanna Dickinson's** life, as one can surmise from this photograph.

Photo courtesy Texas State Library and Archives Commission

OCTOBER 8

1838 In what is now western Navarro County, near Dawson, two dozen surveyors were mapping the territory to prepare it for allocation among veterans of the Revolution, whose service had earned them a land bounty. A band of about 300 Indians, mostly Kickapoos, rode up and asked the white men to get off their land. Before long a very one-sided battle broke out. Although the surveyors reported killing some thirty Indians, they lost all but seven of their party. The survivors escaped to a camp of Kickapoos, where they explained that they had been in a fight with Indians, but told a forgivable lie about what tribe was involved, and these Kickapoos helped them reach Fort Parker. A few days later they returned, with a force of fifty men, to bury the dead.

OCTOBER 9

1929 Near Sour Lake in Hardin County, the subsidence of the ground that had begun on the 7th of the month finally ended. By now the hole was as much as 160 feet deep in places and covered five acres of an area with a radius of roughly 1,000 feet. After nearly thirty years of pumping oil out of the ground at up to 50,000 barrels a day, the underlying salt dome had finally collapsed, sucking down a powerhouse and thirty-five wells. But it did provide a diverting sight for thousands of spectators, including students from local schools, which were closed to allow them to observe what everyone hoped was a rare phenomenon.

OCTOBER 10

1877 In El Paso, Charles H. Howard, a district judge who claimed the land rights to the highly valuable salt lakes 100 miles east of town, methodically butchered his Mexican rival Luis Cardis with both barrels of a 10-gauge shotgun. Howard was indicted for murder but released on bail. On December 17, in San Elizario, a Mexican mob put Howard and two of his business associates to death before an impromptu firing squad. The executioners were not very good shots and had to finish off their victims by machete.

1890 Presbyterian missionary William Benjamin Bloys held an old-fashioned camp meeting for two days in Skillman's Grove in the Davis Mountains, hoping for once to hold services with more than a handful of his flock, scattered as they were among the remote ranches around Fort Davis. Forty-three people met for what has been an annual event ever since. Over a century later, the Bloys Camp Meeting draws 3,000 people together every August for five days of equal parts prayer and socializing, co-sponsored by four Protestant denominations.

OCTOBER 11

1764 After three days of negotiation with Captain Rafael Pacheco, the previous commander of the settlement at Orcoquisac, who had been relieved but refused to relinquish his post, Captain Marcos Ruiz set fire to his quarters to drive him out. But Pacheco escaped by a secret exit and fled to San Antonio. He was eventually cleared and returned to his command. Governor Angel do Martos y Navarrete, who had ordered Pacheco's removal, was arrested as a consequence of the damage to the presidio. His trial dragged on for fourteen years, but eventually he lost and was fined for the cost of repairs.

OCTOBER 12

1929 In Corsicana, as the elephants of the Al Barnes Circus paraded from their rail cars to the circus grounds, a notoriously ill-tempered elephant named Black Diamond suddenly ran amok. He tossed his handler over an automobile, then seized spectator Eva Donohoo, threw her down, and crushed her. (Ironically, "Speed" was literally Donohoo's middle name, but this didn't help her outrun a crazed elephant.) On the 16th, after the circus had moved on to Kenedy, circus owner John Ringling had Black Diamond "humanely" shot to death.

❖

OCTOBER 13

❖

1821 Jacob Friedrich Brodbeck, hypothetical early aviator, was born in Württemberg. He emigrated to Texas in 1846 and settled in Fredericksburg in 1847, where he became a schoolteacher. Brodbeck had always been a tinkerer and also dabbled in winemaking; for two decades he worked intermittently on a flying machine. In 1863, the same year he moved to San Antonio, he constructed a little model driven by a propeller and a wind-up spring. In September 1865, or maybe 1868, in a field east of Luckenbach, or in San Antonio's San Pedro Park, he supposedly flew a full-size aircraft, again powered by springs. The springs unwound after about a hundred feet, and the impact wrecked the airship. Brodbeck realized at last that spring power was inadequate and speculated that a lightweight steam engine (!) would be sufficient. But he was unable to interest investors in the project, and he built no more flying machines before he died near Luckenbach in 1910. If Brodbeck's invention ever existed, then it was just one of the many early designs that failed because they lacked sufficient power—power that would be available only with the advent of the gasoline engine, with which the Wright brothers succeeded in 1903.

1835 Attorney and friend of Texas independence William H. Christy chaired a momentous meeting in the New Orleans arcade owned by Thomas Banks. The attendees resolved to form two volunteer companies to serve in Texas and to organize an attack on Tampico to stir up a rebellion against Santa Anna's Centralist government. Both resolutions ended in disaster. The two companies of the New Orleans Greys were almost all killed, some at the Alamo, the rest at Goliad; their flag was captured and now resides in a museum in Mexico City. The expedition against Tampico was doomed when the schooner *Mary Jane*, bearing 150 rebel soldiers, ran aground offshore; the delay allowed the Centralists to reinforce the city, and the attack failed. The American schooner *Halcyon* evacuated most of the insurgents, but twenty-eight were captured, court- martialed, and shot.

OCTOBER 14

1890 Dwight David Eisenhower was born in Denison, in a two-story frame home only yards from the railroad tracks; the house is now a state historical site. After Ike became world famous there was some confusion, even in his own mind, about the place of his birth; all his military records indicated Tyler, although he had written Denison on his application to West Point. In 1952 the former supreme commander of the Allies in Europe became the thirty-fourth president of the United States, the only man ever elected to the highest office in the land without having previously held any other elective office.

1959 At the Abilene Country Club, James J. Johnson of Fort Worth teed up and drove down the fairway of the first hole. At the same time the following day, he finally quit, having become the first man to play golf for twenty-four hours continuously on a regulation course. In that time he completed 363 holes: approximately 15 holes per hour.

OCTOBER 15

1883 Governor John Ireland called the legislature into special session to address the problem of rampant fence cutting. Some ranchers were fencing in not just their own land, but public lands, public roads, or land belonging to their neighbors. In reaction, an epidemic of wire cutting and fence wrecking spread across half the state. Most of the damage was done under cover of darkness, but still fence-builders and fence-cutters occasionally confronted each other, and several men were shot and killed. In January 1888 the legislature passed a bill outlawing both fence cutting and illicit fencing, although the former was a felony subject to a prison term and the latter was only a misdemeanor. Most of the trouble subsided, but as late as 1888 the Texas Rangers had to put down another rash of fence cutting in Navarro County.

❖ OCTOBER 16 ❖

1902   Prohibitionist and reformer Carrie Nation visited the University of Texas in Austin at the invitation of students who, for a joke, implored her to help rehabilitate the faculty, which they described as a pack of dissolute drunkards. Nation took her famous hatchet to a saloon owned by a city alderman and was thrown out. Then she proceeded to the campus, where she yanked cigars and pipes from the mouths of dumbfounded professors. Apparently she never tumbled to the deception, for she returned in 1904 under a similar false impression. She met the dignified, respectable Dean of Engineering, whom the mischief-makers had branded as the "worst reprobate in the University" and called him an "old booze hound" while the students looked on and cheered.

1923   The trial of Frederick Albert Cook on charges of fraud began in a Fort Worth courtroom. Cook was already notorious for his false claims as an explorer—that in 1906 he had been the first man to climb Mount McKinley, and that in 1908 he had reached the North Pole a year before Robert E. Peary. Now he was accused of using extravagant, phony production figures to attract investors in his Petroleum Producers Association. He was only the most conspicuous of 400 people indicted. After testimony by 283 witnesses, Cook was sentenced to fourteen years in Leavenworth. He served only six before he was paroled, and in 1940 President Roosevelt pardoned him, only months before he died at the age of seventy-five.

OCTOBER 17

1935 Sheriff Frank Hoegemeyer of Columbus arrested two teenage pecan harvesters, Ben Mitchell and Ernest Collins, for the rape and murder of nineteen-year-old Geraldine Kollmann. After hours of questioning, the two confessed to killing the attractive valedictorian of Columbus High School. The townspeople were infuriated when they learned that under state law the two were juveniles, and their only punishment would be placement in a reformatory until they were twenty-one. On November 12, as the two boys were being transported in a police car, a mob of 300 to 500 seized them and strung them up from an oak tree just north of town, which was afterwards known as the Hanging Tree. County Attorney O. P. Moore called the lynching "an expression of the will of the people," and County Judge H. P. Hahn expressed his regret that inadequate laws had made it necessary. The Texas Rangers investigated, but, predictably, no charges were filed.

OCTOBER 18

1927 Charles A. Windus, seventy-six, died in the hospital at Fort Sam Houston in San Antonio. Windus had an unusually varied military career: He fought in the Union army at Petersburg, deserted the cavalry in 1868 and spent a year at hard labor, and won the Medal of Honor fighting the Kiowa at the Battle of the Little Wichita in 1870. In 1877 he acquired another unique distinction while serving as deputy sheriff of Brackettville. In the course of arresting four fugitives, he shot and killed a Black Seminole named Adam Payne, one of several Black Seminoles who had won the Medal of Honor serving as scouts for the U.S. Army. Windus thus became the only known recipient of the Medal of Honor who ever killed another.

OCTOBER 19

1918 At the age of eighty-three, Alejo Pérez Jr. died in San Antonio, having apparently lived there all his life. Pérez was less than a year old when his mother took him with her into the Alamo at the beginning of the siege in February 1836. Thus it is likely that he was the youngest person in the mission at the time, and that on the day of his death he was the last remaining survivor of the Battle of the Alamo.

OCTOBER 20

1867 Comanche chief Ten Bears spoke to a group of commissioners at Medicine Lodge Creek in Kansas, the day before signing another peace treaty with the U.S. government. To answer charges that his people had violated previous agreements, he was invited to state the Indians' case: . . . *My people have never first drawn a bow or fired a gun against the whites. There has been trouble on the line between us, and my young men have danced the war dance. But it was not begun by us. It was you who sent out the first soldier and we who sent out the second. . . When I was at Washington the Great Father told me that all the Comanche land was ours, and that no one should hinder us in living upon it. So, why do you ask us to leave the rivers, and the sun, and the wind, and live in houses? . . . If the Texans had kept out of my country, there might have been peace. But that which you now say we must live in, is too small. The Texans have taken away the places where the grass grew the thickest and the timber* *was the best. Had we kept that, we might have done the things you ask. But it is too late. The whites have the country which we loved, and we only wish to wander on the prairie until we die. Any good thing you say to me shall not be forgotten. I shall carry it as near to my heart as my children, and it shall be as often on my tongue as the name of the Great Spirit. I want no blood upon my land to stain the grass. I want it all clear and pure, and I wish it so that all who go through among my people may find peace when they come in and leave it when they go out.*

❖ OCTOBER 21 ❖

1917 In Eastland County, the McClesky Number 1 well came in, initiating the typical boom cycle in the small town of Ranger. The census of 1920 found 16,201 people there, and the number probably peaked around 30,000, ten times that of 1916. The former agrarian town was soon unrecognizable; oil derricks, cheap housing, brothels, disease, and crime all proliferated. While a few people made fortunes, the bulk of the population just tried to live with the pervasive odor of oil and the intermittent well fires, one of which charred two blocks. The Ranger wells were tapped out by 1921, and the town quickly shrank as the oil gypsies migrated to the next big field. In the 1930 census, Ranger was back to 6,208 people.

1970 At the age of ninety-five, Abraham Lincoln Neiman died in a Masonic home in Arlington. In September 1907, with his wife Carrie and his brother-in-law Herbert Marcus, Neiman founded the Neiman Marcus store in Dallas, and it immediately established a reputation for high quality at a high price. But in 1928, after frequent clashes with Herbert as well as with Herbert's son Stanley, he sold his share of the business to Marcus for $250,000. About the same time, he and Carrie were divorced. Neiman started several other businesses over the years, but some were less successful than others. At the time of his death he was utterly destitute, his only possession a cuff link that he kept in a cigar box.

OCTOBER 22

1994   After more than two years of work by sculptor David Adickes, his 77-foot concrete and steel statue of Sam Houston was dedicated in Huntsville. The stately figure stands on a ten-foot base of Texas granite and is visible for miles; the top of Sam's head is the highest point on a line from Houston to Dallas.

OCTOBER 23

1840   Colonel Samuel W. Jordan and his force of about one hundred Texan volunteers, part of the army of the Republic of the Rio Grande in its revolt against Santa Anna, suddenly found themselves in a desperate fight. Near Saltillo, they were betrayed to the enemy and surrounded by 1,000 Centralist troops. They took cover behind a stone wall at the end of an enclosure, situated so that it was assailable only by a frontal assault, which soon followed. At the end of the day five Texans were dead, but so were more than a hundred Mexican soldiers. Jordan and his men slipped away during the night and were able to retreat to the Rio Grande. In the hyperbole typical of the press in those days, their battle against great odds and their long march across hostile territory were compared to Xenophon's heroic retreat across Persia in the fourth century B.C.

1909   A pointless tragedy marred what ought to have been a pleasant, if mundane, event. The train carrying President William Howard Taft arrived in Dallas, where he was to speak at the State Fair. The National Guard lined the streets from the tracks to the grandstand, expecting to perform only a ceremonial role. But a city employee, who just wanted to catch a streetcar, tried to cross the cordon, and when he persisted a zealous guardsman stabbed him with his bayonet. When the hapless civil servant died, the sergeant was arrested; eventually he was sentenced to life in prison. Oblivious to the absurd life-and-death drama playing nearby, Taft blithely rode on to the fair and gave his speech as planned.

❖ OCTOBER 24 ❖

1930   Jiles Perry Richardson was born in Sabine Pass. By 1957 "Jape" was a disc jockey for Beaumont radio station KTRM, where in May he set a world record for continuous broadcasting by playing more than 1,800 45s over six straight days and nights. His unmistakable voice also started him on a singing career, and that same year, under his stage name "The Big Bopper," he recorded "Chantilly Lace," the number 3 song of 1958. Meanwhile he wrote hits like "Running Bear" and "The Purple People Eater Meets the Witch Doctor" for other performers. But in early 1959 he was killed in the same plane crash that took the lives of Buddy Holly and Ritchie Valens.

1960   At 8:15 in the evening, *The Alamo*, produced by John Wayne, premiered at the Woodlawn Theatre in San Antonio. Wayne and rancher James T. "Happy" Shahan spent two years building the set, a full-size replica of the Alamo in Brackettville, 125 miles west of the original. Naturally the Duke starred as Davy Crockett, and not so naturally Governor Price Daniel's brother Bill played Lieutenant Colonel James Neill. The film was nominated for seven Academy Awards, including Best Picture and Best Supporting Actor (Chill Wills), but the only Oscar it won was Best Sound.

❖ OCTOBER 25 ❖

1693 Driven to despair by crop failures, floods, and hostile Indians, Father Damian Massanet and the two priests of the mission of San Francisco de los Tejas, near modern Weches in East Texas, buried the church bells and whatever else they could not carry with them. They then took torches to the mission buildings and began the journey to Coahuila, 400 miles distant. Their flight ended the first permanent Spanish settlement in Texas, which had been intended to counter France's claims to the region. It could only have added to their frustration that they wasted several weeks wandering in the wrong direction and did not arrive in Monclova until mid-February. Massanet declared that further attempts to establish missions would be futile without proper support from the government. It would be more than twenty years before Spain next attempted to settle Texas.

❖ OCTOBER 26 ❖

1863 Colonel William Clarke Quantrill and his band of 400 brigands reported for duty to General Henry E. McCulloch at Bonham. By the beginning of the Civil War, Quantrill was already notorious as a murderer. In August 1863 he and his men raided Lawrence, Kansas, killing nearly two hundred men and boys and pillaging the town. Three weeks before he arrived in Bonham, he defeated a Union force of one hundred men and killed eighty of them, some after they surrendered. Despite his vicious reputation, Quantrill was assigned the task of rounding up draft-dodgers and deserters, but when he killed most of those he caught, McCulloch set him to defending the frontier from Comanches. Instead his group began preying on Texas citizens, and in March 1864 McCulloch had him arrested. He escaped and led his men north across the Red River, pursued by 300 Confederates. In June 1865, the war all but over, he died after being shot in a skirmish in Kentucky.

1886   The first Dallas State Fair and Exposition opened on eighty acres east of Dallas donated by banker William H. Gaston. A rival Texas State Fair had opened just the day before, on John Cole's farm north of town. Both events were reasonably well attended, although both had problems. The Texas State Fair was still under construction on opening day, and a traveling circus downtown actually drew more people. The Dallas Fair was more popular, but it still lost $100,000. Rather than continue the mutually destructive competition, the two merged on February 10, 1887; beginning that fall, the Texas State Fair and Dallas Exposition would be held at the eastern site, now called Fair Park.

❖
OCTOBER 27
❖

1835   Six days after issuing his "Appeal to the Inhabitants of Texas Residing East of the Guadalupe" from Goliad, Texas patriot Philip Dimmitt wrote to Stephen F. Austin describing his design of a banner for the rebellion: "I have had a *flag* made, the colours, and their arrangement the same as the old one— with the words and figures, 'Constitution of 1824', displayed on the *white*, in the centre." The men at the Alamo fought not under the Lone Star flag, but under this one, which symbolized allegiance to the Federalist government of Mexico, not to an independent Texas.

❖
OCTOBER 28
❖

1835   In the Battle of Concepción, which led to the siege and eventual capture of San Antonio by Texas rebels, Richard "Big

Dick" Andrews became the first Texan to die for the Revolution. He told those around him, "I'm a dead man, boys, but don't let the others know it; keep on fighting to the death."

1963 After serving Texas for thirty-six years in the U.S. House of Representatives and the Senate, Thomas T. Connally died in Washington, D.C. In the 1928 Senate race, incumbent Earle Mayfield, elected in 1922 with powerful help from the Ku Klux Klan, offered to buy a suit for anyone who could show that Connally had ever accomplished anything. Connally had some advice for those who thought about taking Mayfield up on his offer: "Make him give you a good suit and not that old second-hand thing he ran in—in 1922—that sheet and pillowcase. Make him give you a good suit that can be worn in the daytime as well as at night." Connally was elected that year and remained in the Senate until he retired in 1952.

❖

OCTOBER 29

❖

1898 A Mexican child died of smallpox in Laredo, the first fatality in an epidemic that lasted into the following spring. Fewer children might have died if relations between Texas law enforcement and Mexican-Americans had been less hostile. Medical authorities ordered vaccinations for all children and fumigation of homes in poor east side neighborhoods. Feeling they had been singled out because of their social status, residents resisted, and with increased vehemence when Texas Rangers arrived on March 19 to enforce the order. Animosity between the two groups dated back to the Mexican War, and when the Rangers used force to remove people from their houses it looked like the same old abuse. Shouted protests escalated to rock-throwing and then to gunfire in which two Hispanics were killed and several people were wounded on both sides. The disturbances ended after the Rangers were relieved by the 10th U.S. Cavalry on March 21. Whether the emergency measures had worked or the epidemic had just run its course, the deaths from smallpox among the children of Laredo fell sharply in April and ended in May.

❖ OCTOBER 30 ❖

1784 Mary Austin Holley, a cousin of Stephen F. Austin, was born in New Haven, Connecticut. She traveled to Texas five times between 1831 and 1843 but never fulfilled her wish to live there permanently. In 1833 she published *Texas: Observations, Historical, Geographical and Descriptive, in a Series of Letters Written during a Visit to Austin's Colony, with a view to permanent settlement in that country, in the Autumn of 1831*. The book was promoted as "the first book published in English about Texas." With a second, expanded edition in 1836, Holley drew national attention, and she became an informal ambassador for Texas. When she died of yellow fever in New Orleans in 1846, her last words were "I see worlds upon worlds rolling in space. Oh it is wonderful."

❖ OCTOBER 31 ❖

1993 Former General Edwin A. Walker, the original of the military fanatic in Fletcher Knebel's *Seven Days in May,* died in Dallas at the age of eighty-three. In 1961, while Major General Walker commanded a division in Germany, he was relieved of command and reprimanded for spreading John Birch Society propaganda among his troops. In protest of what he considered pro-Communist censorship, he resigned from the army. He made Dallas the headquarters of his crusade against Communism, ran for governor, and was arrested for obstructing the integration of the University of Mississippi at Oxford. On April 10, 1963, someone fired a rifle at Walker in his home in Dallas. Only after the death of President Kennedy did the FBI discover that the unknown sniper was Lee Harvey Oswald, who used the same rifle on both occasions.

NOVEMBER

NOVEMBER 1

1886 With funds raised by the United Confederate Veterans and the United Daughters of the Confederacy, the Texas Confederate Home opened in Austin. Over 2,000 disabled or impoverished Confederate servicemen lived in the home at some time, with a peak residency of over 300 in the 1920s. Then age began to reduce their numbers; by 1938 only 38 were left, five years later they were down to six, and the last man, 108-year-old Thomas Riddle, died in 1954. After 1939 veterans of the Spanish-American War and the First World War filled some of the space no longer occupied by Confederates. The few inmates left in 1963 were moved to a state hospital, and seven years later the old Confederate Home was demolished.

NOVEMBER 2

1929 In a gravel quarry near Malakoff in Henderson County, Cuban native Indelicio Morgado and his brother Teo unearthed, or claimed that they did, a stone carving of a human head. Six years later another head turned up, prompting archaeologists from the University of Texas to search the site for more relics; in 1939 they found the third and last head.

Experts at the time were convinced the heads were genuine artifacts of an ancient native people and estimated them to be as much as 50,000 to 100,000 years old. But today most scholars are extremely skeptical of their authenticity. Most agree that head number three is just a geological oddity, not a carving at all, and it is most likely that the other two are nothing but twentieth-century hoaxes.

NOVEMBER 3

1863 Confederate General Hamilton Bee, aware that superior Union forces under General Nathaniel Banks were approaching from Brazos Santiago with 7,000 men to his 1,200, evacuated Brownsville and Fort Brown, burning all the cotton stores and anything of military value. His men overlooked the four tons of black powder in the fort's magazine, however. When the flames reached it, the explosion unintentionally leveled much of Brownsville.

1897 John Salmon "Rip" Ford—soldier, Ranger, statesman, and historian—died in San Antonio at the age of eighty-two. His nickname had its origins in the Mexican War, where Ford served as adjutant to Colonel Jack Hays. Whenever he found himself obliged to perform the lugubrious duty, as they liked to say then, of notifying a dead soldier's next of kin, he expressed his personal sympathy by writing "Rest in Peace." When he was pressed for time, he would abbreviate it "R.I.P.," and the acronym followed him the rest of his life.

NOVEMBER 4

1806 American general James Wilkinson and Lieutenant Colonel Simon de Herrera of the Spanish army, the respective commanding officers on the border between Louisiana and

Texas, ratified an agreement that U.S. troops would stay east of Arroyo Hondo, and the Spanish would keep west of the Sabine River. The treaty, though unofficial, relaxed tensions over the boundaries of the Louisiana Purchase and averted an imminent war. Wilkinson had been in league with Aaron Burr in his plans to invade Texas and Mexico; instead he informed President Thomas Jefferson of the conspiracy, Burr was arrested, and Wilkinson testified against him at his trial. The region between the two streams became known as the "Neutral Ground." For the next thirteen years, until the U.S. formally relinquished its claims on Texas in 1819, the strip of land provided a refuge for smugglers, robbers, and murderers, and from its sanctuary the lawless plagued the countryside to the east and west.

❖ NOVEMBER 5 ❖

1878 John Peters Ringo, by trade a gunman, was elected a constable of Loyal Valley. After spending most of the last two years in jail, Johnny Ringo had recently been acquitted of the 1875 murder of John Cheyney in the Mason County War, in which Ringo served the faction led by ex-Ranger Scott Cooley. But in keeping with his history of wandering, Ringo didn't stay long in Loyal Valley. The next year he moved on to Arizona, where he continued to straddle the line between lawman and outlaw, siding with the Clantons against the Earps. On July 13, 1882, he was found dead of a pistol shot to the head; whether he was a suicide or a murder victim is still unclear.

❖ NOVEMBER 6 ❖

1891 In her home in Houston, Mary Jane Briscoe hosted the charter meeting of the Daughters of Female Descendants of the Heroes of '36, an organization dedicated to research, preservation, and awareness of the history of early Texas, especially the period from the revolution to annexation. Membership was restricted to women who could prove direct descent from someone who served Texas during the time of the Republic or earlier. Mary Smith McCrory Jones, widow of Texas president Anson Jones, was selected as the group's first president, a position she held for the next sixteen years. They shortly changed their name to the Daughters of the Lone Star Republic. Then in 1892 they switched to the name by which they have been known ever since: the Daughters of the Republic of Texas. Their most conspicuous accomplishment is the rescue and restoration of the Alamo, although this has been accompanied by some controversial decisions as to what should be restored, what should be reconstructed, and what should be razed. We also owe the DRT our thanks for the preservation of the San Jacinto battlefield, the French Legation in Austin, and the Old Land Office, where O. Henry worked for four years.

1914   In San Antonio, Japanese historian Shigetka Shiga donated a granite monument to the heroes of the Alamo. Reading about the battle, Shiga was moved by the courage of the Texas soldiers. It reminded him of another unequal battle, a watershed in Japanese history, that occurred in 1575 at Nagashino Castle, where warlord Oda Nobunaga and 3,000 peasants armed with arquebuses defeated 12,000 samurai of the Takeda clan.

———————— ❖ ————————
NOVEMBER 7
———————— ❖ ————————

1835   In San Felipe the Consultation, a meeting of fifty-eight delegates from most of the settled portion of Texas, adopted a declaration not of independence from Mexico, but of adherence to the republican principles of the Mexican

Constitution of 1824. They offered to join forces with any other Mexican states that would take up arms against Santa Anna's Centralist dictatorship, but they pledged in any case to resist all Centralist forces in Texas, as they already had at Gonzales, Goliad, and Concepción. The declaration didn't take a strong enough position to satisfy some delegates. Still the vote to adopt it was unanimous, and they ordered the printing of a thousand copies to deliver their message to the people. It would be another four months before the delegates took the crucial step of declaring Texas to be an independent nation.

NOVEMBER 8

1932   U.S. Representative John Nance Garner of Uvalde was elected vice president of the United States; on the same day he was re-elected by the Fifteenth Congressional District. Garner had taken a shot at the White House before ceding his nomination votes to Franklin D. Roosevelt, who returned the favor by making him his running mate. On March 4, 1933, Garner resigned from Congress *after* convening the House in his capacity as Speaker. He then walked to the other end of the Capitol and convened the Senate in his capacity as vice president, becoming the first man to preside over both chambers of the legislative branch.

NOVEMBER 9

1807   Six years after the end of Philip Nolan's failed revolt in Texas, orders arrived from the King of Spain regarding the fate of the filibusters still held in a Chihuahua prison. One man in five, determined by rolling dice, was to be executed; the rest would be released. One of the ten prisoners had already died in captivity, so the jailers decided that only one more victim need be chosen. Ephraim Blackburn, the oldest man, went first. He had to wait while eight other men rolled before he knew that his 1 and 3 was the losing roll. Two days later he was hanged.

1881 A clerk set up a temporary stove in a room of the Capitol building in Austin and fed the stovepipe into a hole in the wall, thinking it connected to a flue. But the opening only led to the neighboring room, which was full of papers and books. Not long after the stove was lit, the entire building was ablaze. Low water pressure crippled efforts to fight the fire, and the building was utterly destroyed. Plans to build a new Capitol were already underway, actually, so the loss of the structure was a serious inconvenience at most. Far worse was the loss of the State Library: decades worth of books, documents, maps, and natural history specimens which could never be replaced.

NOVEMBER 10

1914 In Washington, D.C., President Woodrow Wilson pushed a button which fired a cannon in the port of Houston, officially opening the newly completed Houston Ship Channel. The Southern Steamship Company's *Saltilla* began regular service between Houston and New York City the following August. By the 1930s, oil refineries and fueling docks lined the ship channel, and Houston was one of the country's greatest seaports after all, realizing the far-sighted or just far-fetched prediction of the Allen brothers, who founded the city in 1837.

NOVEMBER 11

1885 Fisher became the first town in Fisher County. Roby, four miles to the south, became the second on April 16, 1886.

As in many another Texas county, the two were soon engaged in a no-holds-barred fight over the county seat, despite the fact that the population was so scanty that cattle outnumbered people 100 to 1. When the votes were counted, Roby had the edge, but Fisher supporters always suspected irregularities, especially when Mr. Bill Purp, a registered voter, was revealed to be a Roby resident's pet dog.

1918 At 11:00 in the morning, in the Compiegne Forest fifty miles north of Paris, General John J. Pershing ordered bugler Hartley B. Edwards of Denison to play taps, signaling the Armistice that ended the First World War.

❖ NOVEMBER 12 ❖

1926 To the Texas Federation of Women's Clubs, it was no doubt regrettable that the cotton industry, a major component of the Texas economy, was suffering from a dramatic drop in prices, competition from foreign growers, and inroads by synthetic fibers. Still, this was not sufficient grounds for the degree of sacrifice that one member had proposed. So the ladies of the Federation, unwilling to part with their silk dresses, rejected the motion that members be required to wear cotton. Five years later, the female students at the University of Texas proved that they were made of more patriotic stuff, when they pledged to wear all cotton in support of the cotton farmers of Texas.

❖ NOVEMBER 13 ❖

1863 Josefa "Chipita" Rodriguez, age unknown but around sixty, was hanged in San Patricio for the murder of horse trader John Savage. Records of Chipita's trial are sketchy and contradictory; for that matter, the trial itself appears to have been sketchy and contradictory. Supposedly she killed Savage with an ax to steal his $600 in gold, but the gold was later found in the Aransas River. Her defense consisted of a "not guilty" plea; the jury was stacked with known felons; the foreman was the sheriff who arrested her. Nevertheless county judge Benjamin Neal ignored the jury's recommendation for leniency, and Chipita was hanged from a mesquite tree, then buried in an unmarked grave. The Texas legislature reversed her murder conviction in 1985. Chipita is popularly thought of as the first and last woman to be judicially hanged in Texas, but in May 1853 a slave named Jane Elkins was hanged in Dallas for murder. It is true, however, that after Chipita the state did not execute another woman until Karla Faye Tucker was put to death in Huntsville in February 1998.

❖ NOVEMBER 14 ❖

1954   Roland K. Towery, editor of the *Cuero Record*, printed the first of his Pulitzer Prize-winning reports of fraud in the Veterans' Land Program. His stories touched off an official investigation which eventually led to twenty indictments. Amazingly enough, when Bascom Giles, commissioner of the General Land Office and chairman of the Veterans' Land Board, was sentenced to six years in Huntsville for theft of state money, he became the first elected official in the history of the state to be sent to prison for a crime committed while in office.

❖ NOVEMBER 15 ❖

1983   Billie Sol Estes, convicted of fraud in 1963, was released on parole from the Federal Penitentiary at Big Spring. Estes, once an associate and financial backer of Lyndon Johnson, went to prison after both federal and state courts found him guilty of bilking West Texas farmers of over thirty million dollars by selling them tens of thousands of fictitious tanks of anhydrous ammonia fertilizer. The case made headlines nationwide and caused heads to roll as far away as Washington, DC. Henry Marshall, an employee of the state Agriculture Department who seems to have been the first person to uncover evidence of the gigantic swindle, was found dead on his ranch near Franklin, shot five times with a bolt-action rifle. A grand jury in Frankston concluded that Marshall had committed suicide.

❖
NOVEMBER 16
❖

1840 The Republic of Texas and Great Britain signed a treaty for the suppression of the African slave trade. The navy of either nation was permitted, with cause, to inspect a vessel of the other and to seize it if slaves were aboard. The document also listed in detail the distinctive characteristics which would be considered *prima facie* evidence that a ship was engaged in the slave trade. They give some insight into the grim accommodations aboard a slave ship.

First: Hatches with open gratings, instead of the closed hatches which are usual in merchant vessels;

Secondly: Divisions or bulk-heads in the hold or on deck, in greater number than are necessary for vessels engaged in lawful trade;

Thirdly: Spare plank fitted for being laid down as a second or slave deck;

Fourthly: Shackles, bolts, or handcuffs;

Fifthly: A larger quantity of water in casks or in tanks, than is requisite for the consumption of the crew of the vessel, as a merchant vessel;

Sixthly: An extraordinary number of water casks, or of other receptacles for holding liquid; unless the master shall produce a certificate from the custom-house at the place from which he cleared outwards, stating that sufficient security had been given by the owners of such vessel, that such extra quantity of casks or of other receptacles should only be used to hold palm-oil, or for other purposes of lawful commerce;

Seventhly: A greater quantity of mess-tubs or kits, than are requisite for the use of the crew of the vessel, as a merchant vessel;

Eighthly: A boiler, or other cooking apparatus, of an unusual size, and larger, or fitted for being made larger, than requisite for the use of the crew of the vessel as a merchant vessel; or more than one boiler, or other cooking apparatus of the ordinary size;

Ninthly: An extraordinary quantity of rice, of the flour of Brazil manioc, or cassada, commonly called farina, or maize, or of Indian corn, or of any other article of food whatever, beyond what might probably be requisite for the use of the crew; such rice, flour, maize, Indian corn, or other articles of food, not being entered in the manifest, as part of the cargo for trade;

Tenthly: A quantity of mats or matting, greater than is necessary for the use of the vessel as a merchant vessel.

❖
NOVEMBER 17
❖

1882 At the ceremony laying the cornerstone of the main building of the University of Texas in Austin, Ashbel Smith, president of the board of regents, said "Smite the rocks with the rod of knowledge, and fountains of unstinted wealth will gush forth." Forty years later his figurative prophecy became literal truth: on the Reagan County lands owned by UT, the Santa Rita Number 1 well gushed forth a fountain of unstinted oil. The discovery was the beginning of not just the Permian Basin oil boom, but the steady flow of hundreds of millions of dollars into the Permanent University Fund. In 1940 the Santa Rita drill rig was moved to the UT campus. It stands there as a symbol of the foresight of those nineteenth-century lawmakers who reserved millions of acres of land for the support of higher education.

The Main Building at the University of Texas was unfinished when this picture was taken in 1884. It was demolished in the 1930s.

Photo courtesy Texas State Library and Archives Commission

❖ NOVEMBER 18 ❖

1908 On John B. Armstrong's 50,000-acre ranch in the Gulf Coast county of Willacy, one of the cowhands decided he'd been given one gruff command too many, and shot "Major" Armstrong. Actually a second lieutenant when he left the Rangers, Armstrong recovered from the bullet wound (not for the first time), and saw his man sent to prison for attempted murder.

❖ NOVEMBER 19 ❖

1854 In the consummation of a dream cherished by his wife, Margaret, since their marriage fourteen years earlier, Sam

Houston was finally baptized in the waters of Rocky Creek by Reverend Rufus C. Burleson, president of Baylor University. (This was actually not the first time for Houston: As a formality of Mexican citizenship, he had been baptized into the Catholic Church with the name Samuel Pablo not long after his arrival in Texas in 1832.) A crowd of spectators traveled to Independence from miles around to witness the occasion. Congratulated on having washed away his sins, Houston replied, "Lord help the fish down below."

1911 Robert G. Fowler and his Wright Flyer landed in Midland. Local blacksmith John V. Pliska was enraptured by the sight of the flying machine and decided he had to have one. Before Fowler took off again, Pliska and an automobile mechanic named Gray Coggin photographed the pusher biplane and took notes about its construction. Then, with wood, piano wire, canvas, and the skimpiest of plans, they started fabricating the parts. As an illustration of their inexperience with aeronautical engineering, at first they covered the wings with plain canvas, before they realized that a coating of shellac would block the pores in the fabric and enhance the lift. The finished product, complete with its fifty-horsepower four-cylinder Roberts engine, a tank of fuel, and a pilot, weighed just over 1,000 pounds. Remarkably for a first attempt by two complete amateurs, the plane flew, at times traveling more than a mile before touching down. The first airplane built in Texas was restored in 1965 and is now displayed in the lobby of the Midland International Airport.

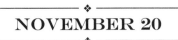

NOVEMBER 20

1837 In his annual report, Robert A. Irion, secretary of state, recommended that the Republic create agencies to issue copyrights and patents. In January 1839 President Mirabeau

B. Lamar signed a bill that allowed citizens to file for a four-teen-year copyright or patent; the fee for doing so was a hefty thirty dollars. Perhaps that is the reason that in its ten-year lifetime the Republic issued only three copyrights, and only one of those works was ever published: George William Bonnell's *Topographical Description of Texas, To Which is Added an Account of the Indian Tribes* is the only book on Earth with a Texas copyright from those ten years. Texas granted a total of fourteen patents to ten inventors: The devices included a variety of machines, a chimney, a lamp, and, inevitably, one patent medicine.

1899 Suspecting a night attack, 2nd Lieutenant E. H. Rubottom, in command of Fort Ringgold, ordered his Gatling gunners to fire into the dark in the direction of neighboring Rio Grande City, in Starr County. Ever since a troop of the 9th U.S. Cavalry, a black regiment, had been stationed at the border outpost, they had suffered racial harassment in town, regardless of the fact that they had just returned from service in the Spanish-American War. Insults grew to threats, and in time the inhabitants of the town and the fort each expected an attack by the other. No one was hurt in the harmless fusillade, and things did calm down afterward. Nonetheless the townspeople were indignant at having hot lead sent their way, and although neither military nor civilian inquiries resulted in any charges being filed, a white cavalry unit was assigned to Fort Ringgold, and the 9th moved to another post.

NOVEMBER 21

1980 After a summer in which the world wondered, "Who shot J. R.?" the prime-time soap opera *Dallas* revealed that it wasn't Sue Ellen, the wife he had betrayed a hundred times, or Cliff Barnes, his archrival in the cut-throat oil business. It was

Kristin, the sister-in-law who was carrying the child of the Ewing clan's sleazy mastermind. The broadcast set a new world record for the number of viewers (300 million), and the figure was not topped until the *M*A*S*H* finale in 1983.

NOVEMBER 22

1898 World-famous flyer Wiley H. Post was born near Grand Saline, in Van Zandt County. In 1931 he and co-pilot Harold Gatty flew around the world, a journey of over 15,000 miles, in under nine days, less than half the previous record set in 1929 by the *Graf Zeppelin.* He repeated the feat in 1933, this time single-handed, and cut nearly a day off the time. Today *Winnie Mae,* the Lockheed Vega in which he made these historic flights, is on display at the National Air and Space Museum in Washington. Wiley Post, with his passenger Will Rogers, was killed in 1935 in a crash in Alaska. With a patch over his left eye, Post was readily recognized around the world, but though flying eventually cost him his life, it didn't directly cost him the eye. He was injured in an Oklahoma oilfield in 1926, working to earn enough to buy his first airplane; ironically, the workman's compensation gave him the money he needed.

1963 At his Uvalde home, John Nance Garner, former Speaker of the House and vice president under FDR, received a phone call from President John F. Kennedy, wishing him a happy ninety-fifth birthday. A few hours later Kennedy was dead and another Texan was president of the United States.

NOVEMBER 23

1969 The Manned Spacecraft Center in Houston hosted the first news conference for men in space. Reporters on the

ground wrote down their questions, and these were relayed to astronauts Pete Conrad, Alan Bean, and Richard Gordon 108,000 miles away aboard *Apollo XII*, on its way home after the second manned landing on the Moon.

NOVEMBER 24

1868   Scott Joplin, composer of the greatest piano rags of all time, was born in Texarkana, son of a former slave (at least this is the date and the place most often cited, although the record is actually sketchy). His music was enormously popular during his lifetime: "Maple Leaf Rag" sold a million copies. After his death in 1917 his music was nearly forgotten. But thanks to the soundtrack of *The Sting*, now his masterpieces like "The Entertainer" and "Maple Leaf Rag" are once again familiar favorites.

1874   Joseph F. Glidden, of DeKalb, Illinois, received patent number 157124 for his innovative new fencing material. Given the shortage of wood on the plains, Texans had tried for years to find a suitable means to separate cattle and crops, such as hedges of thorny plants like bois d'arc. Glidden's invention was in effect artificial thorns: iron barbs spaced along a strand of wire and kept in place by a second strand wrapped around the first. His design, which he called the "Winner," was not necessarily the earliest barbed wire scheme, but it was the most popular. By 1878 salesmen for the Barbed Fence Company were catching the attention of Texas ranchers and farmers with demonstrations of their effective new product, which was "light as air, stronger than whiskey, and cheap as dirt." Before the end of the century, barbed wire changed the Texas landscape, bringing an end to the open range, the cattle drive, and the trademark herds of longhorn cattle.

NOVEMBER 25

1861 After several committees had studied Robert Creuzbaur's plans for an armored gunboat, the Texas Legislature appropriated $500 to send him to Richmond to lay them before the Confederate War Department. Creuzbaur, a surveyor, mapmaker, and draftsman as well as inventor, proposed to build the *Sea King* of wood and iron, with propellers driven by hot air, and armed not just with ordinary guns but with something suggestive of a modern torpedo tube, which he called a "submarine cannon." It is unclear whether he ever showed his ideas to anyone of influence in the Confederate navy. In any case it is unlikely that it affected the design of any Rebel warships. The CSS *Virginia*, the ironclad that sank two wooden Union warships at Hampton Roads, Virginia, in March 1862, was already under construction in November, and the Confederacy built many other ironclads according to the same pattern.

1919 The first play-by-play radio coverage of a football game originated in College Station, where the Aggies played the Longhorns in the annual Thanksgiving Day showdown. Frank Matejka of WTAW, then just a 250-watt ham station with the call letters 5XB, used Morse Code to send out cryptic descriptions of each play. Other ham receivers who had the list of codes could translate his signals and pass on the results to waiting fans around the state.

NOVEMBER 26

1835 The Texas Rangers entered history and legend when Governor Henry Smith signed a bill, passed by the Council two days earlier, to create a small frontier defense force: *An*

Ordinance and Decree to establish and organize a Corps of Rangers... there is hereby created and established a Corps of Rangers, which shall consist of three companies of fifty-six men each, with one Captain, one Lieutenant, and one second Lieutenant for each company; and there shall be one Major to command the said companies...

1905 In Kerrville, "Mr. C. C. Butt Staple and Fancy Groceries" staged its grand opening. The store was named for Charles C. Butt, but the moving force behind the operation was his wife, Florence Thornton Butt. For years the company was purely a Butt family operation; they didn't hire their first employee until 1913, when the store had grown beyond what they could manage. In the 1920s, at the initiative of son Howard, they opened additional stores in other cities. Florence retired in 1935, leaving Howard in charge; he renamed the firm to the H. E. Butt Grocery Company, then in 1942 he streamlined the name to H-E-B. Howard Butt, a Baptist deacon, did not permit his stores to carry wine or beer, and this remained the case until his son took the helm in the 1970s. H-E-B is still the largest privately owned food chain in the United States, with more than two hundred stores, every one of them in Texas.

—————— ❖ ——————
NOVEMBER 27
—————— ❖ ——————

1835 The provisional government at San Felipe authorized the first Texas navy, with the dual object of protecting the supplies coming to Texas from the East and intercepting supplies intended for Santa Anna's army. In January they bought four schooners with varied former careers: a U.S. Revenue cutter, a privateer, a slaver, and a merchantman. Renamed *Independence*, *Liberty*, *Invincible*, and *Brutus*, they performed valuable convoy duty and captured a number of Mexican ships, but none of them lasted long. The *Liberty* was sold when the government could not pay for repairs; two Mexican warships captured the *Independence* off Velasco; *Invincible* and *Brutus* were wrecked on the shoals outside Galveston. By August 1837 Texas again had no fleet.

The second Texas navy was less of a slapdash production. The Republic ordered six ships built in Baltimore, ranging in size from schooners to a sloop-of-war, and they arrived between June 1839 and April 1840. Again their only adversary in combat was the Mexican navy. The schooners *San Jacinto* and *San Antonio* were lost at sea, and the rest of the fleet spent much of its time in New Orleans unable to afford a refit. But in April and May of 1843, the *Austin* and *Wharton*, the two biggest Texas ships, did engage a superior Mexican fleet, including two large steamships, and fought it to a draw. These were the last engagements of the Texas navy. Upon annexation, the remaining ships became part of the U.S. Navy, which discarded most of them as unusable. The third Texas navy, formed by Governor Price Daniel in 1958, is a historical organization dedicated to keeping alive the memory of the first two; in keeping with their traditions, it too has no ships.

———————— ❖ ————————
NOVEMBER 28
———————— ❖ ————————

1861   Adina Emilia de Zavala, one of the two women who rescued the Alamo, was born in Harris County, the granddaughter of Lorenzo de Zavala, the first vice president of the Republic. By the turn of the century, the Alamo church—the most familiar building of the mission—was safe in the hands of the Daughters of the Republic of Texas. But the convent, later known as the long barracks, was in jeopardy. One faction of the DRT, led by Clara Driscoll, did not believe that the building had been part of the mission in 1836 and was determined to demolish it. Zavala led the opposition and in 1908 even staged what today might be called a sit-in to draw attention to her protests. Thanks to her the long barracks was at least partially preserved. Today historians generally agree with her that it was the scene of much of the hardest fighting in the last assault, and that this homely structure ought to be as deeply valued as the more famous church.

In the late 1860s, when this photograph was taken, the Alamo was a supply depot for the US Army Quartermaster Corps.

Photo courtesy the UT Institute of Texan Cultures at San Antonio
The *San Antonio Light* Collection

❖
NOVEMBER 29
❖

1865 Sam Newcomb, a schoolteacher at Fort Davis in Stephens County, recorded another colorful frontier episode in his diary: *A large buffalo was driven into the fort this morning, causing a great deal of commotion and excitement. The animal was immediately attacked by forty dogs and killed in a very few minutes.* Five years later Newcomb died in a measles epidemic at the age of thirty. His diary, now preserved at Texas Tech, is a rare window into the everyday lives of Texas pioneers.

---❖---

NOVEMBER 30

---❖---

1857   In response to formal protests in Washington by the Mexican ambassador to the United States, Governor Elisha M. Pease asked the state legislature for a special appropriation for militia to put a stop to the "Cart War," a terroristic campaign being waged against Hispanics hauling freight in Texas. Mexicans and Tejanos were competing too successfully in the business of carrying goods from Indianola to San Antonio and other inland cities, and in recent months Anglos had been striking back. Sometimes they went beyond just wrecking an offending oxcart and actually murdered the driver, encouraged by local law enforcement that was either powerless or indifferent, and by newspaper editorials that, to the degree that they regretted the violence, did so because it might increase prices. But Congress did fund the dispatch of armed escorts for the beleaguered carters, and by the end of the year the Cart War was over.

DECEMBER

❖ DECEMBER 1 ❖

1913 Singer and actress Mary Martin, creator of the starring roles in the musicals *South Pacific*, *Peter Pan*, and *The Sound of Music*, was born in Weatherford. In recognition of her long career, which brought her two Tony awards, the town erected a bronze statue of Peter Pan in front of the library. After her death from cancer in 1990, Mary Martin's ashes were brought home to Weatherford for burial.

1917 On the advice of geologist Charles N. Gould, the firm of C. M. Hapgood started drilling their first exploratory well in the Panhandle on Robert B. Masterson's ranch, over 200 miles from the nearest known oil field. One year, 2,605 feet, and $70,000 later, they hit a pocket of gas that yielded 10 million cubic feet a day. By the 1920s, as other wells pushed daily gas production over 150 million cubic feet, it was apparent that the Panhandle Hougoton gas reserves were the largest on earth, measured in tens of trillions of cubic feet. The discovery of gas soon led to oil wells. In 1933 the relative abundance of gas led oil lobbyists to push the Sour Gas Law through the legislature. This act permitted well owners to strip gasoline from the gas and "flare" what was left; that is, they simply released the gas into the atmosphere. The profligate and hazardous practice of "stripping and flaring," which wasted a billion cubic feet of gas each day, continued for two years before public protests led to the repeal of the law.

DECEMBER 2

1854   As part of its lengthy effort to clear the debts of the old Republic, the State of Texas granted Elizabeth Crockett $24, her entitlement as the widow of David Crockett, "for Services at the Alamo in 1836." Elizabeth moved to Texas in 1854 and died in Hood County in 1860. In 1913 Texas erected a statue at her gravesite in Acton. The plot is the smallest state park in Texas.

DECEMBER 3

1854   On a wharf in Galveston, a hundred immigrant families from Krakow and southwestern Poland debarked from the *Weser*, nine weeks after they sailed from Bremen. Soon they began their rugged 200-mile journey west, to the land waiting for them fifty miles southeast of San Antonio. The people walked all the way, with hired carts carrying their belongings and the cross from a Polish church. On the trail the settlers lost some of their number to fatigue and exposure, and they gained a few new births. On Christmas Eve they arrived at their destination, which they named *Panna Maria* (Virgin Mary), and celebrated a midnight mass in the first Polish settlement in the United States.

DECEMBER 4

1835   Ben Milam, former filibuster and *empresario* and now a scout for the army of Texans besieging a Mexican army in San Antonio, learned that most of the rebels wanted to abandon the siege for the winter. Milam was sure that this would mean the end of the revolt against Mexico. He implored them not to forsake the cause at this critical moment and then asked, "Who will go with old Ben Milam into San Antonio?" His words moved 300 men to volunteer for an attack on the city the next morning. After four days of house-to-house fighting, the Mexicans surrendered, and the Revolution had won a crucial victory. But Ben Milam was killed by a sniper's bullet on the 7th; he didn't live to see the results of his dramatic intervention in Texas history.

❖
DECEMBER 5

❖

1955 It wasn't anything out of the ordinary in the District Court of Waco when a man named Harry Washburn was convicted of murdering his former mother-in-law and sentenced to life in prison. His *modus operandi*, planting a bomb in Helen Weaver's car in San Angelo, was unusual. But what made this trial unique was the fact that it all happened on television. CBS affiliate KWTX, Channel 10, broadcast all 25 hours of the proceedings, the nation's first televised murder trial.

❖
DECEMBER 6

❖

1832 James Britton Bailey died of cholera on his land east of the Brazos, now known as Bailey's Prairie in Brazoria County. Brit Bailey was one of the more ornery of the original settlers in Stephen F. Austin's colony (known today as the Old Three Hundred), a group not always renowned for their genteel behavior, and his eccentricities carried over into the next life. His will included an unusual provision: He was to be buried standing up and facing west. His reputation led to embellishments of the story; some say that he also took his rifle and a jug with him, and others say that his spirit, manifested as a ball of light, still roams in search of one more drink.

1920   At the request of the U.S. Postal Service, Plehweville in Mason County was renamed Art. Postal authorities in Washington said that the name, chosen to honor the tiny community's first postmaster, Otto Plehwe, was too difficult for people to spell correctly, and much of the town's mail was going to Pflugerville by mistake. In 1920 the local postmaster's name was Ely W. Deckart, and Washington suggested using the last three letters of his name; thus was born Art, Texas.

DECEMBER 7

1955   The board of trustees of the Dallas Museum of Fine Arts, then located in Fair Park, officially stated that they planned to "exhibit and acquire works of art only on the basis of their merit as works of art," and not with regard to the political or ideological affiliation of the artists who created them. It was a time when anything less than militant opposition to Communism was un-American, and, under pressure from a local body of watchdogs called the Public Affairs Luncheon Club, the museum had taken down some Picassos and Riveras. But now they went back on display, and the board took the position that an artist's politics could be left-wing without automatically branding his creations as "Red art."

DECEMBER 8

1958   At Lake Whitney for a few days of fishing, Tristram E. Speaker, one of the greatest hitters ever to step to the plate, died of a heart attack at age seventy. Born in Hubbard, in 1906 Tris Speaker started playing for Cleburne's North Texas League team for fifty dollars a month. He spent seven years with the Boston Red Sox and eleven in Cleveland, where as a player-manager he led the team to its first pennant in 1920. After twenty-two years in the major leagues, he retired in 1928 with a lifetime batting average of .344. In his career he batted .380 or better five times, and below .300 only four times. Speaker may also have been the greatest centerfielder in the history of the game, with an unmatched talent for throwing out disbelieving baserunners; he still holds the record for the most double plays by an outfielder. In 1937 Tris Speaker was the seventh man to enter the Baseball Hall of Fame.

❖

DECEMBER 9

❖

1889 Andrew Jackson Dorn died in Austin on the day after his seventy-fourth birthday. After the Civil War, Dorn moved from Missouri to Bonham, in Fannin County. In 1873, although to the rest of the state he was a mere cipher, the Democratic convention nominated him for treasurer, apparently as a gesture to the North Texas delegation, and Dorn was elected on Governor Richard Coke's coattails. He hung onto the office for six years, in spite of charges of nepotism when he appointed his son as his chief clerk. After that he spent most of his time asking his political friends for jobs. First he went to Washington, where Coke, now a Senator, was unable to get him a position as assistant doorkeeper of the Senate. Coke helped pay his train fare back to Texas, both to assist his colleague and to get rid of a persistent importuner. In 1885 Dorn did win the post of doorkeeper of the state Senate, in which capacity he served the state with distinction for four years.

1916 Nicholas J. Clayton, architect, died at the age of seventy-six in Galveston. Born in Ireland, he emigrated to Cincinnati, Ohio, with his mother when he was a boy, and moved to Houston in 1871. The next year he moved to Galveston, the city with which his name is permanently linked. For the next thirty years he was the city's principal architect, designing homes, businesses, churches, and civic buildings by the dozen. His High Victorian style still sets the distinctive tone of Galveston architecture, and the period is referred to as the Clayton Era. Some of his creations were destroyed in the hurricane of 1900, and others have been demolished over the years. But visitors to the Bishop's Palace or the Strand can still appreciate Nicholas Clayton's impact on the character of turn-of-the-century Galveston.

DECEMBER 10

1838   In Houston, at the inauguration of Mirabeau B. Lamar as the second president of the Republic, his predecessor Sam Houston rose to deliver a "brief" address on the occasion of his "exauguration." Houston intended his parting speech as a parody of George Washington's celebrated farewell address; he even wore a powdered wig and colonial garb to make the jest complete. When he finished talking—three hours later—Lamar was too vexed and agitated to speak. His secretary, Algernon P. Thompson, tried to deliver his speech for him, but, to cap a disappointing day for Lamar, half the crowd drifted off without waiting to hear it.

1878   The steamship *Emily B. Souder*, en route from New York to Santo Domingo, went down at sea. Among those drowned was Jane Cazneau, once the *emprasaria* of a Texas colony and later a self-appointed diplomat, first for the Republic and then for the state. Under her maiden name of McManus, she was named as the correspondent in Aaron Burr's divorce suit in 1834. That same year she tried to found a colony of German immigrants in Texas, but she ran out of funds and they were stranded near Matagorda, where they remained. After Texas won its independence, Jane, now married to Texas politician William Cazneau, became one of America's leading imperialists. She strongly supported annexation; after that was accomplished, she advocated American acquisition or domination of Cuba, the Dominican Republic, and Nicaragua. But it would be hard to say how much of her position had ideological roots and how much was due to the sizable investments the Cazneaus had made in these and other places. They had an estate in Santo Domingo and another in Jamaica, and that was her destination when the *Souder* was lost.

❖

DECEMBER 11

❖

1835 With plenty of land and not enough armed men at their disposal, the delegates to the revolutionary Consultation decreed a bounty of 640 acres to every volunteer; four days later they raised it to 800 acres. In a gracious provision, the land would be granted to the heirs of any volunteer killed in the line of duty. In December of 1837, with independence won, the Texas Congress refined the bounty to 320 acres for every three months of service, up to a limit of 1,280 acres.

❖

DECEMBER 12

❖

1930 Fundamentalist Baptist pastor J. Frank Norris came from Fort Worth to convene a rally on the town square of Canyon, where Joseph Leo Duflot taught sociology at West Texas State Teachers' College. Norris had recently blasted the professor on a radio program from nearby Amarillo, entitled the "Panhandle Church of the Air," for contaminating his students with his skeptical philosophy and for suggesting that evolution might be more plausible than Genesis. Now he invited Duflot to a public debate, which Duflot declined in favor of a pleasant round of golf. Norris carried on without him, calling his absentee opponent "an orangutang, God-denying, Bible-destroying, evolutionist professor" who should be removed from the faculty forthwith. Later, in the inevitable hearing before the school's board of regents, the teacher known by his admiring students as "Jumping Joe" for his animated presence articulately defended himself and was cleared of any improprieties. He also responded to Norris in print, although it is unlikely that Norris could ever have been swayed by Duflot's appeals to intellectual freedom.

❖ DECEMBER 13 ❖

1777   French engineer Luis Antonio Andry sailed from New Orleans on the schooner *Señor de la Yedra*, his mission to survey and map the Gulf Coast from the mouth of the Mississippi River westward to Matagorda Bay. No news of the ship or her crew reached New Orleans until January 1779, when word came from Natchitoches that her burnt hulk had been found near La Bahía. Two months later Tomás de la Cruz, the single survivor of the fourteen men aboard, was repatriated after a year as a slave of the Karankawa Indians; he described the fate of the others. Around March of 1778 they reached Matagorda Bay and completed their survey, but there they were betrayed by Karankawas who offered to help them find food. They secretly murdered two shore parties, then duped Andry into letting them board the ship, whereupon they killed Andry, his young son, and everyone but de la Cruz. These thirteen joined the hundreds of other explorers and adventurers whose lives were lost on the treacherous Texas coast, victims of hurricanes, Indians, or the baffling sandbars.

❖ DECEMBER 14 ❖

1854   Even on his deathbed in the Ake Hotel in Georgetown, attorney Robert Jones Rivers of Columbus retained the sharp wit which had made him an oratorical legend in a time when pungent oratory was a popular art. Georgetown, a small hamlet on the edge of the hill country, was not a grand setting, he conceded, yet he could think of one benefit of being there of all places at this of all moments: "I can die at Georgetown with fewer regrets than any place I know of."

DECEMBER 15

1840 President Mirabeau B. Lamar, worn out both by the financial collapse of the Republic and by his own tuberculosis, was permitted by Congress to take a medical leave of absence. Vice President David Gouverneur Burnet was made acting president. An audacious bill to raise his salary was immediately crushed in light of the monetary crisis. Early the next year, facing expenditures four times the amount of revenue, the legislature effectively disbanded the army by appropriating no funds, and the defense of the Republic was left to the militia. Bankrupt, harassed by Indians, threatened by a Mexican government that still did not concede the loss of its largest state, Texas had reached its darkest hour since Goliad and the Runaway Scrape.

DECEMBER 16

1836 The Republic of Texas issued its first railroad charter to the Texas Railroad, Navigation, and Banking Company (TRRN&B), authorizing them to build a combined rail line and canal from the Rio Grande to the Sabine. But there were reports of corrupt management, and when only a fraction of the anticipated shares were sold, the enterprise collapsed. The Republic tried three more times to establish a railroad, and each attempt failed. Texas did not have its first successful railroad until 1853, when it had been a state for seven years.

❖

DECEMBER 17

❖

1817   The schooner *Huntress* sailed from Philadelphia with about one hundred fifty French exiles led by Baron Charles François Antoine Lallemand, bound for New Orleans and then Galveston, where they arrived in January. In March they left the island and headed for the Texas mainland in boats lent by the Laffite brothers. They proceeded up the Trinity River to a site near modern Liberty; there the band of Bonapartists, mostly army officers, built a fortress which they christened Champ d'Asile (Field of Asylum). Their object in establishing a base in Texas is still uncertain. They claimed that they wished only to work the land in peace, but they invested little effort in agriculture and spent most of their time assembling arms and

This idealistic engraving of the colony of French exiles at Champ d'Asile depicts a utopian agricultural enterprise and ignores the group's military ambitions.

Photo courtesy Texas State Library and Archives Commission

strengthening their fortifications. They may have planned to cooperate with Mexican insurgents against Spanish rule; at least the Royalist government thought enough of the possibility to send an army from San Antonio to dislodge them. When Lallemand learned that Spanish troops were on the way, he ordered his men back to Galveston. There an American agent later arrived to tell him that the United States did not welcome their presence in Texas either. While the French waited for transport, a hurricane struck the island and left them without shelter. Finally the Laffites, who were actually Spanish agents, helped the miserable refugees reach New Orleans. Champ d'Asile was a short-lived failure. But in France, it acquired a noble, almost utopian image, which attached itself to Texas as well. The most significant after-effect was French readiness to recognize the Republic of Texas before any other nation in Europe.

1867 In Galveston, twenty-one-year-old German immigrant Julius Schott opened the J. J. Schott Drug Company, a pharmacy. A couple of years later, Schott was investigating chicle as a potential medicine. It didn't show any promise for that purpose, but he did conclude that if he refined it and added flavoring, it would make a better chewing gum than the paraffin that most people then used. After Schott had been selling his gum for several years, Thomas Adams of New York City sued him for violating his 1871 patent, which described the same idea. In court, Schott was able to prove that his research had preceded Adams's patent, but all the same he got out of the gum business. Incidentally, there was a Texas connection to the Adams Chewing Gum Company: Adams got the idea from Rudolph Napegy, secretary to Antonio López de Santa Anna, when the exiled Mexican leader was in New York to raise capital. Thus, for Chiclets and Dentyne, we owe thanks to a gimpy washed-up tyrant.

DECEMBER 18

1860 Captain Lawrence Sullivan "Sul" Ross led 130 Rangers, cavalry, and civilians in an attack on a Comanche camp on Mule Creek, near modern Margaret. They found the camp consisted mostly of squaws, children, and captives; one squaw stood out, with her blue eyes. It soon transpired that she was Cynthia Ann Parker, who had been captured twenty-four years before at the age of nine. She no longer spoke English, and in her arms she carried her infant girl, the daughter of Chief Peta Nocona, whom the Rangers had killed that same day. She was reunited with her white family but, though the state legislature granted her an annual pension of a hundred dollars and a league of land, she was not happy there. She longed to see her Comanche family again, including her son Quanah Parker, but that was never possible. She died about ten years later, preceded by her daughter Topsannah (Prairie Flower).

After one career as a capable warrior, **Quanah Parker**, son of Peta Nocona and Cynthia Ann Parker, began a second as the leader of the Comanches in their efforts to accept, and prosper under, the dominion of the white man.

Photo courtesy Texas State Library and Archives Commission

❖
DECEMBER 19
❖

1875 Comanche chief Yellow Bear and his nephew Quanah Parker checked into the Pickwick Hotel in Fort Worth. When they retired for the night they turned out the gas lights in their rooms, but Yellow Bear didn't notice that a valve was not completely closed in his. The slowly seeping gas accumulated overnight, and in the morning he was dead.

1959 The last veteran of the Civil War, Walter Washington Williams of Hood's Texas Brigade, died in Franklin at the age of 117. When the last Union soldier had died in 1956, President Dwight Eisenhower had made Williams an honorary general, but he was buried in his old uniform, that of a Confederate enlisted man. Ike declared a national day of mourning to observe the passing of the last participant in the most traumatic struggle in the nation's history.

❖
DECEMBER 20
❖

1835 The Mexican Congress passed a law treating all foreign insurrectionists as pirates, "citizens of no nation…and fighting under no recognized flag." This statute would furnish Santa Anna's pretext for his slaughter of prisoners at Goliad and the Alamo.

1993 Gussie Nell Davis, founder of the Kilgore Rangerettes, died in Kilgore at the age of eighty-seven. In 1928, as a physical education teacher at Greenville High School, Davis started a female baton team called the "Flaming Flashes," the first pep group that went beyond drumming and cheering and actually twirled their batons while they danced. In the following years she added flags and other props, and their dance routines became more intricate.

In 1939 the president of Kilgore College asked Davis to suggest something besides drums and bugles to occupy football fans at halftime; the result was the Kilgore Rangerettes, and Davis directed them for the next forty years. They entertained the crowds at dozens of bowl games, performed on television and in movies, and appeared on magazine covers. Although feminists later deplored the Rangerettes' conservative "Barbie Doll" image, and civil rights advocates wondered why for more than thirty years there were no black Rangerettes, they remain a proud Texas institution. Davis's notion of wholesome halftime entertainment is now taken for granted in virtually every high school and college in the United States.

————— ❖ —————
DECEMBER 21
————— ❖ —————

1836 By act of Congress, it became the law of the Republic that *Every person who shall kill another in a duel, shall be deemed guilty of murder, and on conviction thereof shall suffer death.* Furthermore, *Every person who shall be the bearer of any challenge for a duel, or shall in any way assist in any duel, shall, on conviction thereof, be fined and imprisoned at the discretion of the court before whom such conviction may be had.* All the same, dueling continued to be virtually a sport in Texas, particularly among army officers. The *casus belli* could be as great as a slanderous editorial, or as trivial as the choice of a piece of beef. General Albert Sidney Johnston had to fight a duel to assume his rightful command of the Texas army, and he lost at that. Even Sam Houston received several challenges; he refused each of them and was one of the few men in the Republic who could do so without being shunned in dishonor. The law against duels was never effective, but in time the practice simply went out of favor.

1842 President Sam Houston issued a proclamation reversing a law passed on February 5, 1840, which required "all free persons of color" to leave Texas within two years. On the same day he revoked a law from February 11, 1840, exempting French wine from import duties.

1958   *Tales of the Texas Rangers*, which began its broadcast life on Saturday afternoons on CBS in 1955, was promoted to ABC's Monday evening prime-time lineup; it was demoted again after one season. Like *The Lone Ranger*, another ABC Western, *Tales* had also been a radio series in the early fifties, with Joel McCrea. The television series depicted the exploits of Rangers Jace Pearson and Clay Morgan with an unusual twist: Though the two main characters carried over from week to week, each episode took place in a different historical setting, from the Rangers' origins in the 1830s to Texas in the mid-twentieth century. Whatever the milieu, the program dealt in Ranger myth, not Ranger reality.

DECEMBER 23

1866   Sarah Bowman, the army wife and prostitute known as the "Great Western," was buried in the army cemetery at Fort Yuma, Arizona, with all the honors due a military veteran. Sarah's colorful nickname, which compared her to a famous transatlantic liner of the time, was a tribute to her sturdy, six-foot-two-inch frame as well as her rough-and-tumble personality. She entered history during the Mexican War, in which she traveled as a cook with the first of her many husbands, a soldier in Zachary Taylor's army. Her courage during the Mexican bombardment of Fort Brown, when she continued to run the officers' mess despite several near misses, earned her another nickname, the "Heroine of Fort Brown."

By 1848 she had survived her first and second husbands. She decided she very much needed a third when she was told that only married women could accompany some dragoons ordered to California, so in the presence of them all she unabashedly asked, "Who wants a wife with fifteen thousand dollars and the biggest leg in Mexico? Come, my beauties, don't all speak at once. Who is the lucky man?" When the dragoons moved out, she went with them. In El Paso, in Socorro, New Mexico, and finally in Fort Yuma, she alternated between keeping hotels, cleaning the army's laundry, and running brothels. Twenty-four years after her death, all the remains in the Fort Yuma cemetery were moved to the San Francisco presidio, and she traveled alongside her soldiers one last time.

1927   Santa Claus walked into the lobby of the First National Bank in Cisco. He distracted the attention of customers and staff while his three accomplices took their positions, then all four drew guns and announced that this was a stickup. Mrs. B. P. Blassengame escaped through a side door and raised the alarm. When city police arrived, a blazing gun battle erupted, with over two hundred shots fired. Police Chief G. E. "Bit" Bedford and Patrolman George Carmichael were killed, and six other townspeople were hit, some probably by other townspeople. One of the robbers, Louis Davis, was captured after being fatally wounded, but the other three stole a car and got away, though without their loot. By December 30, after a massive manhunt, they had all been caught; all three men were wounded, and each was carrying at least three pistols when he was arrested. Robert Hill received a life sentence, from which he was eventually paroled. Marshall Ratliff (the man in the Santa suit) and Henry Helms were convicted of the murders of the policemen and sentenced to death; Helms was duly electrocuted. But while Ratliff, previously the beneficiary of one of Ma Ferguson's famous pardons, was confined in the Eastland jail, he pretended to be mentally ill. When his two jailers let down their guard, he killed one of them in an attempt to escape. An angry crowd, hearing what had happened, overcame the remaining guard, dragged Ratliff from the jail, and lynched him from a convenient power pole. A grand jury did not indict anyone involved in the deed.

DECEMBER 24

1877 James Alvis Lynch and his family made camp in Palo Pinto County east of the Brazos River after their trek from Denison in search of a healthier climate. Having bought eighty acres of land, in the spring of 1878 Lynch tried to dig a well, but he couldn't reach deep enough with hand tools. In 1880 an itinerant well digger did the work for him in exchange for a team of oxen. The family thought the water from the well tasted awful, but then the wife's rheumatism cleared up. Lynch's "Crazy Well" became Mineral Wells, an internationally famous spa, whose Crazy Waters promised to cure everything from female disorders to cancer. The Hexagon House, the town's first resort hotel, went up in 1897, and by 1920 there were 400 mineral wells in the town that advertised itself as "the South's greatest health resort."

DECEMBER 25

1834 William B. Travis sold a five-year-old black boy to Jesse Burnham for $225. The transaction was illegal under the Mexican constitution of 1827, which said that no one born in Mexico, even the child of a slave, could be sold into slavery. Another Travis slave, named Joe, was one of few survivors of the Alamo.

1886 Elliott Speer Barker, forester and nature writer, was born in Moran. Barker spent almost all of his life in New

Mexico and worked his way up from forest ranger to state game warden. When he retired in 1953, he became a full-time writer, his best-known work being *Western Life and Adventures, 1889-1970*, which won the Golden Spur Award for nonfiction. But the most memorable action of Barker's life took place in 1950, after a fire in New Mexico's Lincoln National Forest. A five-pound orphaned bear cub, gamely hanging onto a blackened tree despite his terrible burns, was rescued and put in the care of veterinarian Ray Bell, who healed his injuries. Barker and the New Mexico Department of Game and Fish donated the cub to the National Forest Service, and for the rest of his twenty-six years Smokey Bear (officially there is no "the" in his name) was a star attraction at the National Zoo in Washington. In his familiar ranger's hat he is, of course, still the national symbol of forest fire prevention and, in a greater sense, all wildlife conservation.

❖ DECEMBER 26 ❖

1842 At the Mexican town of Mier, on the Rio Grande south of Laredo, a renegade army of 260 Texans under Colonel William Fisher surrendered to General Pedro Ampudia. Despite being outnumbered ten to one, the previous day the Texans had inflicted hundreds of casualties on Ampudia's army to their own thirty, and the Mexican general was himself prepared to surrender if his ruse failed. But he offered the Texans the chance to lay down their arms, and they let themselves be outbluffed; they paid dearly for their mistake. They were an army without government sanction, so Mexico treated them not as prisoners of war but as outlaws and nearly executed them. As they were marched south to a Mexican prison, some were shot after trying to escape, and a lucky few did get away. The rest spent up to two years at hard labor before the last were released in September 1844.

1858 Seventeen Indians from the Brazos Reservation, located on the Brazos River just south of Fort Belknap in West Texas, were camped on Ioni Creek in Palo Pinto County. The agent, Captain Shapley Ross, had given them permission to hunt off the reservation for a week, but white settlers in the area, if they knew that, didn't care. That night some of them attacked the Indian camp without warning and left behind seven dead. Two weeks later Governor Hardin Runnels sent 100 soldiers to protect the 2,000 Caddo, Anadarko, Waco, and Tonkawa Indians on the reservation. On May 23, John R. Baylor, veteran Indian-fighter and editor of the hatred-mongering *White Man*, led several hundred like-minded men to the Brazos and threatened to fire on the troops if they defended the Indians. When the army stood firm, he murdered an Indian woman and an old man, then retreated. A few miles away, a war party caught Baylor's party on the Marlin Ranch and attacked. Chief John Hatterbox and two settlers were killed, while the cavalry, without jurisdiction off the reservation, merely observed. Forced to accept the impossibility of keeping the Indians in Texas, authorities reluctantly moved them north to the Indian Territory.

❖

DECEMBER 27
❖

1836 Stephen F. Austin, the "Father of Texas," died in the Columbia home of Judge George B. McKinstry. After losing in the Republic's first presidential election, Austin was appointed secretary of state, and indirectly this brought about his early death. In the primitive setting of the temporary capital, the office and quarters of the secretary were an unheated shed. Working there day after day, determined to obtain diplomatic recognition of his new country, Austin caught pneumonia and died at the age of forty-three.

1875   The ten-year-old Sutton-Taylor feud ended in Clinton when a posse of Sutton men surrounded Jim Taylor and two of his friends at the home of Martin King. In March of the previous year, Jim and his brother Bill had caught William Sutton on the waterfront of Indianola as he was boarding a steamship and brazenly shot him and a companion to pieces. This time the Suttons had the advantage, and they killed all three men without hesitation. Jim was the last Taylor to press the war against the Suttons; with his death the feud, which had raged across several counties and cost at least twenty-five men their lives, finally subsided.

❖

DECEMBER 28

❖

1920   George W. Brackenridge, eighty-eight-year-old philanthropist and benefactor of the University of Texas, died at Fernridge, his estate on the San Antonio River. He was buried with Masonic rites in the family cemetery near Edna, in Jackson County. This family plot was an unusual arrangement: 150 feet square, surrounded by a four-foot stone wall in which there were no gates. By Brackenridge's direction, the grounds were not groomed; the land was left to natural growth. In 1924 his beloved sister Mary Eleanor, a leader in women's suffrage and social reform who had lived with him since 1866, died at age eighty-six and became the last family member buried there.

❖

DECEMBER 29

❖

1845   U.S. President James K. Polk, nominated and elected largely on his pro-annexation platform, signed the Texas Admission Act after the Senate and the House of Representatives accepted the new Texas state constitution, which Texans had approved by popular vote on October 13. Interest in annexation had been lukewarm in the United States since

Texas won its independence in 1836. But now Great Britain was doing all it could to enhance its influence over the Republic, hoping to create a barrier to further U.S. expansion westward, and Americans felt they had to accept Texas as a state to keep it from becoming a tool of the British. Although the formal ceremonies would wait until February 1846, now Texas was legally the twenty-eighth state of the Union.

❖ DECEMBER 30 ❖

1842 President Sam Houston, fearing that Mexican forces under Santa Anna would overrun Austin, attempted to have the state records moved to the temporary capital in Houston. But Mrs. Angelina Eberly spotted a wagon behind the Land Office and raised the alarm. Austin diehards intercepted the wagon at Brushy Creek and recovered the papers, in the final skirmish of the "Archive War."

1917 Three troops of U.S. Cavalry from Fort Duncan tracked a band of Mexican goat rustlers from the Indio Ranch, near Eagle Pass. The trail led across the Rio Grande to a tiny Mexican village in Coahuila named San José. There they discovered several recently slaughtered goats and a cow bearing the Indio brand. When Mexicans fired on them, the Americans dismounted and returned fire, then brought up their machine gun and raked the houses where the thieves had taken cover; that brought the fighting to an end. There were no casualties among the 150 U.S. troops, whereas there were at least a dozen dead Mexicans. As in other incidents where American forces had pursued bandits across the river, the Mexican government protested the violation of their sovereignty, but the governor of Coahuila took the more pragmatic step of organizing a state ranger company to patrol the border on the Mexican side.

❖

DECEMBER 31

❖

1835 A theater in New York City presented a melodrama entitled *The Triumph of Texas, or, The Siege of San Antonio de Bexar.* The performance was standing room only, with audience members crowding the edge of the stage, and hundreds of people were turned away. The show took in a whopping $1,700 that first night. It was only three weeks since Texas rebels had captured the city, and the rapid production of a play based on events in distant Texas is one measure of the United States' widespread approval of the rebellion. In those days the American Revolution was still a living memory, and the struggle of the outnumbered Texans must have reminded many Americans of their own foolhardy and glorious undertaking fifty years before.

1980 In Austin, Armadillo World Headquarters staged its last concert on New Year's Eve, shortly before its lease expired and the building was torn down. Converted from a National Guard armory in 1970, the Armadillo was at the center of rock and country music in the city that was becoming the musical heart of Texas. Austere budgets, tolerant creditors, and volunteers kept the place alive through ten years in which it hosted not only recognized stars but promising regional performers. Many of them went on make the next generation of Texas music famous around the world.

Index

A

Acequia Madre, 101-102
Adams-Onis Treaty, 35-36
Alamo, 87
 last survivor of, 204
 monument to defenders of, 24
 preservation of, 230-231
America's first military air flight, 42
"Archive War," 253
Armadillo World Headquarters, 254
Armstrong, John Barclay, 101
Arredondo, General Joaquín de, 161
Art, Texas, 236
Astrodome, 69
Audubon, John J., 82-83
Aurora mystery airship, 76
Austin, Moses, 110
Austin, Stephen F., 85, 251
Autry, Orvon Gene, 188

B

Bache, Richard, 49
Bailey, James Britton, 235
Baker, Cullen Montgomery, 4-5
barbed wire, 227
Barrow, Clyde, 63-64, 104
Bartholomew, Susan Emily, 186
baseball, Texas Rangers, 183
Bass, Sam, 140

Battle of Glorieta Pass, 60
Battle of Juarez, 91
"Battle of Keating's Saloon" 74-75
Battle of Palmito Ranch, 94
Battle of the Alamo, 45
 last survivor of, 203
Bean, Judge Roy, 34
Bee, General Hamilton, 214
Behrens, Ella, 19-20
Bell, Peter H., 46-47
Bellisle, François Simars de, 157-158
Bewley, Anthony, 177-178
Bickerstaff, Benjamin F., 66
"Big Bopper, The," 173, 207
"Big Freeze of 1899," 28
Black Seminole scouts, 82
Black Seminoles, 203-204
"Black Sunday" dust storm, 73-74
Blackburn, Ephraim, 218
Bloys Camp Meeting, 199
bluebonnet, 47-48
Bonfoey, David B., 153
Borden, Gail, 8
Bowie, Jim, 11-12
Bowles, Cherokee chief, 138
Bowman, Sarah, 247-248
boxing championship, heavyweight, 34
Brackenridge, George W., 252
Bradley, Carl "Bigun," 92
Branch Davidians, 80

Brann, William Cowper, 195-196
Brodbeck, Jacob Friedrich, 200
Browning, David (Skippy), 50-51
Burnet, David Gouverneur, 73
Burning Bush colony, 75
Byers, Chester (Chet), 12-13

C

Cabet, Étinne, 22-23
"Cactus Jack," *see* Garner, John
    Nance
camels in Texas, 165
Camp Ford, 98-99
Camp Logan, 143
Cantú, José, 112
Capitol building, 44, 96-97
Carswell, Major Horace S. Jr., 39
"Cart War," 232
Castroville, 171
Cazneau, Jane, 238-239
Chambers, Thomas Jefferson,
    51-52
Champ d'Asile, 242-243
Chicken Ranch, 149
"Chicken War," 7
Chief Buffalo Hump, 153-154
Chief Ten Bears, 204-205
Chief Yellow Bear, 244
Chisholm Trail, 172
Civil War, last veteran of, 245
Clyde, Vander, 152
Cody, Samuel Franklin, 46
Coke, Richard, 10-11, 117
Columbus Hanging Tree, 203
Columbus slave uprising, 172
"Come and Take It flag," 49
Confederate Air Force, 172-173
Confederate reunions, 154-155

Confederate Woman's Home, 110
Connally, Thomas Terry, 64, 210
Consultation of Texas, 239
Cook, Frederick Albert, 202-203
Córdova Rebellion, 151
Coronado, Francisco Vázquez de,
    106
Corps of Cadets, 194
Corrigan, Douglas "Wrong Way,"
    139
Corsicana, 199
Cortez, Gregorio, 115-116
Cortina, Juan, 188-198
Costilla, Father Miguel Hidalgo y,
    180
Courtright, Tim "Longhair Jim,"
    25-26
Coxey's army, 57-58
"Crash at Crush," 179
Crockett, Davy, 36, 104
Crystal City, 59

D

Dallas State Fair and Exposition,
    209
Dallas, 225-226
Daniel, Price, 92
Darden, Ida, 48
Daughters of the Republic of
    Texas, 215-216
Davidson, James, 133
Davis, Governor Edmund, 10-11
Dayton sidewheeler explosion, 177
de la Cruz, Tomás, 240
De León, Martin, 72-73
Dealey, Samuel David, 164
Dickinson, Susanna, 196-197
Didrikson, Mildred "Babe" 126
Dimmitt, Philip, 162

Dobie, J. Frank, 178
Doolittle, Jimmy, 62
Dorn, Andrew Jackson, 237
Dr Pepper, 122
Drennan, Lillie, 103
Dumas oil tank fire, 147
Dust Bowl, 73-74

E

earthquakes in Texas, 159
Eastland, 11
Ebsen, Buddy, 36
Eisenhower, Dwight David, 201
El Chico restaurants, 107
Elissa, 141
Ernst, Johann Friedrich, 75
Esparza, José María (Gregorio), 37-38
Estes, Billie Sol, 220-221
Ezekiel Airship, 154

F

Fairchild, Olive Ann, 56
fence cutting, 201-202
Ferguson, Governor Jim, 26, 163
Ferguson, Miriam A. "Ma" 163
first air-conditioned building, 1
first airplane built in Texas, 224
first all-female rodeo, 30
first all-woman state supreme court, 20
first artificial heart, 65-66
first automobile, 194
first battle of the Mexican War, 81
first book about Texas in English, 211
first circus, 192

first document printed in Texas, 35
first dry community in Texas, 174-175
first elected official sent to prison for crime committed while in office, 220
first female sheriff, 149
first German to settle in Texas, 75
first golf ball on the Moon, 25
first hotel built over a pier, 128
first hotel with a heliport, 101
first indoor rodeo, 53
first jackrabbit roping contest, 124
first known airborne wedding, 108
first man to die flying for the Army, 93
first man to fly over Texas, 32
first man to play golf for 24 hours, 201
first news conference for men in space, 226-227
first nonstop flight around the world, 38-39
first overland mail coach, 134
first permanent Spanish settlement in Texas, 208
first play-by-play of football game, 228
first Polish settlement in Texas, 234
first prisoner in Huntsville, 191
first professional theater in Texas, 114
first public institution of higher learning, 193-194
first public laundromat, 76-77

first railroad charter, 241
first steam locomotive, 140
first televised murder trial, 235
first Texan to die for the
    Revolution, 209-210
first Texas navy, 229-230
first Thanksgiving, 85
first trainload of Texas cattle, 172
first U.S. minister to Mexico, 8-9
first word spoken from Moon,
    140-141
Folk Saint of Falfurrias, 130
Ford, John Salmon "Rip," 214
Fort Worth, 111
Fort Worth Stockyards, 144
French, Parker, 181-182
Frontier Battalion, 88
Fry, E.W., 36-37
Fullingham, Archer Jesse, 178

G
Galveston architect, 237-238
Galveston hurricane of 1900, 27,
    173-174
Gálvez, Bernardo de, 92-93
García, Macario, 125
Garner, John Nance, 47, 217, 226
Givens, Lieutenant Curd, 67
Glenn Spring Raid, 90
Goliad, 24
Gonzales, cannon at, 48-49
Governor's mansion privy,
    169-170
Goyens, William, 122
"Grave of the Confederacy," 132
Grayson, Peter, 133
Grenier, Chevalier, 184

Guitérrez, José Bernardo
    Maximiliano, 61

H
Hallettsville, 117
Hamilton, James, 185
Hamilton, Jeff, 65
"hanging tree," 203
Hardin, John Wesley, 161
Hays, John Coffee, 113-114
helium, 129-130
Henderson, James Pinckney, 68
Herzog, Sofie Dalia, 141
Hidden Canyon, 54
Hobby, William P., 163
Hogan, Ben, 100
Hogg, James S., 13, 43
Holly, Buddy, 173, 207
Hopkins, Sam "Lightnin'," 52
Houston, 87, 167
Houston, Andrew Jackson, 79
Houston, Sam, 5, 20, 72,
    223-224, 238, 246-247
Houston Ship Channel, 218
Houston, Temple Lea, 158-159
Howard, Charles H., 198
Hubbard, Richard B., 13-14
Huddle, William Henry, 58
Huey, Arthur, 168
Hughes, Howard R., 155
Hurricane Carla, 176
Hurricane Celia, 150
Huston, General Felix, 99

I
Ikard, Bose, 3
illegal duel, 195
"Immortal Ten," 14

Indianola, 181

J
Japanese attack on Pearl Harbor, 163-164
Jarrott, Mollie, 166
Johnson, Jack, 62
Johnson, Lady Bird, 84-85
Johnston, Albert Sidney, 24
Jones, Anson, 32-33, 119
Jones, Captain Frank, 128
Jones, Carolyn Sue, 84
Jones, Frank Albert, 30
Jones, Major John B., 76, 87-88
Jones, Rose Myrtle, 106
Joplin, Scott, 227
Jordan, Samuel W., 206
Juneteenth celebration, 121

K
Karnak, 187
Keene, Texas, 5-6
Kelly, George, 93
Kickapoos, 197-198
Kicking Bird, 89
Kilgore Rangerettes, 245-246
King, Billie Jean, 183
"king of the oil-well firefighters," 123

L
La Bahia, 23
La Réunion, 18
La Salle, Rene-Robert Cavalier, 1
"Lady in Blue," 22
Lamar, Mirabeau B., 241
Langtry, Lillie, 3
Lanham, Governor S.W.T, 11

Laredo, 77
Laredo smallpox epidemic, 210-211
largest privately owned food chain, 229
Larn, John M., 124
last survivor of the Battle of the Alamo, 203
last veteran of the Civil War, 245
Lea, Margaret Moffette, 92
Lee, Nelson, 64
Lee, Robert E., 30-31
Liendo, 17
Lincoln's birthday, 28
Lindbergh, Charles, 55-56
Lone Ranger, The, 179
Lone Star flag, 6, 16, 88, 209
Long, James, 123-124
Long, Jane Wilkinson, 142-143
longshoremen strike, 50
"Lost Battalion," 47
Love Field, 171-172
Lucas, Anthony, 7

M
MacKenzie, Col. Ranald, 187
Marlboro Man, 92
Martin, Anna, 129
Martin, John, 16
Martin, Mary, 233
Mason County War, 125
Masonic lodge, first in Texas, 17-18
Masterson, Bartholomew (Bat), 15-16
Matagorda, 76-77
Maverick, Samuel Augustus, 170-171
McCormick, Frenchy, 9

meteorites, 150
Milam, Ben, 234-235
Miles, Nelson A., 175
Mineral Wells, 249
Mitchell, Roy, 146-147
Mittie Stephens sternwheeler, 27-28
Moody, Governor Dan, 122
Moore, Bessie, 15
Moore, Edwin W., 161-162
Morse, Samuel F.B., 83-84
Munson, Thomas, 186
Murphy Jim "Judas," 112
Murphy, Audie, 105-106

N
Nameless, Texas, 7
Nation, Carrie, 202
National Mother-in-Law Day, 45
Natural Bridge Caverns, 60
Neiman Marcus, 20-2065
"Neutral Ground," 215
Neville, Edwin, 59
New Braunfels, 57
New London school explosion, 54-55
New Orleans Greys, 200-201
Newcomb, Sam, 231-232
Ney, Elisabet, 16-17
Nimitz, Chester William, 37
Nocona, 41, 146
Nolan, Philip, 43
Norris, J. Frank, 139-140

O
O. Henry, 84
Odessa, 124
official mascot of Texas, 192
Old Glory, Texas, 137

Old Rip, 11, 13
Olive, Prentice "Print," 160
only Northern memorial in a Confederate state, 155
Orbison, Roy, 80-81
Orozco, Pascual Jr., 166-167

P
Pacheco, Rafael, 199
Parker, Bonnie, 63-64
Parker, Cynthia Ann, 244
Parker, Fess, 36
Parker, Quanah, 127, 244, 245
Parrilla, Diego Ortiz, 52-53
Paulhan, Louis, 32
Pecos High Bridge, 61-62
Permanent University Fund, 222
peyote, 29
Pinckney, John McPherson, 81
"Pitchfork Smith," 135
"Plan of San Diego," 33-34
Poinsett, Joel R., 8-9
Popeye the Sailor Man, 12, 59-60
Porter, Sophia Suttenfield Aughinbaugh Coffee Butt, 165-166
Porter, William Sydney, 84
Post, Charles W., 162-163
Post, Wiley H., 226

Q
Quantrill, William Clarke, 208-209

R
race riot of 1943, 118-119
Racer's Storm, 194
Randolph Field, 122

Ranger oil boom, 205
Recknagel, Friedericke, 40
Reconstruction Acts, 61
Red River Telegraph Company, 29
"Red River War," 131
Reeves, Jim, 147
Rice, William Marsh, 184
Richardson, Jiles "Jape" Perry,
    173, 207
Rickard, George "Tex," 38
Ringo, Johnny, 215
riverwalk, 174
Robinson, James W., 67
rodeo, first all-female, 30
Rodriguez, Josefa "Chipita,"
    219-220
Roe v. Wade, 14
Rogers, Will, 31
"Rope Walker," 145
Rothschild, Abraham, 15
"Rough Riders," 89-90
Ruby, Jack, 51
Rutersville College, 21

S
Saibara, Seito, 71
Sam Houston statue, 206
San Antonio, 116-117, 174
    hailstorm, 100
    mutiny, 83
San Jacinto, 78
Santa Anna, Antonio Lopez de,
    109
Santa Claus bank robbers, 248
Satank, Chief (Sitting Bear), 113
secularization of missions in
    Texas, 70
Seeyle, Emma, 108

Selman, John, 66
"Semicolon Court," 3-4
Shamrock Hotel, 53
Shelbyville, 158
Shephard, Alan, 25
Sheridan, Phil, 58
Sherman, William Tecumseh,
    99-100
Shiga, Shigetka, 216
Sibley, Brigadier General Henry,
    34
silver mine, 31
Simpson, Jim, 114
Siringo, Charles Angelo, 25
Six Flags Over Texas, 151-152
slave trade, 221-222
smallest state park in Texas, 234
Smith, George Washington, 193
Smith, Lonnie, 65
Smokey Bear, 250
Sneed, John Beal, 9-10
Sour Gas Law, 233
Sour Lake sinkhole, 198
Speaker, Tristram E., 236-237
"Spinach Capital of the World,"
    59-60
Spindletop, 7-8
Spring Palace, 107
Stafford Opera House, 36
Starr, Belle, 23
State Fair and Exposition,
    208-209
Steele, Alpnonso, 134
Stilwell, Arthur, 59
Stinson, Katherine, 136
Stockdale, Fletcher, 115
stone carving of human head,
    213-214

Sublet, William Caldwell, 5
Sutton-Taylor feud, 252

T

Taft, William Howard, 206-207
Tascosa, Texas, 9
telegraph office, first in Texas, 29
Ten Bears, chief, 204-205
Terry's Texas Rangers, 142
Texas Admission Act, 252-253
Texas Brigade, 71-72, 181, 182
Texas Centennial Exposition,
   112-113
Texas City ship explosion, 75-76
Texas Confederate Home, 213
Texas Consultation, 216-217
Texas Declaration of
   Independence, 41
"Texas Horse Marines," 110
Texas navy, 169, 229-230
"Texas, Our Texas," 103
Texas Rangers, 228-229
Texas Rangers baseball team, 183
Texas
   copyrights and patents,
      224-225
   dueling, 246
   first minister to the U.S., 51
   official mascot, 192
   smallest state park, 234
   state bird, 20
   state Capitol building, 44,
      96-97
   state song, 103
   supreme court, first all-woman,
      20
   tornadoes, 90-91, 182
Texas Tech, 63

"Texas Troubles," 134
The Alamo, 207
The White Man, 146
"The Eyes of Texas," 94
Tin Hat Brigade, 124
Toepperwein, "Plinky," 18
tornadoes, 90-91, 182
Travis, Charles Edward, 167-168
Travis, William B., 249
Troutman, Johanna, 6
"truth serum," 137
Tubb, Ernest, 26
"Twelfth Man," first, 1-2
Twin Sisters cannon, 70-71

U

Urrea, Teresa, 156-157
USS *Harmon*, 144
USS *Texas*, 78, 127

V

Valens, Ritchie, 173, 207
Valentine, 30
Van Cliburn Piano competition,
   185
Vergara, Clemente, 28-29
Vernon public library, 77
Victoria, 12
Victorio, 152-153
Villa, Pancho, 2

W

"Waco Horror" of 1916, 96
Walker Colt, 192
Walker, Edwin A., 211-212
Walker, Samuel H., 192
Walters, Lemuel, 135
Wharton, William Harris, 51

"Whiskey Rebellion," 91
white buffalo, 196
Wichita Falls tornado, 70
Wigfall, Louis Trezevant, 32
Wills, Bob, 95
Windus, Charles A., 203-204
Woman's Commonwealth, 98
Women's Airforce Service Pilots
  (WASPs), 95

"world's greatest woman pilot,"
  136
WW I Armistice, 219

Y
Yellow Bear, chief, 245

Z
Zavala, Adina Emilia de, 230-231
Zavala, Lorenzo de, 230